MURDERED JUDGES
Of the Twentieth Century
And other mysterious deaths

Susan P. Baker

EAKIN PRESS ✦ Fort Worth, Texas
www.EakinPress.com

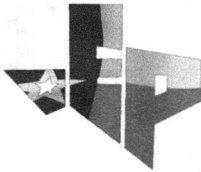

This book is dedicated with love to Dianna Sue Baker, my best friend, for her assistance in the research and for years and years and years of friendship and support. Sisters-in-law by chance. Sisters by heart.

Contents

Questions that Beg an Answer   vii

Foreword   ix

Chapter 1: Judge Hargis: Kentucky, 1908   1

Chapter 2: Judge Massie: Virginia, 1912   7

Chapter 3: Judge Knowles: Rhode Island, 1915   20

Chapter 4: Judge Lawler: Alabama, 1916   25

Chapter 5: Judge W.H. Parker: Mississippi, 1920   30

Chapter 6: Judge Price: Mississippi, 1921   32

Chapter 7: Judge Morning: Nebraska, 1924   43

Chapter 8: Judge Smith: Alabama, 1926   46

Chapter 9: Judge Crater: New York, 1930   51

Chapter 10: Judge Keith: New Jersey, 1933   60

Chapter 11: Judge Rabenau: Missouri, 1934   62

Chapter 12: Judge & Mrs. Pierson: Texas, 1935   65

Chapter 13: Judge Johnson: Tennessee, 1937   71

Chapter 14: Judge Trueman: Utah, 1943   74

Chapter 15: Judge Jackson: Missouri, 1948   79

Chapter 16: Judge Wade: Pennsylvania, 1954   84

Chapter 17: Judge & Mrs. Chillingworth: Florida, 1955   96

Chapter 18: Judge Parkinson: Illinois, 1959   102

Chapter 19: Judge Colasanto: Virginia, 1970   105

Chapter 20: Judge Haley: California, 1970   108

Chapter 21: Judge Kegley: Virginia, 1970   115

Chapter 22: Judge Williams: Virginia, 1974   119

Chapter 23: Judge Lawless: Washington, 1974   123

Chapter 24: Judge Crescente: New Jersey, 1974   125

Chapter 25: Judge Cunningham: Virginia, 1975   128

Chapter 26: Judge Sullivan: Connecticut, 1975   132

Chapter 27: Judge Prizzia: New Jersey, 1976   134

Chapter 28: Judge Helfant: New Jersey, 1978   136

Chapter 29: Judge Travers: Virgin Islands, 1978   140

Chapter 30: Judge Wood: Texas, 1979   141

Chapter 31: Judge Fishman: Maryland, 1980   147

Chapter 32: Judge Partridge: New York, 1982   150

Chapter 33: Judge Gentile: Illinois, 1983   154

Chapter 34: Judge Bailey: Florida, 1987   157

Chapter 35: Judge & Mrs. Sherry: Mississippi, 1987   162

Chapter 36: Judge Daronco: New York, 1988   175

Chapter 37: Judge Irons: Michigan, 1988   181

Chapter 38: Judge Dooley: Texas, 1989   187

Chapter 39: Judge Fairbanks: New Hampshire, 1994   190

Chapter 40: Judge Vance: Alabama, 1989   199

Chapter 41: Judge Bunnell: New Hampshire, 1997   202

Chapter 42: Judge & Mrs. Taylor: California, 1999   205

Acknowledgments   207

Bibliography   213

Questions that Beg an Answer

- What could have compelled these children to strike down their parents? See chapters 1, 8, and 12.
- Who fired the first shot at the Carroll County Courthouse? See chapter 2.
- Who killed Judge Willis Knowles in 1915? See chapter 3. Judge Moody Price in 1921? See chapter 6. Judge Bill Williams in 1974? See chapter 22. Judge Jack Prizzia in 1976? See chapter 27. And Judge and Mrs. H. George Taylor in 1999? See chapter 42.
- What government officials took the law into their own hands? See chapters 4 and 17.
- How did the cow kill the judge? See chapter 5.
- Why did the judge have to pay? See chapters 7, 16, and 34.
- Where is Judge Crater? See chapter 9.
- Was it murder or suicide? See chapters 10 and 39.
- Were these killers criminally insane, or just plain criminals? See chapters 11, 21, and 33.
- Was this a case of justifiable homicide? See chapters 13, 15, and 22.
- What made Austin Cox so mean? See chapter 14.
- Was it murder, or an accident? See chapter 18.
- How did the dog kill the judge? See chapter 19.
- Who failed to follow orders outside the Marin County Courthouse? See chapter 20.
- Was it a prank, or intentional murder? See chapter 24.
- What made the judge's friend do him in? See chapter 25.
- Was it a suicide pact, or murder? See chapter 26.
- Was this judge killed because of his mob connections? See chapter 28.

- Was robbery the motive, or was the stabbing a hit? See chapter 29.
- Who was "Maximum" John? See chapter 30.
- Where is Lawrence Fishman? See chapter 31.
- What made Edward Meyers go berserk? See chapter 32.
- How did a scam turn to murder? See chapter 35.
- Who was the second federal judge killed in the twentieth century? See chapter 36.
- What made Michigan women so angry? See chapter 37.
- Whom did Nga Duc Nguyen intend to execute? See chapter 38.
- Which judges were killed by a mail bomb? See chapters 23 and 40.
- Who was only the second female judge to be murdered? See chapter 41.

Foreword

Although there have been individual books published about famous murder cases, collections about serial murders, seventeenth-, eighteenth-, and nineteenth-century murders, regional murders, unsolved murders, female murderers, badmen, gunfighters and outlaws and almost every other kind of murder collection one can think of, *Murdered Judges of the Twentieth Century* is the first collection of its kind.

I began this project because I was concerned by the prevalence of violence in our American courthouses in the 1980s and '90s. I had always thought of a courthouse as a safe haven, a place where one went to resolve differences through peaceful means, a sanctuary, if you will. I imagined that people had respect for the judiciary, for lawyers, for bailiffs, and for other folks who worked in the legal business. Although I knew of Federal Judge John Wood's assassination, I assumed it was a fluke. It was related to a drug case. Those people knew no bounds.

Suddenly, or so it seemed, a man took a gun into an appellate court in Fort Worth, Texas, shot two justices, and killed two lawyers. Another man shot and killed four women who worked in a New York child support collection office. In Florida, a man shot and killed a judge, a lawyer, and his wife's sister because he didn't want to pay alimony. In Austin, Texas, the husband in a divorce case shot and killed the attorney representing his wife during property settlement negotiations.

Before taking office in January 1991, I requested security measures be taken in our local county courthouse. Our county commissioners refused to vote on it. I wrote letters, drawing their attention to events around the country, requested a security study by the local federal marshal, and showed them videotapes on security. Finally, several years down the road, the commissioners acquiesced. The reason it was so difficult to convince them was that no one wanted to believe that it could happen.

I received no support from the other sitting judges because no one believed that anyone other than a family law judge and family court participants were at risk. It was not important to them that all kinds of people were being killed at courthouses around the country.

My curiosity got the better of me. I started casually looking for information about judges and others who had been killed at courthouses. I wanted to prove that the murders weren't related only to family law. Even though we had gotten some security, I wanted to be able to defend the commissioners' decision should the subject arise again. (This actually happened in 1995, when Texas passed a concealed handgun law. Our state senator wanted people who were licensed to be free to take their guns past the metal detectors as long as they didn't take them into the courtroom proper.) I wanted to be able to demonstrate that paying for security was a sound decision based on real events.

I had no system of research in the beginning. Browsing through a used bookstore, I discovered a book about a judge and his wife who had been kidnapped from their vacation home in Florida and drowned. This "hit" occurred in the 1950s. My interest piqued by that and too many other occurrences for one book, I decided to narrow my subject while at the same time making a firm commitment to formalize my efforts and end up with a finished product.

I realized that it would be an impossible task to identify every municipal, county, state, and federal judge (or former judge) in the United States who fit my criteria. I thought that by including those I discovered after a year's research, I would have a representative sample to demonstrate the dangers inherent in our profession. That goal was not easily accomplished, because the information was not readily available. For a book that started out to illustrate the dangers to sitting judges, other employees, and court participants, including those involved in litigation other than family law, research revealed a plethora of other circumstances surrounding the judges' demise.

Reading this book will be like traveling through the history of the twentieth century. One continuous thread will be identified by the observant: the unchanging nature of human beings. People kill today for the same reasons they did 100, 200, or 5,000 years ago.

Judges are people with normal human failings. Judges' families have the same problems as do other families, including mental illness. Many cases demonstrate a misunderstanding of the role of the judge in our system of government. After reading these cases, one will see that this misunderstanding is not restricted only to the disgruntled party to a lawsuit. After reflection, one will see that the misunderstanding also lies in some of us who assume the role of judge.

Justice Frankfurter said in his dissenting opinion in *Board of Education v.*

Barnette, 319 U.S. 624, 646-647 (1943), "The duty of a judge who must decide which of two claims before the Court shall prevail ... is not that of the ordinary person. It can never be emphasized too much that one's own opinion about the wisdom or evil of the law should be excluded altogether when one is doing one's duty on the bench."

The Preamble to the *Texas Code of Judicial Conduct,* 1995, says that "judges, individually and collectively, must respect and honor the judicial office as a public trust and strive to enhance and maintain confidence in our legal system."

In other words, judges are to carry out the law, not make it. Now more than ever, it is important for this truth to be taken to heart.

Chapter 1

Judge James Hargis
Jackson, Breathitt County, Kentucky
February 6, 1908

Retired County Judge James Hargis, once known as "the King of Breathitt County," was raised in the hills of Kentucky. He was one of many descendants of Scottish clans who were reared on feuds and fights that raged for decades. Jackson, Kentucky, a little town built alongside a running river, should have been obscure but gained fame as the site of the Hargis-Cockrell feud, or the Hargis-Cockrell-Marcum-Callahan War. Many of the feuding families were united by marriage.

John Hargis arrived in Jackson, Kentucky, in 1835. He married Nancy Weddington, who bore seven children, six of them in Virginia and the youngest in Kentucky. They lived in a log cabin by the river. Modern times led to the building of a highway parallel to the river, but there were no roads, only paths, in 1835. Until about the twentieth century, there were no paved roads in Breathitt County.

Eliza Hargis, the youngest child of John and Nancy, was born in 1837. Around the time of the War Between the States, she married Captain William Strong, a notorious feud chieftain of Breathitt County. He earned the rank of captain in the Union Army during the Civil War after having served in Tennessee and Georgia. Transferring to the Home Guards, he became a "scout" on patrol duty. He engaged in bushwhacking and pillaging the homes of Rebel sympathizers.

Breathitt County was a border county. Sympathizers on both sides of the

war lived on land next to each other. This divided sympathy led to major feuding between the families.

Captain Strong fought with the Callahans, Cockrells, and Littles, among others. In 1874 he took over the courthouse in Jackson, the county seat. The governor sent in state guards to restore order. In 1878, the state troops were called to Jackson when Strong and John Aikman (or Akemon), with their factions, were fighting once more.

Strong and Ed Callahan were enemies whose various supporters fought to the death. Callahan headed up the Ku Klux Klan, also known as the White Caps, which people said was supposed to be a policing organization made up of "respectable" citizens. The opposing faction was called the "Red Strings." The feuding continued until both Strong and Callahan died.

Strong died first. Even as an old man in 1897, people feared having a confrontation with him. One day when he was out in the countryside riding his mule with his little grandson sitting behind him, he came upon six armed men who ambushed him. Two men shot the mule, two shot Captain Bill's legs, and two shot at his chest. When the mule was hit, it fell on top of the little boy. Once Captain Bill was shot to death, one of the men pulled the crying grandson out from under the mule. After assuring the boy that they weren't going to hurt him, the bushwhackers sent him to get his granny to fetch his grandfather for burial.

Eliza Hargis Strong's sister, Mollie Hargis, was the mother of John S. Hargis (though she never married). John S. Hargis married Evaline Britton Sewell. They had five children, the third one being James Hargis ("the king").

In 1898, James B. Marcum, a Republican lawyer and nephew of Captain Bill Strong, accused James Hargis, a former school superintendent, of voter fraud. He alleged that Hargis tried to get a minor to vote in a school board election. Both James Marcum and James Hargis had bad tempers and drew their weapons on each other. Luckily, cooler heads prevailed. Neither man fired upon the other. No one was hurt or killed that day, but the accusation was not forgotten. Former friends, and distant relatives, Marcum and Hargis became avowed enemies until the day they died.

In 1902, James Hargis ran as the Democratic candidate for county judge. Ed Callahan ran on the same ticket for sheriff. Some Democrats crossed over and voted for Republicans in what they called a "Fusionist" ticket. Hargis and Callahan won, but only by a few votes. They were quickly accused of election fraud, not such a far-fetched idea. Marcum and his longtime law partner, O. H. Pollard, split up over this election. Marcum represented the "Fusionists" and Pollard the Democrats.

Though Breathitt County had been Unionist (Republican) during the

Civil War, the tide seemed to be turning, with more and more locals becoming active Democrats. This change may have been related to the KKK. It grew in membership because of post–Civil War policies that included rather high-handed practices by Union officers in the treatment of folks who had been loyal. Also, many people were unhappy that their slaves had been freed without the federal government compensating them. That, coupled with the bad behavior of the former slaves and the Union commanders, may have been another cause of the political shift.

At any rate, Democrats Hargis and Callahan were having their depositions taken in Attorney Marcum's office concerning the alleged election fraud when their lawyer, Pollard, Marcum's former partner, made an objection. Marcum took offense at Pollard's objection. The two men argued vehemently and came close to fisticuffs. The two Democrats drew their guns, but neither fired. Marcum terminated the depositions and ordered everyone to leave his office. Police Judge T. P. Cardwell issued arrest warrants for everyone who had drawn a weapon. Marcum went to court and paid a fine for drawing his gun, but James Hargis, who was also an avowed enemy of the police judge, refused to be tried for the offense.

The town marshal was Tom Cockrell, a young man still under the age of twenty-one. Cardwell, the police judge, ordered Tom to bring in Hargis. Tom and his brother, Jim Cockrell, went after James Hargis. When Tom placed Hargis under arrest and told him he had to take him in, Hargis went for his gun. Tom beat him to the draw. The sheriff, Ed Callahan, stood close by and drew his gun on Tom. Jim Cockrell then drew down on Callahan. Hargis and Callahan gave up. By the time the party got back to Judge Cardwell, Marcum had dropped the charges. The case was thrown out, but there were still hard feelings all around.

In spite of Marcum's apparent effort to settle things, a few months later, Marcum and Callahan had another argument, this time about a school election. Just after they had settled the new argument, Callahan was accused of killing Marcum's uncle. In return, Callahan accused Marcum of assassinating his father.

Events continued to escalate. Town Marshal Tom Cockrell and Ben Hargis, one of County Judge James Hargis' brothers, got into an argument in an illegal saloon, called a "blind tiger." (Breathitt County had been dry since 1871.) The shootout took place just like those depicted in the movies years later. The two men drew down on each other, and Ben Hargis was killed. Judge James Hargis and another brother, State Senator Alex Hargis, brought murder charges against Tom Cockrell.

Dr. D. B. Cox now found himself involved in the escalating feud. The legal guardian of all of the Cockrell children, it fell to Cox to hire a lawyer for Tom Cockrell. Dr. Cox was married to Police Judge Cardwell's sister. There is a story that John Hargis had also been in love with Cardwell's sister. Jerry Cardwell, a cousin of Judge Cardwell's, shot and killed John Hargis in 1897. Jerry Cardwell had been a railroad detective. When he tried to arrest "Tige" Hargis on the train for disorderly conduct, a gun battle ensued. John Hargis ended up dead. Though the trial judge sentenced Cardwell to two years in prison, the governor pardoned him. Jerry Cardwell moved to Wolfe County as soon as he was freed.

Some people say the Cox/Cardwell/Hargis love triangle had started the feuding, not the election contest. Still others thought the feuding started over a piece of land, with a Hargis half-brother being killed by Jerry South in 1900.

When Dr. Cox found himself in the position of having to hire an attorney, he turned to none other than the Republican James Marcum, who agreed to represent Tom Cockrell *pro bono* (for free). Marcum, an avowed enemy of the Hargis family, representing Cockrell, who had killed a Hargis, did not sit well with the Hargis side of the feud.

In this feud, relatives were pitted against relatives. Senator Alex Hargis was married to J. B. Marcum's niece. Tom and Jim Cockrell's maternal uncle was Curtis Jett's father. Jett's mother was a half-sister of the Hargis brothers.

Curtis Jett turned out to be the wild card in the equation. He engaged in violence for the fun of it. He was also one of Ed Callahan's deputies.

Two weeks after John Hargis was killed, Elbert Hargis, a half-brother of County Judge James Hargis, was ambushed and killed in his own yard. A few days later, Dr. Cox received a message to go to a sick woman. He was ambushed and killed on the corner across from the courthouse, opposite Judge Hargis' stable. Judge Hargis and Sheriff Callahan stood watching from the second floor of the Hargis house. They claimed not to have heard or seen anything.

Jim Cockrell became town marshal after his brother Tom was charged. One night he and Curtis Jett had words in the Arlington Hotel. There was a shootout. Although the hotel was badly damaged, neither man was injured. A few days later, though, Jim Cockrell was assassinated by a shot from a second-floor window of the courthouse. Some say Judge Hargis and Sheriff Callahan were standing on the second floor of Judge Hargis' general store and saw Cockrell get shot. If they did, they took no action to help him.

Curtis (known as Curt) Jett was reputed to have committed the murder of Jim Cockrell and hidden in the courthouse until late at night, when friends brought him a horse and supplies so he could get away. Jett, a tall, blue-eyed redhead, had a record of arrests for shootings, disorderly conduct, and two rapes, but had never been seriously punished.

Because Judge Hargis was related to the deceased Ben Hargis, a motion to recuse him from Tom Cockrell's murder trial was filed. Another judge, Ira Julian of Frankfort, Kentucky, granted a change of venue. The case was tried in Campton, Wolfe County, where Jerry Cardwell had moved. Judge Hargis and his brother, Senator Alex Hargis, refused to travel to Campton for the trial. Wolfe County was quite a distance to travel on horseback. The countryside was dense and desolate in areas. The two men knew they would be ambushed along the way, so they didn't go. Judge Julian dismissed the murder charges against Cockrell.

In 1903, J. B. Marcum, who had heard a rumor that he was to be killed, used to take his little grandson (or son, this is unclear) to work with him every day so that no one would shoot at him. On May 4, however, he went to the courthouse to file some papers and afterward, as he stood talking to a friend, Curtis Jett shot him to death. Jett, not being sure he had killed the man, ran up to Marcum and put a final bullet directly into his head while Marcum's friend, Captain Benjamin Ewen, ran for cover. Across the street, Judge Hargis and Sheriff Callahan sat in rocking chairs inside the Hargis store and watched.

Jett and another man were arrested, indicted, and tried for Marcum's murder. Both were sentenced to life in prison. Hargis and Callahan were charged for complicity in Marcum's murder but were acquitted. Mrs. Marcum sued them in civil court for her husband's death and won a judgment for $8,000, which Judge Hargis paid before he died.

Judge Hargis was as violent at home as he was in his political life. He often beat his son, Beauchamp Cooper Hargis, known as "Beach" (sometimes misspelled Beech), not only when Beach was a child but even after he grew up. Judge Hargis had been known to pistol-whip the young man, beat his head on the floor, and whip him with a rope. Beach hated his father. He was his mother's favorite child. She spoiled him rotten as he was growing up, and the judge couldn't discipline him without getting violent. Judge Hargis' favorite child was their daughter, Evaline.

Early in February 1908, after Judge Hargis had retired, he and Beach, now twenty-two, got into another fight. Beach drew a gun on his father. The old man beat him severely. Shortly afterward, on February 6, 1908, Beach went out and got drunk before going to the family store. James Hargis, enraged that his son would come to the store drunk, argued with his son once more, this time about his heavy drinking. Beach pulled out a pistol and shot his father five times, killing him right in front of customers. The town marshal arrived after it was all over. Beach raged and fought with Marshal Smith, but he was eventually arrested and dragged, kicking and screaming, to the jail.

Judge Hargis had special-ordered his own coffin not a month before his death. Either he'd had a premonition or else he knew the odds were against him. After thirty-eight killings in the county during his tenure as county judge, his number would have to be up soon.

Beach was permitted to leave the jail and view his father in his coffin. He kneeled next to it, sobbing and crying out, "Lord, have mercy," and his mother came and kneeled beside him. Judge Hargis was buried next to his three brothers, who had all died from gunshot wounds inflicted by their political enemies.

Hargis' tombstone. (Photo by author)

Mrs. Hargis raised $89,000 to pay for her son's defense. A long list of reputable attorneys, including a former governor, a judge, and four other lawyers, defended Beach. The first trial ended in a hung jury. Beach was released to his mother on a $25,000 bond, which his mother, her brothers, and several friends signed for him.

During his freedom, Beach drank and terrorized the town. He threatened to kill one of his cousins. Eventually, early in 1909, his bondsman surrendered him. He spent the rest of the time before his second trial in jail. Upon retrial, Beach was convicted and sentenced to life in prison. When paroled, Beach went home to Jackson to live.

In 1913, Ed Callahan was ambushed outside his home, thus ending the era of feuding in Bloody Breathitt County.

Chapter 2

Judge Thornton L. Massie
Hillsville, Carroll County, Virginia
March 14, 1912

The hills of Virginia are full of stories of historic feuds between families and political factions. One of the oldest families is the Allen family, which can be traced back to 1476 in Ireland. William Allen, Sr., who was born in 1725 and died in 1788, sired the early Virginia family. His youngest son, William Allen, Jr., moved to Carroll County (formerly Henry County), Virginia, and got a land grant of 400 acres in 1791.

In 1912, the Republican Party dominated Carroll County. The Allens were Democrats, though many of their friends were Republicans. The Allens were business owners and farmers, and some had been soldiers. Floyd and Jasper Allen often ran for and were elected to township offices such as constable and supervisor even though they were Democrats.

The Allens also had their share of enemies. There were folks who were envious of the family's stature in the community, including some who would take every opportunity to publicly embarrass them. Two such persons were the county prosecutor, W. M. Foster, and the court clerk, Dexter Goad.

On one occasion in the spring of 1911, on a Saturday night, Wesley Edwards, a nephew of Sidna and Floyd Allen, and a boy named Thomas had an argument. The following Sunday morning, Wesley was at his uncle Garland Allen's church services, which were held in a schoolhouse. Wesley was singing hymns when another boy beckoned to him and called him out. Wesley went outside, walked thirty or forty yards from the schoolhouse, and met up with the Thomas boy and two other boys (making four in all). Another argument started, and all four boys jumped Wesley. Wesley's brother, Sidna Edwards, heard the ruckus, went outside, and jumped into the fight. Subsequently, the Thomas boy and his three friends filed charges on

Wesley and Sidna Edwards for disturbing religious services and fighting. The prosecutor, W. M. Foster, the enemy of Floyd Allen, got Floyd's nephews indicted by the grand jury. The other four boys had no charges filed on them.

Floyd Allen was the family patriarch. He had helped raise the two young men, who were in their early twenties at the time. Since their father had died, they had developed a close relationship with their uncle Floyd. When the boys found themselves in trouble, they went him, but he was sick. Unable to help them with their problem, he told them to leave the state until he could make their bond. The boys rode south of Hillsville, down to North Carolina.

When Floyd got better, he rode into Hillsville, made the boys' bond, and headed down to fetch the boys. On his way, Floyd came upon Deputies Pink Samuels and Peter Easter, who had ridden across the state line and taken the boys into custody without proper "requisition" papers, making it an illegal arrest. Not only that, but the deputies had tied up Floyd's nephews like common outlaws when neither of them had ever been in trouble before. The charges against them were merely misdemeanors. Floyd was offended and angry at the deputies who had handcuffed his nephews and tied them to the buggy in which they rode. It was clear to Floyd that the way the boys were being treated was designed to humiliate the Allen family. The officers were hostile to Floyd. Additionally, it was clear that the deputies had deliberately taken the Fancy Gap Road, which ran in front of Sidna Allen's store, just to be sure that Sidna and other Allens would witness the humiliation. When Floyd Allen saw how the boys were being treated, he told the deputy to untie and unmanacle the boys, that there was no call to treat them so badly. After Floyd asked them a second time, the deputies released the boys but then refused to take them into town. One deputy pulled a gun on Floyd, but Floyd took it away from him and smashed it to pieces. The deputies rode into town and charged Floyd with interfering with a peace officer.

Floyd posted his bond and was indicted, and the trial was scheduled, setting the scene for tragedy. Sidna Allen, in front of whose store this whole event took place, was also indicted, though he had no part in the incident. Barnard Allen, who was working for Sidna Allen that day, was also indicted, though he was later tried and acquitted. The charges on Sidna were specious, and thus he was never tried for them.

Before Floyd ever came to trial for the charge of interfering with a peace officer, both Wesley and Sidna Edwards were tried on their misdemeanor charge. They received thirty days in jail, which was considered pretty stiff, but had completed their sentence by the time of Floyd's trial.

Judge Thornton L. Massie, age forty-eight, presided at Floyd's trial.

Judge Massie had been appointed to the 21st Circuit Court by the governor in 1908 to succeed Judge R. C. Jackson. He had moved to Pulaski, Virginia, around the time he began to practice law, and made a home there with his family. His wife, the former Mamie Nicholson of Kentucky, two sons, P. Cabell Massie and Wilbur Massie, and a daughter, socialite Mary Bentley Massie, all lived in Pulaski. His brother, Robert W. Massie, was a prominent citizen of Lynchburg, Virginia, and the owner of Massie-Pierce Lumber Company. Another brother, Withers Massie, lived in Massie's Mills. According to *The Roanoke Times*, Judge Massie was being considered to fill a vacancy on the Virginia Supreme Court left by Justice Buchanan.

The case was tried on March 13, 1912. Floyd's enemy, W. M. Foster, prosecuted, while Dexter Goad officiated as clerk of the court. Floyd Allen's lawyers were Judge D. W. Bolen and Walter Tipton. When he testified, Floyd admitted requesting that the boys be released but denied using any force on the two deputies. At the end of the day, the jury could not reach a verdict, so the trial was recessed until the following day. Floyd stayed the night at his brother Sidna Allen's home.

The next morning, Floyd and Sidna overslept. By the time they arrived at the courthouse, the jury had reached a verdict. Judge Massie asked Floyd to stand and, when he did, Judge Massie sentenced him to one year in prison.

Floyd's attorneys asked the judge set aside the verdict; they were going to file a motion and would like to argue it the next morning. They requested that the judge set a bond for Floyd so that he wouldn't have to spend any time in jail. Judge Massie said that he could not release Floyd on bond now that he'd been convicted and sentenced, even though Floyd had always presented himself for every court appearance. The attorneys told the judge that they would file a motion for a new trial based on newly discovered evidence—some witnesses that Floyd had wanted to call hadn't testified. Judge Massie, who had always been a fair man, said that he would like to hear from the witnesses. Claude Allen, Floyd's son, went over to Floyd's table, where Floyd and he discussed which witnesses Claude should fetch. Claude turned and walked away.

Sidna Allen recalled that he was talking with a man by the name of John Moore, with whom he did business. Just after Claude had walked past John and him, a shot rang out. The shot came from where Dexter Goad and the sheriff, Lew Webb, stood. Guns glinted in their hands. They were aimed at Floyd. Sidna was left-handed, and John Moore was on his left. Moore later made a statement that Sidna didn't pull his gun, which was on his left side, until the shooting had already started.

Floyd took a bullet in his thigh and fell to the floor. The day had dawned

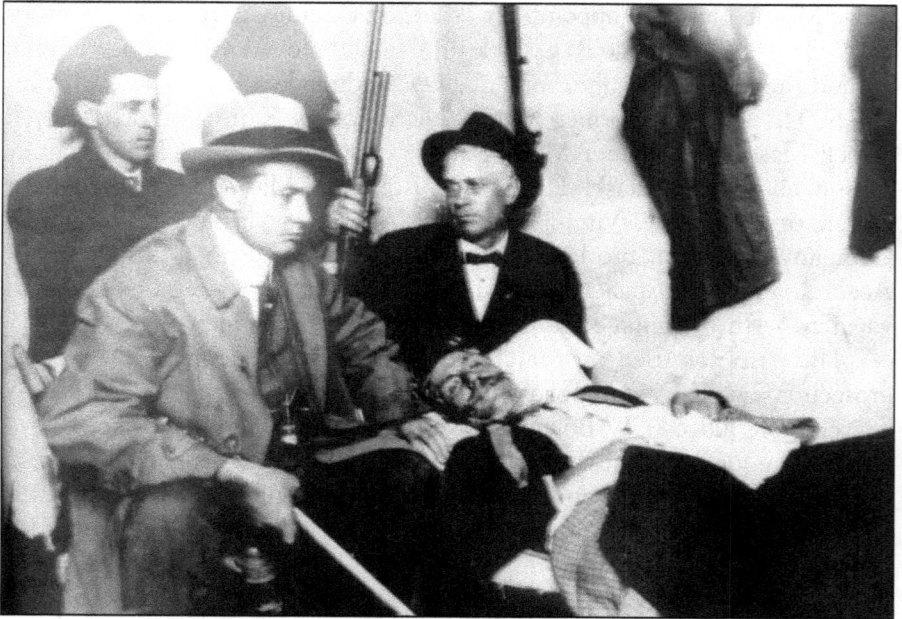

Authorities and Floyd Allen after shootout.

overcast and gloomy. Gunfire flashed all over the courtroom. Clouds of smoke filled the room. Sidna recounted, "When guns were fired long streams of flame flashed out from their muzzles, lighting up the courtroom as lightning illuminates cloud banks at night."

Sidna fired at Dexter Goad, who seemed to be shooting at him, though neither hit the other. Sidna reloaded at one point when the shooting seemed like it would never stop. Finally, it did stop. He turned to run out of the building. A deputy sheriff fired at him, and Sidna fired back. When he got outside, someone else started shooting at him. It was Dexter Goad. Again Sidna fired back but didn't think he ever hit him.

When the shooting stopped, Judge Thornton L. Massie, Sheriff Lew Webb, Commonwealth Attorney W. M. Foster, Juror C. C. Fowler, and a witness, Betty Ayers, lay dead. Several other people were wounded.

Floyd Allen dragged himself out into the courtyard. His brother Sidna, Sidna's son Claude, Wesley Edwards, and Friel Allen, brother Jasper's son, joined him. They held a powwow and realized that no Democrat, especially an Allen, would receive justice in Hillsville, Virginia. They decided to flee. Floyd, unable to mount his horse, was left in the arms of his sister, Alvirtia Edwards, Wesley and Sidna Edwards' mother. Her son, Victor Edwards, who had taken no part in the shootout, also remained behind. The rest of the

Allen family headed for the hills. They were immediately blamed for shooting first and killing all five people. Authorities immediately arrested Floyd. It is questionable whether he ever fired a shot.

The four Allens who fled decided to separate and meet at Jasper Allen's that night. Three of them appeared and stayed with Jasper, but Claude Allen never showed. They agreed not to turn themselves in, knowing they would not get a fair trial. Sidna Edwards had not fled with the others. He never fired a shot but was also blamed. He eventually turned himself in. Claude stayed in hiding for seven days and was captured.

Immediately after the shooting, the Republicans blamed the Democrats. The Allens were portrayed as villains, outlaws, and gangsters. The press had a field day, printing wild, mostly untrue stories. Posses roamed the hills for months looking for the Allens. The Baldwin-Felts Detective Agency of Roanoke, Virginia, headed one such posse. Huge rewards were offered for the "outlaws." So many armed "deputies" were brought into Hillsville that the village began to look like an armed garrison.

At noon, two days after the shooting, a special train full of prominent citizens from Pulaski, Virginia, left that city and traveled to Hillsville. There they retrieved the body of the revered judge and took him home for burial.

Sidna Allen and Wesley Edwards stuck together. They knew the hills and, with the assistance of their friends and relatives, managed to hide out for weeks. Sidna Edwards and Friel Allen grew tired of hiding and surrendered after a week. Although only seventeen, Friel was later tried and sentenced to eighteen years in prison. Sidna Edwards was sentenced to fifteen years in prison.

Sidna Allen related later that he and Wesley had watched the posses as they circled the hills looking for them. They evaded capture in the hills surrounding Hillsville for five weeks before taking a train and ending up in Des Moines, Iowa. They moved into a boarding house and got jobs as carpenters. Sidna assumed the name of Tom Sayers. Wesley assumed the name of Joe Jackson. After a few months, Wesley got lonely for his girlfriend and decided to sneak back to Virginia to see her. Sidna advised against it, feeling that it would lead to their capture, but Wesley couldn't resist the urge.

It wasn't long before Wesley returned all aglow. His girl was soon going to join him in Des Moines so they could be married. Sidna knew they were doomed. One day, while writing a letter, Sidna heard a commotion from the landlady and someone in the hall. He looked up to find a Baldwin-Felts Detective Agency operative who immediately placed him under arrest. They arrested Wesley a few hours later on a streetcar. The pair found out later that Wesley's girlfriend betrayed them to the detectives and led them to Des

Moines. For that, they paid her a few hundred dollars that she quickly used to marry another man.

In the meantime, Floyd and his son, Claude, were tried and sentenced to death. They never had a chance with the trial being scheduled so close to the time of the shooting. Sentiments ran high. The Republicans in control of the courthouse gave their versions. The convictions were quick and easy. Many of the Allens' friends intervened on their behalf, trying to save them from the electric chair, but it wasn't to be. Even though their friends appealed to the governor, he refused to grant a reprieve. They had been convicted of conspiracy, and a conspiracy charge carried the death penalty.

Authorities housed Sidna and Wesley in the Roanoke jail. In the days be-

Photo of Judge Massie and two other court officials.

fore automobiles, the distance was too great for their families to visit. Neither man had money to pay for his defense, including witness expenses. Friends and relatives hired some well-known lawyers to represent them, but the county attached Sidna's property, including his home, for costs. When the government took Sidna's house, his wife and two daughters were thrown out into the street. Both men felt rather hopeless in light of Floyd's and Claude's sentences.

The first bit of good news the pair received was that their case had been transferred to Wytheville, Virginia. They felt that they had a better chance of a fair trial there, where their enemies in Hillsville didn't control the courthouse. The government charged Sidna and Wesley with conspiracy and with the death of each of the decedents. A conviction for the conspiracy charge could result in their execution in the electric chair.

On September 22, 1912, the two were taken to Hillsville and arraigned.

On November 6, 1912, they were taken to Wytheville for trial. Judge Waller R. Staples of Roanoke presided. The first trial was for the death of Judge Massie. The jury was chosen from Giles County rather than Carroll County. Sidna later said that he was very happy with the panel chosen for this trial. The trial hadn't begun, though, when one of his lawyers (in fact one who had been selected against his wishes by the others representing him) stood in open court and made a motion to have the jury dismissed. The prosecutor agreed, and even after objections by Sidna and the other attorneys, the judge granted the motion. Sidna's wife and some of the lawyers were told later that the Giles County people had come to Wytheville in the hopes of being selected for jury duty because they were going to make sure that at least one Allen got a fair trial. The general sentiment in Giles County was that Floyd and Claude had gotten a raw deal.

The second venire was from Grayson County. A jury was selected. After evidence was taken, the jury deliberated for two days and returned with a compromise verdict of fifteen years. Sidna, thinking there was not enough evidence to convict, was shocked by the sentence. The next trial against Sidna was for the killing of William M. Foster. Seventy-five veniremen from the northeastern counties of Virginia were summoned. Trial was set for December 2. Jury selection was completed by December 3. The trial took until December 10, when it went to the jury at 2:30 P.M. The jury deliberated until the afternoon of December 11, finally returning a verdict of voluntary manslaughter and a sentence of five years. Again Sidna was surprised, for again, he thought he would be acquitted.

The third trial, for the killing of Sheriff Webb, was scheduled next. Even though Sheriff Webb had stood across the courtroom from Sidna, and Sheriff Webb had been shot in the back, Sidna was charged with his murder. Sidna already had twenty years stacked against him and, figuring he wouldn't live to do the twenty, offered to plead guilty. For the killing of Sheriff Webb, he was sentenced to fifteen years, making a total thirty-five years. (The judge ordered that the sentences run consecutively, which is called "stacking" the sentences, like pancakes. In modern times most sentences run concurrently, but there is no hard-and-fast rule about this.)

To avoid the same fate as Sidna, and certainly of Floyd and Claude, Wesley Edwards pled guilty to everything. He was sentenced to twenty-seven years in prison.

Both Sidna and Wesley were sent to the same prison as Floyd, Claude, and Friel Allen and Sidna Edwards. They were all able to see each other in prison. Many thousands of Virginians petitioned the governor to commute Floyd and Claude Allen's sentences. They were first sentenced to die on

November 22, 1912, but Governor Mann granted a stay of execution until December 13. That stay was extended until January 17, 1913, and then again until March 7. On March 6, the governor refused to commute their sentences and set their execution date.

Nothing any of the family and friends could do stopped the execution. Floyd and Claude were executed on March 28, 1913. They were buried next to each other at the foot of the Blue Ridge Mountains. Thousands of people attended the funeral. Claude's casket was opened, and a medal, awarded to him by the ladies of southwest Virginia "For Bravery in Defending His Father," was removed from Claude's lapel and given to his girlfriend. Floyd's wife moved away from Virginia and never returned.

Four days after he arrived at the prison, Sidna Allen was named foreman of the carpentry shop. Later, when the prison opened a woodworking shop, he was made foreman of that shop. The prison allowed Sidna to work on his own projects in his spare time. He constructed wooden objects. At first, he gave these novelties away as gifts. Later, he sold them. He used the money to pay the debts he owed when he entered the prison and to support his wife and children. He was even known to send money to the needy. He became quite famous for intricately made furniture.

As many as 100,000 people petitioned the governor to pardon the Allens. In 1922, the governor pardoned Friel Allen and Sidna Edwards. He said that he didn't pardon Sidna Allen and Wesley Edwards because they had served very little of their much longer sentences. People were outraged. In 1923, more petitions and letters were written to the governor. Many stressed that grave injustices had been brought upon the Allen and Edwards families, that the shootout had been nothing more than a political feud, and that the Allens had suffered enough.

Eventually, the political tide turned. A new governor, Harry F. Byrd, was elected and took office. Finally, April 29, 1926, Governor Byrd pardoned Sidna Allen and Wesley Edwards. Wesley Edwards went to Richmond, Virginia, where his widowed mother lived. His mother, Mrs. Alvirtia Edwards, had held her brother, Floyd, in her arms after the shootout. Sidna Edwards had also moved there. Victor Allen and his mother, Floyd's widow, moved to New Jersey. Friel Allen moved to California. Sidna Allen first went to Leaksville, North Carolina, to stay with his older brother, Victor Allen.

Leaksville is about eighty-six miles south of Hillsville, Virginia. When Sidna arrived, his wife and his grown daughters arrived from Hillsville to meet him. On the advice of friends, he never moved back to Hillsville. He made his home in Leaksville.

Soon after his pardon, Sidna made his living by showing his handmade furniture, considered works of art. His collection consisted of twenty pieces: four tables, one suitcase, ten treasure boxes, four cups, and a vase. One table contained seventy-nine varieties of wood and took 3,544 hours to make. The wood came from scraps such as hairbrushes, chairs, window sashes, umbrella handles, butter boxes, hoe handles, and gateposts. Another table contained more than 75,000 separate pieces of wood. The suitcase had 386 pieces. The cups each had 130 to 140 pieces. It took eleven years of Sidna's life to make all twenty pieces, which were often referred to as the eighth wonder of the world.

In 1929, Sidna finished his manuscript for *Memoirs of J. Sidna Allen: A True Narrative of What Really Happened at Hillsville, Virginia.* Subsequently, he continued to travel the country and show his collection.

In 1964, two Hillsville, Virginia, men, Randolph F. Surratt and Sam Marshall, signed an affidavit before a notary in which they stated that they had heard a statement made by Woodson Quesinberry, who was deputy clerk of the Circuit Court of Carroll County, Virginia, at the time of the Hillsville tragedy. Quesinberry said that he went to the courthouse on March 12, 1912, with the intention of killing Floyd Allen. He fired the first shot. He further

Carroll County Courthouse. (Photo by author)

stated that he shot Floyd Allen in the hip with a .25 automatic pistol. When all hell broke loose, Woodson Quesinberry fell to the floor.

Today, the Sidna Allen house, which was confiscated by the county (probably illegally), is still in the public domain and may be seen south of Hillsville on the highway to North Carolina. A collection of photographs and news articles may be seen in town at a local museum.

Allen home. (Photo by author)

Ballads

CLAUD ALLEN

Claud Allen and his dear old father
Have met their fatal doom at last.
Their friends are glad their troubles are ended
And hope their souls have gone to their rest.

Claud's mother's tears will gently flow
For the loss of two she loved so dear.
It seems no one can understand her troubles,
No one can feel 'em but her.

Claud Allen's pretty little sweetheart
Is mournin' the one she loved.
But she will meet him beyond the river
She will sure meet him in heaven above.

Claud was young and very handsome,
And he still had hopes up to the end,
That he might in some way or another
Escape his death at Richmond pen.

But the governor being so hard-hearted,
And not caring what his friends might say,
He finally took his sweet life from him
And they laid his body in the clay.

High up on yonder lonely mountain
Claud Allen sleeps beneath the clay.
No more we'll hear his plea for mercy
Nor see his face till Judgment Day.

Come, all you young men, and take warning,
Be careful how you go astray;
Or you might be like poor Claudy Allen
And have that awful debt to pay.

SIDNEY ALLEN [sic]

(Sung to the tune of "Casey Jones")

Come all you people if you want to hear
The story of a cruel mountaineer;
Sidney Allen was the mountaineer's name,
At Hatfield courthouse he won his fame.

Judge called the jury at half past nine;
Sidney Allen was the prisoner, so he was on time.
He mounted to the bar with cocked pistol in his hand
And he sent Judge Massie to the Promised Land.

In just a moment the whole place was in a roar,
Men dead and dying were a-lying on the floor;
With a thirty-eight gun and a thirty-eight ball
Sidney backed the sheriff up against the courthouse wall.

The sheriff saw that he was in a might bad place;
Sydney Allen was a-staring him right in the face;
He turned to the window and then he said,
"Just a moment later and we'll all be dead."

He mounted his pony and away he did ride;
His friends and his neighbors they were riding at his side;
They all shook hands, took an oath that they would hang
    Before they would give up to the sheriff's gang.

Sidney Allen got away and he wandered all around,
    Until that he was captured in a western town.
He was taken to the station dressed in ball and chain
And they put poor Sidney on the east-bound train.

They arrived at Sidney's home about eleven forty-one;
There he met his wife and daughters and two little sons;
    They all shook hands and then they began to pray.
And they prayed, "Oh, Lord, don't take our papa away."

The people gathered 'round from far away and near
    Just to see Sidney sentenced to the electric chair;
        But to their surprise, the judge just said,
    "I'm sending him to the penitentiary instead!"

Chapter 3

Judge Willis Sidney Knowles
Johnston, Providence County, Rhode Island
September 6, 1915

Willis S. Knowles was the second of five children born to Horace and Sophia (Hingington) Knowles on June 30, 1868 (some records say July 1). The Knowles family dated back to early times in America. The descendents of the pioneers moved to Ohio, where many of them remained.

Willis S. Knowles served as a captain for forty years on the steamboat line he owned. It ran between Pittsburgh and Cincinnati. He was a Republican, a bachelor, and a judge for small towns near Providence, Rhode Island. He was educated in the public schools of Ohio, spent three years at Ohio University at Athens, and moved in 1890 to Boston to study law for three years with the Simon Davis law firm. Later, he moved to Providence, where he studied with attorney E.C. Pierce. When Knowles was admitted to the State Bar of Rhode Island in 1898, he opened his own law office. In 1908, he was elected justice of the court.

Judge Knowles presided over the 8th Judicial District, which included the city of Cranston and the towns of Johnston, Scituate, and Foster, today commonly called the Justice of the Peace. He lived in Johnston on the east side of Moswansicut Lake with his housekeeper, Cora Wardwell. Cora was also his sweetheart, though this was not well known. Every morning, Cora walked him out when he left for work. He rode the trolley to and from court.

Over the course of the summer of 1915, Judge Knowles mentioned to several people that he feared there might be trouble over some of the liquor cases that were set for trial in his court. The cases had been filed as criminal matters. A certain element in the county didn't want the cases prosecuted.

Around the beginning of August, when the judge was on his way to catch the trolley, someone fired at him from the bushes that lined the path.

The bullet whistled past him as he walked to the trolley car. That evening when he arrived home, he told Cora the story of the near miss but wrote it off as a stray bullet from a hunter's rifle. It was not hunting season, but he wanted to put on a brave front so as not to alarm her.

Judge Knowles' cottage rested on a knoll about 300 feet from the roadway. Shrubbery hid the roadway from view. The nearest neighbor's house was the town barber's, which had a hill between it and the road.

A bit later in August, rumor had it that the judge received death threats. Because of those threats, when his brother Horace was visiting for the summer, they walked together to and from the trolley stop. When Horace was not present, the judge asked a neighbor to accompany him. That pattern went on for about three weeks. Locals also said that the judge usually wore a sidearm, but others said that wasn't true. It would not have been unusual for those times (and even more recent times).

After Horace Knowles went home, when there had been no other incidents or threats, Willis decided that it was safe to make the trek alone. On September 6, the first day he was to walk by himself, Cora walked him to the gate, kissed him goodbye, and he walked away. Newspapers later quoted her as saying that Judge Knowles was about halfway between the house and the trolley stop when someone fired a shot and called out, "There, you ———."

It is pretty much confirmed that Cora heard the shot and a voice, followed by two more shots. She ran to the gateway and saw Willis Knowles lying on the ground. Running back to the telephone inside the house, she called the farm that was up the lane and told the owner, William Watson, about the shooting. Watson, his daughter, and his son hurried over. They saw no one on their way there. Soon, all the neighbors within hearing distance came running. The judge had been shot twice in the chest and once in the fourth finger of his right hand. He was dead at forty-seven.

About fifty yards from the judge's body lay his satchel full of legal papers and his handkerchief. His hat was in between his body and his briefcase. He had been unarmed. It appeared that a struggle had ensued between the murderer and the judge and that the first bullet went wild, striking the judge in the finger. The second and third bullets were only half an inch apart in his chest.

While the neighbors waited for the police, they kept people from trampling the scene or touching anything that might be a clue. Carrying a basket of fruit, two Italians walked up from the north, and the neighbors detained them. (There had been a lot of immigration around that time, and people were very suspicious of Italians, just as many people are of other minorities today.) When the police arrived, they interviewed the Italians but decided they probably didn't have anything to do with the murder. They arrested the Italians anyway for stealing fruit and one of them for carrying a concealed .38 caliber revolver. Police examined the revolver. Though it was missing one bullet, it had not been fired recently. The Johnston chief of police and a constable, the Cranston chief of police, an inspector, and a deputy sheriff all searched the vicinity of the scene but never located any evidence of value.

The autopsy revealed that the two bullets had caused the death of the judge. One of the bullets lodged in a lung while the other exited the body near the right shoulder blade. The recovered bullet was a .32 caliber. The medical examiner rendered an opinion that the same bullet that struck his finger was the one that lodged in the judge's right lung.

A friend of the judge, former clerk H.T. Bodwell, immediately offered a personal reward of $100. He also revealed that the judge had mentioned to him three times in the recent past that he had concerns about an attack on himself due to some liquor prosecutions currently taking place. Bodwell expressed hopes that someone would come forward with information that would be helpful in the investigation. Unfortunately for the investigators, the judge didn't tell Bodwell specifically which cases he was worried about.

Sheriffs' deputies, acting independently of local town authorities, had raided a number of liquor locations in the judge's judicial district by orders from the governor's office. Friends of the defendants in those raids were rumored to be seeking leniency and hoping the cases would come up when Judge Knowles wasn't on the bench, perhaps when on vacation, but Judge Knowles continued the cases until he knew he would be there. He was well known for enforcing the law to the full extent possible, which is exactly what the defendants were afraid of.

When interviewed, Horace Knowles (the brother), who lived in New York City, said that during the five weeks that he had spent with Willis, he had never heard anything to give credence to the rumors of threats. He said there were many days when Willis walked alone to the trolley. Horace only accompanied Willis partway on the days that Horace went fishing. He also denied that Willis ever carried a weapon. Horace told police investigators that he and his brother had spent a great deal of time talking during his visit. Never had his brother mentioned any concerns about his safety.

Judge Knowles' brothers claimed his body and took it to Torch, Ohio, where their father lived, for burial. They also hired two private investigators, who were to begin work as soon as the burial was done.

The acting governor offered $1,000, and with other rewards offered the total came to $2,100—quite a sum for 1915. During the investigation, Marshal Salisbury, a friend of the decedent's who was assisting in the investigation, received threats that if he didn't cease and desist from investigation, he would "get his." Salisbury refused to divulge the source of the threats to the press; however, the authorities checked it out.

A few days after the murder, police returned to the murder scene for another examination and discovered that someone had trimmed the bushes and cut down three saplings on the path that the judge would have to take to the trolley. The assassin would have been able to lie behind the bushes with a clear view all the way to the judge's house. The assailant would also have a clear avenue of escape over a hill without anyone being able to see him or her from the road behind the screen of bushes.

Upon another examination of Cora Wardwell, they learned that the voice she had heard issuing an expletive had actually been the judge's. She had been misunderstood during her first interview. When the judge realized that he was about to be shot, he said a word that ordinarily would not be repeated publicly by an official.

Another part of the investigation revealed a discrepancy of about fifteen minutes between the time Cora said the shots were fired and the time of the phone call she made to the neighbor.

On September 13, police pulled Cora in for questioning again. Ms. Wardwell, who was divorced for many years, had worked for the judge for a long time. The police told her that Judge Knowles was engaged to another woman. Cora reportedly burst into tears, saying that she couldn't believe he could have treated her the way he had all those years she worked for him and be engaged to another woman. She denied that she knew he was in such a relationship and admitted her love for the judge. She stated that on the morning of his death she walked him down to the gate and kissed him good-bye. She had walked back to the house, heard the shots, and rushed back, finding his body lying on the ground. She then ran back to call the doctor. Her original story was that she called the neighbor first. Upon this last examination, she stated that on the day of the murder she was so upset that she was confused about who she had called first.

When Judge Knowles' estate was settled, it turned out that he had left a will dated September 14, 1911, four years before his murder, leaving his farm to Cora Etta Wardwell. He also left her "all the household 'goods furniture' farming implements wagons buggies harness boats and all my property located at my farm on said Hopkins Avenue in said Town of Johnston . . ." This address is where they both resided at the time of his death. It appears unlikely that there was actually another fiancée. The police most likely used the ploy of telling Ms. Wardwell the story of the fiancée to see if they could extract more information from her.

The remainder of the judge's estate, which was set out in an inventory filed in the probate records at Cranston City Hall, consisted of a small amount of cash, some jewelry, and office furnishings. These things were left to his father, brothers, and sister. Additionally, there was an accidental death insurance policy of $5,000, which his brother Horace, as executor of the estate, filed suit upon. The court ruled against the family, finding that the death was not accidental.

Per the July 17, 1937, edition of *The Providence Journal*, more than twenty years after Judge Knowles' murder, this case remains one of Rhode Island's "great unsolved" mysteries.

Chapter 4

Judge W. Thomas Lawler
Huntsville, Madison County, Alabama
June 14, 1916

Just after the Democratic primary election of May 9, 1916, in Madison County, Alabama, a grand jury was empaneled. The grand jury's charge: to investigate whether longtime probate judge W. T. Lawler engaged in election fraud in the defeat of his opponent, David D. Overton. Overton was the second most powerful man in the county.

The office of probate judge was said to be the best job in the county. Judge Lawler had been the probate judge for twelve years. Besides collecting fees which amounted to more than $60,000 a year, the probate judge controlled the disposition of road contracts, was chairman of the Board of Commissioners, and was the official in charge of directing the maintenance of the roads. Additionally, Judge Lawler handled estates, wills and probate, deeds, notes, mortgages, and other instruments recorded on the county books.

David D. Overton campaigned against Judge Lawler on the basis that Lawler engaged in numerous voter fraud offenses, including vote buying. He alleged that Madison County was the rottenest county in the state. Lawler charged Overton with being the head of the bootlegging operation in the county. He said he had evidence that one Chattanooga shipping house had supplied Overton with $90,000 worth of liquor in 1916 alone.

Overton was in charge of the election machinery. On the night before the election, many of the official ballots that were stored in the courthouse disappeared. Judge Lawler figured that this was an attempt by Overton and his men to stuff the ballot boxes. Lawler had new ballots printed in a different color.

The grand jury was ready to hand down ten true bills against Judge Lawler and recommend his impeachment when Judge Lawler turned up

25

missing. His family last saw Judge Lawler on Wednesday evening, June 14. Mrs. Lawler reported that she and her husband had been engaged in some social activities, including visiting his sister, each evening. On Wednesday, Judge Lawler told her that he had a meeting uptown and would hurry, meet the man, and then catch up with her. He didn't return, and, as he was a person of regular habits, Mrs. Lawler thought it unusual, but she was not alarmed. She thought he had probably gone off with some of his relatives who were visiting the city and would soon let her know where he was.

Mrs. Lawler remembered that Judge Lawler had received a note asking him to go to the county courthouse. He didn't show up the following day, so a search ensued. His car stood where he had left it. His glasses case lay on the paved street.

Several days later, the sheriff received an anonymous note that said that if the creek (at that time often called a "slough" or a "bog") were dragged, they would find something interesting. Three days after he was missed, Judge Lawler's body turned up ten miles south of Huntsville. He had two bullet holes in his heart and his skull was crushed. As it turned out, he was shot to death on June 14. The perpetrators weighted down his body with railroad iron and threw it into the mouth of a creek that empties into the Tennessee River.

David D. Overton, the former circuit court clerk and former chief of police of Huntsville, disappeared next, but authorities didn't suspect foul play. He had fled the jurisdiction of the court. The district attorney impaneled a special grand jury that indicted Overton as the principal in the judge's murder. The grand jury also indicted Charles M. Nalls, Madison County circuit clerk, and Percy Brooks, a ferryman and prominent farmer, as accessories to the crime. Both were promptly arrested and kept separated from the public so that no one knew their stories. Nalls and Brooks testified to the grand jury, but, since those proceedings are secret, the evidence they gave was also kept secret.

On June 21, Shelby S. Pleasants, a prominent member of the bar and former assistant district attorney, was linked to the case and committed suicide. Two days later, on June 23, 1916, Sheriff Robert Phillips shot and killed himself at the county jail. The sheriff left a note saying that he had been suspected of the murder but that he was innocent. The contents of the note were as follows:

Dear Wife—The day this horrible crime was committed that night I went to serve a summons and Marcus and I stopped and went on

26

Brooks' new boat. I suppose they suspect me in this dirty act and it is more than I can stand and live under.

This man I thought a gentleman has had me fooled so long. I don't want the stain on my children. I can't stand to be accused of such a crime. I like Judge Lawler, although I worked for the other man, but I was fooled in him and the people blamed me because he fooled me.

I want Lonnie to wind my business up and after paying the bank out of my estate, I want you to do the best you can for Marcus and the baby and all the rest and don't grieve after me, for I hope I will go to rest for the good God knows I am free from doing any harm to Judge Lawler. I pray that the guilty be brought to justice—those who brought me this trouble—and it is more than I can stand. Well, good-bye. I hope to meet you all beyond. I can't afford to live here and be looked at as a murderer, when God knows I am as innocent as the angels in heaven. Will say good-bye once more. Be good and try to raise the sweet ones right— God bless them. May the good Lord forgive me, for this is my prayer. Good-bye, dear wife, children and friends.

Subsequent to the sheriff's suicide, A. D. Kirby, Huntsville chief of police, resigned from office because the grand jury accused him of allowing his cab line to be used to haul whiskey from the Tennessee River to Huntsville for the "bootleg" trade in the city. There was not enough evidence presented for the grand jury to indict Kirby for illegal bootleg activity. Evidence was presented, however, that David Overton was the leader of the bootleggers. The Alabama Attorney General's Office took over the investigation, assigning three attorneys to the case, including the grand jury investigation into the murder, suicides, and bootleg operations.

In order to keep the peace in Huntsville and in Madison County as a whole, two companies of state militia were stationed in Huntsville during the grand jury investigation. Several times, squads of soldiers accompanied detectives out into the countryside in search of Overton, but there wasn't ever any violence in the countryside or any real danger of mob violence in the city against the defendants.

DeKalb County, Tennessee, sheriff G. C. Pucket captured David Overton in Smithville, Tennessee, after Overton had been on the run for more than three months. Although he claimed to be an insurance agent, had about ten days' growth of facial hair, and had lost about forty pounds, he fit the description of Overton down to the scar on his left cheek. He told Sheriff Pucket that he recognized someone else as David Overton, who had hired a horse and buggy to flee. Once detained by the sheriff, he submitted to arrest but then tried to make a break when he was being transferred to the sheriff's vehicle. The sheriff fired at him but missed. Overton, fleeing the sheriff, ran into a tree and was stunned long enough for the sheriff to overpower him. He had no identifying papers on him but did have $315. He said, "Well, I guess you have the right man."

The new Huntsville police chief, Alex Dyas, went to Smithville and identified the defendant. The sheriff refused to turn Overton over to Alabama authorities until he was paid the $1,500 reward that had been offered for Overton's arrest. Meantime, Overton resisted extradition (which at the time in Alabama was called "requisition"). He was eventually taken to the Montgomery County Jail, where he was held until trial.

Judge B. M. Miller, a judge from another jurisdiction, was assigned to the case. Out of concern for the safety of the citizenry, he made a rule that everyone would be searched for weapons before being admitted to the courtroom.

The state arraigned Overton in mid-November. The trial took place shortly thereafter. His sentence: death by hanging on January 12, 1917. Overton immediately filed a notice of appeal to the Alabama Supreme Court.

Subsequent to his trial and sentencing, Overton and a group of jail inmates, including an "Italian murderer," escaped the Jefferson County Jail on March 20, 1917. It was a planned escape, with Overton overpowering a deputy at the point of a pistol, locking him in a cell, and walking out of the jail to a waiting automobile. Posses comprised of sheriff's deputies, police officers, and detectives gave chase, dividing up and going to all the nearby towns and cities.

Overton's group split up at one point. Some of the fugitives were in a Ford, which was found abandoned near Odenville. Overton and his wife rode in a Packard that disappeared north of Odenville while heading toward Gadsden. Eventually they were hunted down and found in Birmingham. A huge gun battle lasting several hours took place in a thicket behind Birmingham College. David Overton was shot to death in the shootout, which continued with the other convicts for quite a while. "The Italian murderer, Malino," also was killed, and "the forger, Latham" was wounded and later died. Several of the others were wounded and hid out for days. Police eventually recaptured them. The escape turned out to be an inside job by jail guards, including the sheriff's brother.

An interesting side note to the whole issue of corrupt government officials in Huntsville, Madison County, Alabama: After the indictment and murder of Judge Lawler, the citizens of Huntsville held several meetings on "good government." They discussed the commissioner form of government that they had at that time, as opposed to the mayor/alderman (councilman) form and the council-manager form. They held an election and changed their government to the mayor/alderman form. The voters cleaned house. All office holders were defeated. Completely new faces took over as mayor and eight aldermen. When it came time for the newly elected officials to assume office, the changeover was done peacefully, much to the pleasant surprise of most folks.

Chapter 5

Judge W. H. Parker
Collinsville, Lauderdale County, Mississippi
November 6, 1920

Former justice of the peace W. H. "Bill" Parker of Collinsville, Mississippi, agreed to go with his friend Walter Gibson to the home of identical twins Paul and Claude Houston. Parker hoped to help settle a dispute over some cows.

The Houston twins alleged that Gibson's brother's cows had encroached on their property and caused extensive damage. The Houstons had penned up the cows on their lot until the Gibsons paid for the damage. Two of the younger Gibsons, Sam and Tom, had gone to a neighbor's home to find out whether the Houstons had borrowed a shotgun from the neighbors. If they had borrowed a shotgun, then the Gibsons would have known to expect trouble. When they found out that the Houstons hadn't borrowed the shotgun, the Gibson boys opened the pen and freed the cows. These younger Gibsons were on their way back home by a back road when they heard an argument and cursing and ran toward the commotion. Their brother Walter had asked Judge Parker to go with him to help resolve the disagreement, something Parker had experience in doing all the years he was a justice of the peace. Bill Parker and Walter Gibson were walking to the Houston home when they came across Claude and Paul Houston in the road, trying to pen up the cows again. They got into an argument.

The Gibson side thought that the dollar amount of damages the Houstons asked for was excessive. The Houstons alleged that the cattle had done a lot of destruction and the dollar amount would just cover the damages.

Claude Houston grew overly excited and began cursing wildly. Judge Parker cursed Claude back. Claude used words so vile that they offended the judge. Parker asked Claude not to repeat some of the words that he had used.

Claude yelled the words again, at which time Judge Parker turned and reached into his hip pocket as if to draw a weapon. Paul Houston witnessed the event. When he saw the judge appear to draw a weapon, he called out a warning to his brother Claude. Claude pulled a knife and stabbed Judge Parker in the neck. The knife pierced the judge's jugular vein. By the time Sam and Tom reached their brother Walter, he was walking toward them, carrying Judge Parker's dead body.

Judge Parker was sixty when he died. His survivors included his wife, three daughters, and three sons.

Sheriff Martin arrested both Houstons, who were forty at the time of the incident. They went peacefully. Claude Houston was charged with murder. Paul Houston was charged as an accessory. At a trial held in March 1921, Claude Houston was tried for murder and found guilty. The judge sentenced him to life in prison. The following day, Paul Houston went to trial. The prosecution presented the same evidence, except that Walter Gibson testified that Paul Houston egged his brother on, while Paul testified that the only thing he had said was "Look out!" The jury found Paul not guilty.

The irony is that the twins looked, talked, and acted so much alike that, except for their relatives, most people could not tell them apart. But for the fact that the eye-witness to the altercation was the Houston twins' nephew, Walter Gibson, the prosecution might have had difficulty making their case.

Chapter 6

Judge Moody C. Price
Meridian, Lauderdale County, Mississippi
January 14, 1921

Something awakened Mary Price in the middle of the night to a room so dark that not even a hint of light filtered through the shuttered windows. She could hear the winter wind as it rustled the magnolia leaves outside the master bedroom. Her husband, Moody, lay next to her, on his side so he wouldn't snore. She recalled having elbowed him earlier and told him to turn over. His breathing came mostly even.

What had roused her? Opening her eyes wide, Mary saw a flash of a light. The hair on the nape of her neck rose. The light flashed again and Mary saw two men standing at the foot of the bed. A third flash reflected off an axe blade. The tool's handle seemed to extend from the shoulder of one of the men.

Terrified, Mary shrieked and attempted to leap out of bed. Her head reeled as someone knocked her to the floor. Fear tasted like a dirty penny on her tongue. Seconds later, the two attackers viciously assaulted her husband, Judge Moody C. Price, well known as a former police sergeant, constable, justice of the peace, and most recently as deputy clerk of the federal court and United States commissioner in and for Meridian, Mississippi.

Mary heard a horrifying slicing noise and Moody howled. One blow. Then a second. Grunts and labored breathing followed the blunt cracking sound as the axe met his skull and split bones open. Blood splattered across the bed covers and wallpaper. A warm splash stained her cheek, the smell reminding her of the odor in the butcher shop where she purchased meat for their dinner table. After nine (by some accounts, ten) whacks and what seemed an interminable period, the two assailants disappeared into the night.

Reportedly struck dumb either by the blow that knocked her to the floor or by fear and shock, Mary Price was unable to give details of the attack for several hours. When eventually she could recite the facts, they, and the events of the days and weeks that followed, sounded like something from a silent movie about the Keystone Kops.

Judge Price lay suffering in his bloody bed until five in the morning, when he gradually slipped away. Robert Yarbrough, the couple's son-in-law, who lived on the second floor of the home with his wife, Mollie Price Yarbrough, discovered the judge and his wife, whose bedroom was on the first floor.

Moody Price home. (Photo by author)

Robert stated to the police chief that he had heard screams coming from the floor below and went down to see what was the matter. Mrs. Price had been dragged from her bed into the hallway. A huge bump had risen on her head, and several bruises covered her face. Robert found his mother-in-law in a semi-conscious state on the floor outside the master bedroom. Judge Price lay in his own blood; the spatter stretched across the covers and speckled the wall at the head of the bed. Alongside the bed lay the axe.

Upon arrival at Judge Price's home, Chief L. C. Monette, of the Meridian Police Department, immediately called Deputy Sheriff Bob Gant, from Crystal Springs, to come to Meridian with his bloodhounds to track down the murderers. Deputy Gant took the next train out.

In the meantime, the chief began his investigation. The bloody axe still lay next to the bed on the floor. The chief ordered it removed for safekeeping until it could be determined whether the intruders had brought it or it belonged to the Prices. At the rear of the house outside, a barrel with a box on top of it sat under the bathroom window. Inside the house, police found the judge's pants, two old pistols, and Mrs. Price's purse by the gallery at the rear door.

Initially the police assumed the perpetrators had gained entrance to the house by climbing through the bathroom window and had made their exit through the back door by the gallery. But the front door was found open.

Deputy Gant arrived in Meridian at noon on the Alabama and Vicksburg passenger train. He brought several other officers. They went directly to the Price residence, where already more than 500 residents had gathered in their Model T's and on foot to watch the dog. The citizens of Meridian had never before seen a hound sniff out a criminal.

Picking up a trail from the back of the Price home, the dog led them on a course through what was then known in the neighborhood as "the Negro quarters." The crowd followed. People abandoned their "tin lizzies" in the middle of the road to follow the deputy and his dog.

The chase wound roundabout the city and ended up at the Union passenger station. After sniffing around a moment, the dog headed east toward the Acme Planing mill, then across the road, over the Sowashee Creek, then north across the old brickyard common toward the waterworks reservoir, and around the dam on the east side toward the reservoir's upper end. At the upper end, they ran in circles for a while and ended up going back the way they had come until about halfway the length of the dam. There they went east, across the Vimville Road near the Oak Grove Church. Until the middle of the afternoon, they traveled east, ending up about four and a half miles out of the city.

During the deputy's and the dog's wending and winding, crowds of people followed. Though many of the hundreds of folk crowded the streets and remained a distance behind them, quite a number of people loudly expressed their lack of faith in the dog. Deputy Gant, however, remained confident that he and his dog would solve the most heinous of Mississippi's murders. In some places, cars jammed together and formed a blockade. In other places, the drivers were so anxious to be part of the chase scene that they didn't watch where they were going and sideswiped each other.

While Police Chief Monette accompanied Deputy Gant, word got out that the chief was in possession of a clue that would lead to the solution of the case. The chief remained mute. There was no question that if the guilty parties had been caught during that chase, the mob would have lynched them.

Besides his wife and his daughter, Mollie (Mrs. Robert E. Yarbrough), Judge Price left behind a son, Moody Price, Jr., two other daughters, Mrs. J. A. Snapp, and Louise Price, one brother, three sisters, and his father, B. D. Price. The pastor of the Fifteenth Avenue Baptist Church conducted the funeral at the Price home the day after the murder. Judge Price was buried in the Magnolia Cemetery.

Price headstone. (Photo by author)

Late on the day of the murder, the coroner, Mr. C. D. Hobgood, empanelled an inquest jury to investigate every identifiable circumstance. Witnesses were testifying before the jury in the evening of the same day up until adjournment, something that wouldn't happen in modern times. Summonses went out to a number of people to give evidence the following morning.

Among those testifying was Deputy Sheriff Bob Gant. His bloodhound had lost the perpetrators' scent in the middle of the Vimville Highway, several miles east of town. He concluded that the guilty parties must have gotten a ride with someone. Late in the evening, another effort was made when the dog picked up a trail at the judge's home, but the trail was quickly played out. Since he could be of no further use, Deputy Gant and his dog took an early train out of the city and headed to Louisiana, where they had been summoned to help locate the killers of an entire family. The case was reportedly similar to Judge Price's murder in that the perpetrators had axed the family to death.

Deputy Gant was not apologetic over his dog's failure to locate the killers. Before he departed, he said that his dogs were not often fooled. In the Meridian situation, the dog's ability to track the responsible parties was greatly diminished because of the large crowd of people who milled around, tramping over the killers' path. He insisted that both trails the dog took were legitimately those of the murderers. One of the men, Gant believed, boarded the train at the crossing near the Standard Oil Company plant. The other caught a ride either by design or with a passerby on the Vimville Highway.

The police chief and the sheriff investigated two men who were arrested at York, Alabama, on the afternoon of the murder. They arrived at York by freight train. The York officials took the men into custody at the request of Chief Monette because two suspicious-looking strangers had been seen boarding a train leaving Meridian on the day of the murder.

Meridian citizens were very nervous and frightened. Many of them volunteered to help with the manhunt in any way they could. Judge Price was well known and well liked. Hundreds of people attended the funeral.

The coroner's jury, led by District Attorney Martin Miller, adjourned subject to being called back by the coroner. Members of the jury were split in their opinions about a motive. Some believed that the perpetrators bore a vendetta against Judge Price dating back to when he was justice of the peace or U.S. commissioner. Others believed that burglars caught in the act of robbery had committed the killing.

Rumor had it originally that Judge Price had withdrawn a sizable sum of money from the bank the day before the murder with which to pay his property taxes, but that rumor turned out to be unfounded. Another rumor was that an individual had deposited a large sum of money in a bank on the morning after the murder and that one twenty-dollar bill had a bloodstain on it. That was investigated, and the party who had deposited the money proved that the stained bill had no connection to the murder.

The axe found on the floor, which still bore the judge's blood and hair when the authorities arrived, was, in fact, the Price household axe. The "Negro" girl who worked for the Prices identified the axe. She used it to chop kindling. Ordinarily it was left in the back yard and was last seen there on the afternoon before the murder.

As was often the case at that time, people jumped to the conclusion that "Negroes" committed the murders. The police didn't give much credence to that theory. They said that if that had been true, the two pistols from the sleeping apartment of Judge and Mrs. Price would not have been left lying around at the rear of the house in the gallery. In fact, the investigators believed that the perpetrators were white men who took the pistols, trousers, and Mrs. Price's purse to the rear of the house to the gallery to make it look like robbery when in actuality they were covering up a deeper motive.

The jury of six men worked diligently but at the end of the second day were forced to conclude that the murder of Judge Price was at the hands of a person or persons unknown.

District Attorney Martin Miller thoroughly investigated the two white men who were arrested at York, Alabama, after having boarded a train in Meridian on the afternoon of the murder. Their activities while they were in

Meridian revealed that the two men were unemployed and their where-abouts for the entire length of their stay were accounted for. They were released at the end of the day.

By January 17, the authorities had run down many leads, questioned several "Negroes" to no avail, and were generally frustrated at finding absolutely no clues to the murder. As the hours passed, the powers-that-be were coming to the conclusion that either there was a deeply laid murder plot accomplished by persons who bore an intense dislike for the judge or that there was an insane person who was just lucky that he had left no hard evidence.

After scouring the grounds around the judge's home, the authorities concluded that the perpetrators did not, in fact, gain entry to the house by the bathroom window. It turned out that the box placed on top of the barrel was too weak to support a man's weight. Also, no mud was on the barrel or the box and there had been heavy rainfall the afternoon and early evening before the murder. Lastly, there were no marks or other indications on the house or windowsill that showed that anyone gained entry through the window.

The inquest jury said the perpetrators gained entry by either the front or the back door. The barrel and the box under the window, as well as the purse, the pistols, and the trousers found on the back gallery, were arranged merely to create the impression that the motive was robbery. The motive was something else altogether. Everything was designed to prevent the authorities from detecting the identity of the real criminals.

On the morning of January 18, Mrs. Price testified. The jurors hoped she would be able to remember more clearly the events of the morning of the murder since a few days had passed.

She had given a statement at the time of the event in which she said that she and Judge Price were awakened at about the same time and as both sat up in the bed a light was flashed in their eyes blinding her. She could distinguish only the dark forms of two men. She could not remember much more when picked up from the floor by her son-in-law, Robert Yarbrough, who rushed down the stairs upon hearing screams or groans after the murder.

At 11:00 A.M. on the 18th of January, the jury, county attorney, attorney Hardin Brooks, the chief of police, and the circuit clerk went to the Price home to make a closer examination of the master bedroom and anything else that might shed some light on the mystery. During the visit, Mrs. Price was again asked to make a statement but was unable to add anything to her original statement. She recited the horrible experience she had undergone when the murderers entered the room, aimed the flashlight in their faces, and attacked the judge.

During the jury's view of the house, bloodstains were found on the wallpaper in the bathroom and on the facing of the rear door leading to the back gallery on which the bathroom also opened. The discovery of the stains led to the belief that the murderers, after murdering the judge, visited the bathroom and washed their hands, showing "coolness and deliberateness almost unparalleled in the history of such murders," the police said. Further, the discovery bore out the theory that the murder was the culmination of a carefully laid plan. Again, the purpose seemed to be to make it appear that a robbery had been in progress.

Wednesday, January 19, 1921: authorities cut a square of bloodstained wallpaper from the bathroom wall and, together with the axe handle, the county attorney turned it over to fingerprint experts. At a citizens' meeting held at the Board of Trade on the afternoon of Tuesday the 18th, a more than $1,000 reward was posted.

The decision to call in fingerprint experts was made on Tuesday afternoon after the county attorney and the jury left the Price home. They had carefully scrutinized the premises and found bloodstains in the bathroom and on the facing of the rear door close by the door leading into the bathroom. Investigators had previously overlooked those blood marks. They decided that the killing being a premeditated act, the murderers took the time to enter the bathroom and wash the blood from their hands at the bathroom "hydrant" before departing. The prints found on the wallpaper appeared to have been made in the darkness of the room by some bloody hands in feeling for the bathtub's "hydrant" faucet.

The county attorney stated that the jury took statements of Mrs. Moody Price, Miss Louise Price, and Mrs. Robert Yarbrough (daughter Mollie) and then adjourned subject to recall at any moment if further evidence was available. According to reports given out by the authorities, Mrs. Price's statement was that she was awakened by an unusual noise in the room. She sat up in the bed to discover that one man stood at the foot of the bed on the side on which she was lying, and another stood at the foot on the side on which Judge Price was sleeping. One, she said, held a flashlight. She could distinguish the forms by the aid of streetlights reflected through the windows but not sufficiently to determine the intruder's race. By then she was so frightened that she fell back, pulling the covers over her, and knew nothing else until picked up in the hall by her son-in-law, Robert Yarbrough, and her daughter, Mollie, who stated they rushed down the stairs upon hearing groans.

Although Mrs. Price did not know the amount of money that Judge Price might have had, he did have a roll of bills. She indicated the size of the roll with her thumb and forefinger. She said that he intended to pay his taxes the next morning.

January 20, 1921: two "Negroes," Rosa Walls and a man by the name of Ed McElroy, were arrested on orders of the chief of police and the district attorney. Walls had been taken into custody because her house, which was only about a block away from the Prices', was the house into which Deputy Gant's bloodhound had run. The dog, upon entering Walls' house, went to a certain bed, trailed back outside and thereafter to the point on the highway where the trail ran out.

The man, Ed McElroy, was held because he was one of the most notorious "Negro" crooks and confidence men known to police. Other than that, no reason was given, though the public presumed that the chief of police must have a clue he didn't want to divulge.

A second "Negro" woman, Annie Ingley, was held and questioned, about what, nothing is known, and was released but kept under surveillance.

One of the most curious aspects of the case was the question of how much money Judge Price had on him at the time he retired for the night, why he had it, and where he got it. The authorities believed that if they could figure that out, they would at least have a motive. Although it was known that he was leaving town on the morning train to begin a new position with the railroad, the description of the roll of bills made it sound like a lot more than he would have needed. Investigation determined that Judge Price drew no money from any Meridian bank and had not received what was owed from the government for his job as deputy clerk of the federal court and United States commissioner on the first of the month. Although the government had sent him a letter acknowledging and thanking him for his final report and his service to the government, the amount due him for the work acknowledged in the letter had not been paid to him before the time of his murder. The authorities appealed to the public for information about the source and amount of money in hopes that a citizen who knew about it would come forward.

At this point, two famous detective agencies became interested in the murder, the Pendleton-Stillson Bureau of New Orleans and the Pinkerton Agency. When both agencies sent an operative, the city became optimistic that the murder might finally be solved.

Fingerprint photos on the bloodstained wallpaper cut from the bathroom of the home and those which might appear on the handle of the axe were expected to reach Meridian from New Orleans on the 21st or 22nd of January. Investigators firmly believed by then that the murderers stopped in the bathroom to wash up after the murder.

Governor Lee M. Russell committed $300 toward the reward money. The committee in charge of raising the reward money set their goal at $2,500 and, with the governor's commitment, only needed $200 more.

On January 21, 1921, the authorities released information that new bloodstains were discovered. Some were outside the Price home on the front yard "hydrant." Across the street, south of the Price home, several pieces of blood-stained wallpaper were found.

At this point, several people espoused the theory that the murder was deliberately planned and executed by persons who "had no fear of detection immediately following the commission" of the crime. If the bloodstains on the front yard "hydrant" came off the hands of one of the murderers in an effort to wash up in the front yard, it was an unequaled act of coolness. The "hydrant" was only a few feet from the front steps and directly lighted by a large streetlight, which reportedly burned all night on the night of the murder.

Others believe the blood on the "hydrant" and on the scraps of wallpaper found across the street got there by the servants using the "hydrant" to clean up the blood from the bedroom floor (there was considerable loss of blood by Judge Price). The blood could have easily gotten on one or more of the servants' clothes, and that person could have brushed against the "hydrant." There was no other explanation, since the home and the property were thoroughly searched on the morning of the murder and the blood on the "hydrant" would have been just too plain to see. Also, there was no logical explanation for the bits of wallpaper found across the street, since there was no report of any wallpaper missing from the bathroom.

On January 23, it was reported that the amount of money Judge Price had on him on the night he was murdered was about $200, though no one ever confirmed it. Ed McElroy was released from jail for insufficient evidence. Rosa Walls was still being held, though authorities would not say why. All leads and clues were for naught.

On January 24, police sought information about two men who were standing catty-corner across the street on a store gallery about 11:00 P.M. on the evening of the murder. Also, a prominent Mobile and Ohio Railroad conductor came forward with information that on the night of the murder when he was on the way to the passenger station to take out his train at 2:00 A.M. he had heard men running on the paved street about five blocks from the Price home. His attention was attracted to the runners because of the early hour, but he couldn't see who they were.

On January 26, not only were two men seen on the store gallery across the street from the Price home the night of the murder, but two men were also seen near the Price home two other times that day, once early in the evening and the other around 9:00 P.M. The citizens who reported the information were of good reputation and could not be doubted. The first time two men were seen, they were near the front of the Price home. The second, they were on the 14th Avenue side, near the rear part of the house. The third time, they were under the store shed, diagonally across the street. No one could say whether it was the same two men each time or what their race was. There having been was no reason at the time to scrutinize the men, and it being dark, no one had a clear idea of what they looked like.

Citizen 499: An anonymous letter addressed to the district attorney arrived on the morning of January 26th. "Citizen 499" claimed to have information about the identity of the murderers and offered to give information to help capture them provided the reward would be paid to him immediately. The district attorney replied that if the information led to the arrest and conviction of the persons involved, the reward would be paid, but he had little faith in the writer. He figured it was a hoax made up by someone wanting the reward.

January 27–29: the detectives who had come from the famous agencies departed for their headquarters, unable to make any headway in the investigation. Authorities concluded that their only hope was that the fingerprints on the bloodstained wallpaper and axe handle would reveal some information as to the identity of the killers. Lastly, perhaps the new grand jury, to be convened by the circuit judge on February 7, might be able to turn up something in its investigation.

The chief of police received an anonymous letter from Winchester. If he would send officers to a small house near the end of the switch north of Winchester, they would uncover valuable information that might lead to the identity and the capture of the men responsible for the murder. Two officers, Motorcycle Officer Pat Allen of the Meridian Police Department and Special Agent Jack Jordan of the Mobile and Ohio Railroad went to the location but found only a woman with no knowledge other than that two white men, "resembling Italians," were seen in a boxcar that had come from Meridian the day of the murder.

On January 30, Judge Price's murder was on the docket for the February 7 grand jury.

On February 14, the grand jury summoned a large number of witnesses. Included were each immediate member of the Price family, a number of close neighbors and relatives, all of the officers from the police and sheriff's department who had worked on the case, several physicians, and a large number of other people who were close acquaintances and friends of Judge Price. After several weeks of examination, nothing new was known and no indictments were handed down.

On August 5, a new grand jury convened and began an investigation into the Price murder. People thought there must be something new, but no indictments were ever handed down.

On January 15, 1922, one year and one day after the murder of Judge Price, a newspaper article stated that nothing was ever discovered that would lead to the arrest of the perpetrator(s).

As far as is known, the murder remains unsolved to this day. No report of fingerprint findings was ever revealed. The police department records were so badly kept that no one knows where the Price case file could be. Various persons throughout the city who did not wish to be named made statements that the corrupt government of the 1920s contributed to such muddled records. Additionally, his own great-granddaughter denied having ever heard of him, much less the circumstances of his death.

Chapter 7

Judge William McClellen Morning
Lincoln, Lancaster County, Nebraska
February 18, 1924

Wallace G. Wallick, fifty-nine, made his living as a small-time well digger and cement contractor. He lived in a suburb of Lincoln. Wallace's first wife, Malinda M. Wallick, divorced him on July 2, 1923, on the grounds of cruelty and non-support. She testified that he had held a gun on her and choked her on at least one occasion. They were the parents of two children.

Judge William M. Morning, fifty-six, was serving his second term on the district court bench. A native of Pennsylvania, he had been born and raised on a farm and received a country education. From age eighteen to twenty, he taught school for two years while studying law. In 1886, he began practicing law. Later, he served as county attorney for one year. His second wife was Grace Stewart, a teacher. He had one daughter, Mildred Morning, also a teacher, by his first wife, who had died in 1913. In 1921, Judge Morning, a veteran, served as Nebraska State Bar president. He was very popular with other attorneys.

After Wallace and Malinda Wallick were divorced, Wallace refused to support her and his children. After four months of no support, Malinda was compelled to return to court to enforce the decree. On October 23, 1923, Judge Morning committed Wallace to jail for contempt of court for nonpayment of alimony and child support of $25 per month. Wallick remained in jail for four days and finally paid $100 before being released.

Everyone thought that Wallace had turned over a new leaf when on January 29, 1924, at Council Bluffs, Wallace married Ethel May Hansen, sixty-one. He gave his address as Yuma, Colorado, and hers as Andres, New York. But Wallace had recently told his brother-in-law that he would never pay what he owed his ex-wife; he didn't care what they did to him, she was never getting any money. Later, Wallick's brother-in-law reported that Wallick always carried a gun.

Wallick continued to refuse to support Malinda and the children. Malinda was once again forced to take him back to court. At 9:40 A.M. on Monday, February 18, 1924, during what looked to Judge Morning like a routine contempt action for failure to pay court-ordered support, the judge asked Wallace Wallick, "Are you ready for trial?"

Wallick replied, "Yes."

"Have you an attorney?" the judge asked Wallick.

"No," said Wallick.

Judge Morning said, "Then take a seat and we will proceed."

In reply, Wallick fumbled inside his coat, bringing out a sheaf of papers. He laid the papers on the counsel table and fumbled around his person again while eying everyone in the room. With his other hand, he reached around his back and pulled out a gun. Moments later, Wallick stretched out his arms full length, took aim, and shot Judge Morning just above the heart. Spectators fled screaming into the hall.

Wallick then fired a shot at Minor Bacon, the court reporter. Swinging around toward the back of the courtroom, Wallick took aim at the specta-tors, including his ex-wife, her brother, and her attorney. They searched for cover. He fired a shot in their direction that went between the two men and lodged in the window shutters.

He yelled, "Have you got enough?" and turned back to the court reporter.

Bacon, the court reporter, cried, "Yes."

Wallick then pulled out another .38 revolver, stuck the muzzle in his mouth, and pulled the trigger. He collapsed on the courtroom floor, dead.

Judge Morning swayed in his chair for a few moments and got to his feet. He stag-gered from his bench and was

Judge Morning.
(*Courtesy Nebraska State Historical Society*)

44

assisted to his chambers. He gasped a request to his domestic relations' investigator to call his former law partner, John Ledwith, and collapsed near the sofa. Bailiff A. A. Lang assisted the judge to the couch, where he died a few minutes later. When the doctors arrived, it was already too late.

After Wallick fell down dead, Bacon, surprised that he hadn't suffered more injury, examined himself and discovered that the bullet that had hit him had lodged in a leather card case that he carried in his vest pocket. The bullet pierced Bacon's clothing but only inflicted a slight flesh wound under his right arm.

It was ironic that Judge Morning should have been killed because of a "domestic relations" case. Domestic relations and juvenile law held great interest for the judge. He was a frequent speaker on the subjects and had gained a national reputation as one who was a friend to small offenders and a help to families.

Chapter 8

Judge Lamar C. Smith
Wetumpka, Elmore County, Alabama
August 30, 1926

A series of strange and confusing events began at the home of Lamar and Sallie Smith during the spring of 1926 that made Judge and Mrs. Smith uneasy. Though they had not alerted the authorities, the Smiths had sought help from their neighbors.

It all began on April 1 at about 11:00 P.M. when a "Negro" man came knocking at their door. When Sallie Smith answered the door, the man stammered and stated that he had a telegram for Judge Smith. She asked for the telegram, but the man searched his pockets and was unable to locate it. He told her that he was going to go search for it and would return. Concerned, Mrs. Smith called the telegraph office about the message. They told her there wasn't one. Mrs. Smith thought it was an April Fool's joke and accused the cook, but the cook denied it.

Some weeks later, Judge Smith got up one morning to find that several of the screen doors were blocked open. He could find no reason for it. No one in the household would admit to doing it.

One night in June, Mrs. Smith opened her bedroom door to find a "Negro" man standing in the room with a large club raised in his hands as if to strike her down. Mrs. Smith screamed, and the man slammed the door in her face. Judge Smith, who had been right behind her, called the neighbors to help conduct a search. When the group entered the bedroom, they found it empty. One electric wire attached to the light socket had been cut so that the room was in complete darkness. They searched outside and heard a noise like the closing of a door. When they went back indoors, they found that the man had escaped through the window by raising the screen. Upon further examination of the home, they found that the telephone wires had also been cut.

On a second occasion, they again found their screen doors had been blocked open but could find no reason for it. No one admitted to it.

Subsequently, someone fed the Smiths' dogs poison, killing them.

Lamar Cantelou Smith was born in Montgomery Alabama on February 12, 1871. His father died when Smith was an infant, and the family moved to Wetumpka. He grew up with the people in Elmore. He and Sallie Evans were married on April 21, 1890. They raised two children. Lamar was described as "a faithful and kind husband, an indulgent father, and ever loyal to his friends." He was a deacon in the Presbyterian Church, of which he was a lifelong member. He also was a Mason. He had served as postmaster at Wetumpka under President Cleveland, circuit clerk of Elmore County, and judge of the Probate Court of Elmore County, and had just retired. He had also been a farmer and had owned a mercantile business. He had served as vice president of the Bank of Wetumpka and lately had been with the Land Department of the Alabama Power Company. As far as anyone knew, Lamar and Sallie Smith had no enemies.

At about 8:00 P.M. on August 30, a hot summer Monday night, Judge Smith was lying in his bed reading the newspaper. His wife was lying nearby thumbing through a magazine. Although the porch windows stood open in hopes of a breeze to cool down their room, the pair didn't hear anyone approach. The stillness of the evening was broken by a blast from the porch. Someone had sneaked up and fired twice from an automatic shotgun through a window. The buckshot shattered the judge's skull upon impact.

Neighbors Lovick Allen and Penton Cousins were driving down the street when they heard the shots and Mrs. Smith's screams. They pulled over and ran toward her voice. Mrs. Smith staggered out of the house. The buckshot had left a huge, bloody gash in her forehead. Her nightclothes were splattered with blood. Lovick Allen caught her just as she fell. Penton Cousins ran into the house to see if Judge Smith needed assistance. With the judge's face mostly shot away, he could tell that there was nothing that he could do for the man except go for help. Cousins ran to call Sheriff Golden. Lovick Allen left Mrs. Smith with the other neighbors when they arrived and ran to another telephone to call Speigner prison and ask them to send bloodhounds right away.

Some of the neighbors told authorities that they saw an automobile parked near the victim's home. Right after the second charge was fired, a white man and a black man came running, jumped into the vehicle, and drove away. Upon inspection of the premises, authorities found that the telephone wires had been cut.

When Mrs. Smith was able to collect herself, she told of the events that had transpired over the past several months. As she related the story, she realized that the window the man had escaped through in the earlier trespass was the same window through which the shotgun was fired that night. She went on to relate what she saw just after the shooting:

> I looked at my darling husband. He had not moved. He did not moan. I saw that his head was covered with blood and I rushed to the door, unlocked it, and then unlocked the front door. Then I discovered I was wounded, and the blood blinded me. I could not see anyone, but screamed for help. If my husband had an enemy in the world, I know he would have told me. I can think of nothing he has ever done that would cause anyone to bear him any ill will. He was a kind and generous husband. Oh, how could they have done such a thing. I wish it had been me instead of my darling husband.

In spite of the buckshot having entered the judge's head on the right side, tearing away fragments of his skull and burying them in the wall on the opposite side the room, friends and medical personnel who arrived on the scene insisted on rushing him to the hospital in an attempt to save his life. He died on the operating room table about three hours after the attack.

His wife, daughter, son, George B. Smith, and twin brother, George Smith, another brother, Ed Smith, a sister Mrs. M. E. Cain, four grandchildren, and other extended family survived Judge Smith. More than 400 people from across the state attended the funeral services.

After investigation, just after the judge's funeral, police arrested Clyde Reese Bachelor, twenty-six, who was married to Judge and Mrs. Smith's daughter Elizabeth. Hayes Leonard, an old "Negro" laborer who worked for Clyde Bachelor on his farm, confessed that the two of them committed the murder.

According to Leonard's confession, Bachelor had promised him $400, that he would cancel a debt, and that he would pay the balance on Leonard's Ford. He stated that on the night of the shooting, Bachelor stood real close and held a pistol on him to get him to shoot the judge. Leonard was also supposed to shoot Mrs. Smith, but "my nerve failed me and I couldn't pull the trigger on Mrs. Smith."

Leonard also admitted that he had been the person who had been in the Smith house with the "big stick."

At first, Clyde Reese Bachelor refused to give a statement. Later, on his way from Montgomery to the Mobile County jail for safekeeping, he talked to deputies. When he arrived at the jail, he talked to newspapermen, other inmates, and the sheriff. Although denying that he held a pistol on Hayes

Leonard, Bachelor, in his statement, confessed that financial difficulties caused him to spend the previous three months planning the killings. He thought that if his wife could get her part of her father's estate, all of their money woes would be solved. Clyde Bachelor was from a very prominent Elmore County family. He and his wife were the parents of an infant.

Bachelor further admitted that he stood at the window when Leonard fired the fatal shot using Bachelor's .12-gauge automatic shotgun loaded with buckshot. He said that he and Leonard ran the two blocks to his automobile, and that the two of them drove back to Bachelor's plantation, which was about ten miles from the Smiths' home.

Bachelor said that he approached Hayes Leonard three months earlier to kill the judge and his wife but that he did not promise Leonard anything in exchange for the murder. He said that on two occasions before August 30 they went to Judge Smith's home to kill him, "but my nerve failed me."

On September 3, the grand jury indicted both assailants, and the case was set for trial on September 7, just eight days after the murder. A hundred men were empanelled for the twelve-man jury. Solicitor John W. Bateman, assisted by several private law firms hired by the Smith family, Holley & Milner, Huddleston & Glover, and Tate & Reneau of Wetumpka, prosecuted. For the defense of Clyde Reese Bachelor, his family hired Ray Rushton of Wetumpka and the firm of Rushton, Crenshaw, & Rushton of Montgomery. The court appointed Fred Farnell and C. S. Melton of Tallahassee for Hayes Leonard. Bachelor pled "not guilty by reason of insanity." Leonard pled simply "not guilty."

On the first day of the Bachelor trial, people came not only from Elmore County but also from surrounding Alabama counties. The courtroom was filled to overflowing with more than 450 people. When Bachelor arrived in the courtroom, he was allowed to greet his father, who had tears flowing down his face. Defense Attorney Ray Rushton immediately made a motion for continuance for at least a month, since it had been little over a week since the shooting, but the judge denied the motion.

Testimony brought out by cross-examination of Mrs. Smith detailed the night of the shooting. After that line of questioning, the defense began its attempt to make a case for Bachelor's insanity. They questioned Mrs. Smith about the day after a "Negro with a club" was in their home. Judge and Mrs. Smith were summoned to their daughter and son-in-law's home, where their daughter told them of her husband's extreme nervous condition. Mr. Rushton's purpose was to show that Bachelor was working under the illusion that he had to kill in order to maintain the lifestyle he wanted for himself, his wife, and their baby.

Mr. and Mrs. Bachelor and Clyde's brother, Dr. Elmer Bachelor, testified that Clyde had changed within the previous few months "from a son and a brother to a mere acquaintance who steered clear of them." His mother said that Clyde had always been crazy about money. She said that she had done everything she could do for him and "dishonesty crept into his life." She further stated that he had been borrowing for his farm from the bank and from his father, who had been very generous with him financially. She said that one time he asked her, "Mother, do you think I am going crazy?"

His father said that Clyde's mind had been off since the previous June. He said that his son had never done anything in good faith and that he was a crybaby. His son never followed through on anything he promised to do. When he would reprimand Clyde for it, Clyde would begin crying. He said that before that year, Clyde had been happy, jovial, and fond of telling funny stories. Lately, that hadn't been true.

Clyde's wife, Elizabeth (Smith) Bachelor, came to the courtroom to testify under subpoena, but when the judge told her she didn't have to give evidence, Mrs. Bachelor asked to be excused and went back home.

The jury, on the third ballot, found Clyde Reese Bachelor guilty of first-degree murder and sentenced him to death. The judge ordered that on October 22, 1926, the sentence of death by hanging be carried out.

As for Hays Leonard, the poor old farmhand, his trial was even swifter than Clyde Bachelor's. His court-appointed counsel fought hard. He argued that "the crime of the Negro was committed under duress and compulsion." He said, "Leonard was a tool in the hands of a mastermind . . . an unfortunate victim of circumstances." Hays Leonard was also sentenced to death by hanging.

Eleven days and thirteen hours after the murders, the trials were over. An article in the *Weekly Herald* of Wetumpka, Alabama, read as follows: "Perhaps the most pitiful sight in the closing hours was the 'Negro,' Leonard. He had obeyed the command of his 'white folks' and for it he was being sent to his death. Halting, stammering, pleading, trembling, he could not understand."

Clyde Reese Bachelor appealed his conviction, but all of his pleas were denied. Before his execution, the method of administering the death penalty changed and Clyde's execution date was delayed because of the appeals and the technicality of having to be re-sentenced. A last minute request to the governor to commute the sentence was also denied. In his last hours, he was allowed to spend some time with his four-year-old son, whom he had not seen in a year, as well as his parents. He was finally executed on July 15, 1927, in the electric chair at Kilby prison.

Chapter 9

Judge Joseph F. Crater
New York City, New York County, New York
August 6, 1930

The roaring twenties brought short skirts and the Charleston, prohibition and gangsters. In New York City, there was Tammany Hall. Tammany Hall, an organization that originated for social and patriotic activities, had, in the previous century, evolved into one of corruption. The political boss, Mayor Jimmy J. Walker, who in a few short years would be forced to resign by the Seabury Commission, ruled like an emperor. Joseph Force Crater had joined up with Tammany Hall while still a young attorney.

Joe Crater led two lives, as many men did in the early part of the twentieth century before the women's liberation movement, *Mr. Mom*, and the sharing of responsibilities in the home. There was the life he led with his wife, Stella, with whom he shared a posh New York apartment in addition to their home in Belgrade Lakes, Maine. And there was the life he led at Tammany Hall. It wasn't long after he became a member of Tammany that he progressed to the position of secretary to Supreme Court Justice Robert F. Wagner. From the work and contacts he made there, he was able to secure his appointment by Governor Franklin D. Roosevelt on April 8, 1930, as a New York State Supreme Court justice.

Undoubtedly the folks at Tammany Hall knew a lot about Stella Crater, but Stella Crater knew little about Tammany Hall. Perhaps had she made it her business to find out the truth about her husband, both before and after his disappearance, she wouldn't have suffered as she did all the remaining days of her life. Stella Crater was a naive soul. She loved and trusted Joe implicitly and never questioned a thing he told her.

Joe not only worked in Tammany Hall for Justice Wagner, but he was a political activist. He raised money, organized meetings, and got out the vote. He paid his dues—so to speak. The question becomes, did he "pay" for his appointment to the bench with cash, promises, or otherwise?

Earlier in the summer of 1930, the district attorney launched an investigation into the appointment of George F. Ewald as magistrate. It was alleged that Ewald paid $10,000 to Tammany leader Martin J. Healy for the magistrate appointment. Ewald and Healy were never convicted. Charges were dismissed after three trials and three hung juries.

On May 27, 1930, Crater withdrew $7,500 from his bank accounts and sold securities worth $15,779, asking that his broker pay him in thousand-dollar bills. Did Crater pay for his appointment? Was it trouble with Tammany that caused Joe Crater to disappear?

On August 3, 1930, Joe and Stella Crater vacationed at their summer home in Belgrade Lakes, Maine. They enjoyed the peace and quiet, the solitude. There was no telephone and no Tammany Hall. Only a few friends occasionally dropped by for a visit. They were relaxed and enjoying the day when Joe received a message that there was an "urgent" phone call for him at the neighbor's home. He went next door to take the call, and when he returned, he said, "I have got to go into the city, Stella. There are some problems there that I must attend to immediately."

Stella immediately let her displeasure at the vacation interruption be known. "Oh, no, Joe. Must you? We've been having such a lovely time, and you need the rest."

Joe had only been on the bench since his appointment the previous April, but it was well known that he was a hard worker. He was sure to be elected for a full term. He reassured his wife that there was no way to avoid going into New York, much as he would have liked to remain with her. He went inside to pack.

A while later, bag in hand, Joe Crater kissed his wife goodbye. "I promise I will be back on Saturday. You know I never miss your birthday."

"All right, darling," she said. "I look forward to seeing you then."

On August 4, Crater was at the couple's New York apartment, where their maid, Almeda Christian, saw him. He went to the office (court was in summer recess) in the Supreme Court Building between ten and eleven in the morning on Tuesday, August 5, and had lunch with one of the other judges. Later, he traveled to the home of a doctor friend for dinner, left around midnight, and returned to the apartment, where he spent the night.

On August 6, 1930, Joe worked in his office at the courthouse in Manhattan on Foley Square. Alone in his office, he selected papers to put into two leather briefcases and five cardboard portfolios. Late in the morning, he called in his court attendant, Joseph L. Mara.

"Joe, I have some banking I need you to do for me," he said, and gave him two checks: one for $3,000 on Crater's account at Chase National Bank and the other for $2,150 on his account at Empire Trust Company. Both checks were made out for cash. Mara asked no questions. He cashed the checks and returned to the office with the money in two envelopes. He gave the envelopes to Judge Crater, who stuffed them into the inside pocket of his coat without even looking at the contents.

Later that morning, Crater called Mara back into the office and asked him to package the portfolios, which were stuffed with various documents. He asked his secretary, Frederic A. Johnson, to close the office. Crater and Mara took a taxi to the judge's Fifth Avenue apartment, where Crater had Mara place the briefcases on a chair before leaving.

"You may go now, Joe," Crater told Mara. "I'm going up to Westchester for a swim. I'll be back tomorrow." Mara left.

Early in the evening, Crater arrived at the Arrow Theater Ticket Agency on Broadway. He wore a high-collared shirt, a pinstriped dark brown suit, and a Panama hat. He requested a ticket for that evening's performance but was told there weren't any. The operator told him that if he could get one, he'd leave it for Crater at the box office.

Judge Crater then went to Billy Haas' restaurant, where theater people liked to hang out, at 332 West Forty-fifth Street. He had dinner with friends, Sally Lou Ritz, a showgirl, and William Klein, a Shubert Theater lawyer. Joe told them that he was going back to Belgrade Lakes for Stella's birthday and a vacation before court reconvened on August 25. After curtain time, Crater left to go to the theater. He said goodbye to his friends on the sidewalk at about 9:15 P.M., hailed a tan-colored taxi, and departed in the direction of Ninth Avenue.

The ticket Joseph Grainsky left for Joe at the box office was subsequently retrieved by someone that evening, but no one knows exactly what time or by whom.

Stella Mance Wheeler Crater waited for her husband to appear on her birthday on August 9, 1930, but he never showed up. She had no knowledge that he was in trouble. He hadn't called, but he often didn't. When her birthday came and went and he made no appearance other than previously having had made arrangements for a canoe to be delivered, Stella began to worry. Joe had never missed her birthday. Finally, on August 11, Stella phoned Simon Rifkind, the man who had succeeded Joe as Justice Wagner's secretary. Rifkind hadn't seen Joe Crater but agreed to ask around after him.

Four days later, when Stella still hadn't heard anything, she sent the chauffeur, Fred Kahler, to New York to search for him with instructions to look everywhere he could think of. On August 22, Fred returned. He said the apartment was all right. People had seen Joe just after he arrived in New York, but later the judge was nowhere to be found. Some of the judge's friends had even asked Fred not to hang around because if the newspaper people found out it might hurt Joe's election efforts.

Justice Louis Valente called from New York on August 25. Joe had not shown up for the reopening of court.

Stella mostly stayed out of the search in the beginning. Had she been more assertive in searching for her husband herself, undoubtedly more would have been discovered. What is known is very little. It would be several weeks before the police, the newspapers, and Stella pieced together Joe Crater's actions during the three days following his departure from Belgrade Lakes.

On August 29, Stella finally had Fred drive her to New York. As soon as she got to the apartment, she telephoned everyone she could think of, including the infamous Jimmy Walker, Marty Healy, and Rifkind. The next morning, New York City police detective Leo Lowenthal, who was Senator Wagner's bodyguard whenever the senator was in New York, showed up at the door. He informed Stella that he'd checked all the hospitals and morgues and there was not a trace of Joe anywhere. He asked Stella to check Joe's closet. Of thirty suits, a brown pinstripe was missing although the vest still hung on a hanger. It was unusual for Joe to wear a suit without the vest. All suitcases were present. Also present on his dresser were his monogrammed pocket watch, pen, and card case, all of which he ordinarily carried on him. The police officer remarked that maybe Joe left them because of the heat of the summer. When Stella's mother arrived, Lowenthal suggested that they go back to Belgrade Lakes and wait until Senator Wagner returned from Europe and they, Wagner and Lowenthal, would try to find out what really happened.

The story finally broke in the press on September 3. On September 4, Rifkind asked Missing Persons to search for Crater. On September 8, Missing Persons issued a flyer with Crater's picture and offering a reward. It read as follows:

$5000 REWARD
MISSING SINCE AUGUST 6, 1930
Justice of the Supreme Court, State of New York

DESCRIPTION—Born in the United States—Age, 41 years; height, 6 feet; weight, 185 pounds; mixed gray hair, originally dark brown, thin at top, parted in middle, "slicked" down; complexion, medium dark, considerably tanned; brown eyes; false teeth, upper and lower jaw; good physical and mental condition at time of disappearance. Tip of right index finger somewhat mutilated, due to having been recently crushed.

Wore brown sack coat and trousers, narrow green stripe, no vest; either a Panama or soft brown hat worn at rakish angle, size 6 5/8, unusual size for his height and weight. Clothes made by Vroom. Affected colored shirts, size 14 collar, probably bow tie. Wore tortoise-shell glasses for reading. Yellow gold Masonic ring, somewhat worn; may be wearing a yellow gold, square-shaped wristwatch with leather strap.

EDWARD P. MULROONEY, Phone Spring 3100, Police Commissioner.

In October, the district attorney requested Stella sign a power of attorney so that the Crater safe deposit box could be searched. She sent it but didn't have a key, so the district attorney had the box drilled. It turned out to be empty. The bank officials insisted that Judge Crater was the only one who had access to the box.

Judge Crater's name was linked with a Ziegfeld girl, Elaine Dawn, who had been in *Showboat*. The newspapers said they'd visited the Club Abbey, a nightclub with a dubious reputation. Joe had told Stella that he'd gone there for political reasons. Miss Dawn admitted she knew him but said that was all there was to it.

Four weeks after Crater disappeared, a showgirl, June Brice, A.K.A. Jean Covell, also disappeared. Their names had been entwined when the district attorney said he had an anonymous letter that said she was an intimate friend of the judge's. Miss Brice denied that she knew Judge Crater, but when she disappeared, it raised questions, since she was soon to go before the grand jury.

Stella was in denial. She refused to believe that Joe could ever be involved with another woman, though from all evidence he appeared to have been on very good terms with several showgirls. Once again she missed a chance at an immediate followup to his disappearance.

In 1939, Stella's attorney, Emil Ellis, filed a suit against the life insurance companies to obtain the proceeds of the policies, and hopefully, double indemnity. To do so, Stella had to prove that Judge Crater was dead and that his body had been disposed of in such a way that it could not be produced. As part of his preparation for the lawsuit, Ellis had been following up on several leads even though it was nine years since Crater had disappeared. He had a theory that Crater visited June Brice the night of August 6 to offer a settlement for some claim she had on him. In an effort to raise the price of the settlement, she may have had two gangsters waiting for Crater's arrival to "convince" him to pay a higher price. The convincing may have led to his death. He may have been disposed of in a crematory in New Jersey that it was rumored several gangs had a contract with. (These were the last days of Prohibition, a relatively lawless time in New York.)

In October 1939, Ellis went to Cuba to interview the former managing editor of the *New York Mirror*, who had attempted to interview June Brice on the night she disappeared. Emile Gauvreau told Ellis that early in September 1930, he received a call from a friend of his who had a girlfriend living in the same building as June Brice. His friend said that he thought he'd found Judge Crater. A tailor's delivery boy had told his girlfriend that he had delivered a suit to Brice's apartment with the initials J.F.C. in the lining. Another girl had also told the girlfriend that she had been in the apartment and had seen a watch bearing the initials J.F.C. Gauvreau reported that he and his friend went to Miss Brice's apartment that night. A woman inside the apartment refused to open the door even though Gauvreau and his friend identified themselves as police and demanded she let them in. She told them to "Get lost," so they went to the girlfriend's apartment to regroup. While they were there, Gauvreau saw someone run down the front steps and jump into a black limousine. It was nighttime, the lighting was bad, and he couldn't tell whether it was a man or a woman or more than one person. When they went back upstairs, the apartment was empty. The only thing left was a photograph of a girl, not June Brice, with a photographer's name stamped on the back. Gauvreau told Ellis that no one had seen Brice since.

Ellis, however, didn't stop his investigation there. He followed up on the name of the photographer and the girl in the picture, as well as June Brice. On November 7, 1939, Ellis located June Brice in the Pilgrim State Hospital at Brentwood, Long Island. She had an active case of tuberculosis and reportedly was suffering from "dementia praecox," a mental illness. Ellis was unable to obtain any statement from her, as she was totally incoherent. He did learn, however, that she had a trunk at the hospital. Thinking that there might be something inside that would reveal the answer to Crater's disappearance, he petitioned the court for permission to examine its contents, but the court refused, citing "invasion of privacy."

Brice's mother was quoted in the *New York Mirror* as saying that June had told her Crater was a friend not only of hers but of all show people. He used his influence to obtain roles in plays for them. She also said that June refused to discuss his disappearance. The *Mirror* also reported that June Brice, since disappearing in 1930, used many aliases and had been a patient in Neurological Hospital, Columbus, Ohio State Hospital, Bellevue, and Manhattan State. She'd made many suicide attempts after destroying papers and letters believed to have some bearing on Judge Crater's disappearance. June Brice died in 1948 with no one ever learning more about what she knew.

Ellis was also able to locate the girl whose photograph had been found in June Brice's apartment. She told him that she and June had been friends for a long time. One night in September, June came to her and asked her to stay with her because she was afraid of being murdered. She knew a terrible secret. She told her friend that newspapermen had tried to question her about Judge Crater, but she had run from them in fear for her life. The friend went on to say that they had moved from hotel to hotel and June was afraid to go out. Finally, the girlfriend could see that June had grown sick with fear. Her health and her mind were failing. Fearing that she would end up like June, she left June to fend for herself.

Ellis persuaded the insurance companies that Joe Crater would never return, so the lawsuit was settled for the face value of the policies minus the overdue premiums.

In 1956, the *American Weekly* carried an article entitled "How Judge Crater Was Murdered" by Camilo Weston Leyra, a convicted murderer. Leyra got the story from a man named Harry Stein the night before Stein was executed for a robbery-murder.

In 1929, a man named Joe Lesser was indicted for forgery. He wanted to get his case "straightened out" and thought Crater, who at that time was a lawyer and active with Tammany Hall, could get it done. Crater sometimes used a private investigator named "Chowderhead" Cohen. Cohen was approached by two men close to Lesser. Cohen went to Stein for help. Neither Cohen nor Stein thought they could approach Crater, so Stein went to a Lower East Side Democratic powerhouse who could be had for a consideration. He got to Crater through an attorney friend of Crater's. Crater quoted a price of $5,000. The money was paid, but Lesser was convicted and imprisoned anyway.

Stein and his cohorts were unhappy that Lesser wasn't cut loose. Cohen and Lesser's friends put pressure on Stein to get their $5,000 back. Stein was associated with a Philadelphia racketeer named Boo Boo Hoff and paid a visit to Philadelphia, where he met up with two men who agreed to help make Crater pay, but Stein had decided to make Crater pay not only the $5,000 but $20,000 for double-crossing him. The two gangsters would get a percentage for their part.

Stein knew someone who was in a position to watch Crater's every move: Vivian Gordon, a well-known prostitute. Judge Crater was reputed to be a regular customer. (She was strangled in 1931 the day before she could testify to the Seabury Commission about the corruption at Tammany Hall. Harry Stein was cleared of this murder.) Stein and the two thugs were tipped off that Crater would be having dinner at Billy Haas' Restaurant on August 6. Stein got a cab from a buddy. One fellow drove, and one sat in the back. Stein waited on the sidewalk. When Crater came out of the restaurant, Stein fingered him; one of the thugs stuck a gun in his ribs and forced him into the cab. At Eleventh Avenue, the hoods made Judge Crater get into the rear of a 3/4-ton panel truck and drove him to an apartment in Philadelphia where they held him for two days.

The kidnappers told Crater they wanted $25,000. He laughed. He told them they couldn't do anything to him because he was a judge and every cop in the country would be looking for them. The two hoods called Stein and told him Crater wouldn't take their demands seriously. Stein told them to keep Crater there. The next morning, Crater was reportedly still laughing. They called Stein again and again. Finally, when they convinced Stein that the police in Philadelphia were rounding up their mob, Stein instructed them to take Judge Crater in the back of the panel truck to a Clifton, New Jersey, abandoned paper mill. Crater was still laughing at their demands.

Stein called Cohen, who spoke to Lesser's people, and between the lot of them, they decided that although it wasn't public yet that Crater had disappeared, sooner or later it would be and the people on the street would be squealing to the cops. They decided that they would have to get rid of Judge Crater. They couldn't let him go, because he was too hot and too powerful and besides, Stein was convinced that Crater had seen him on the street outside the restaurant.

The two gangsters had the judge kneel and say his prayers and then, while he still didn't believe they'd do anything to him, they executed him gangland-style by shooting him twice in the back of the head. It was 2:00 P.M. on August 13, 1930. Then, on the orders of Stein, the Philadelphia thugs got an old bathtub from outside the paper mill, put Crater in it, and poured either muratic or hydrochloric acid over his body. Both of these would decompose flesh, teeth, and bones. The bathtub was then loaded onto the panel truck and driven to a secluded spot on the banks of the Passaic River, outside Clifton, where it and its contents were thrown into the water. As soon as it sank, the hoods fled to Philadelphia.

Stella Crater refused to believe that her husband would have ever had anything to do with the likes of Vivian Gordon, much less be on the receiving end of graft and corruption. She went to her death in 1969 publicly defending him as a decent and honorable man. To this day, no one knows what really happened to Judge Joseph Force Crater.

Questions to ponder:

1. If the first theory of June Brice's involvement is taken as true, then: If his monogrammed pocket watch was found in his apartment, how could it have been in Miss Brice's apartment?

2. If the second scenario is taken as true, then: What papers was Judge Crater packaging up in his office? What did he need the large amounts of money for?

3. Who picked up the theater ticket on the evening of August 6?

4. Who was on the other end of the August 3, 1930, "urgent" phone call, and what was "urgent"?

5. Why was the safe deposit box empty? Why have an empty box—why not turn it back to the bank?

6. What happened to the $23,229 Judge Crater cashed on May 27, 1930?

7. If Ellis could track down Brice and Gauvreau, why couldn't the police?

8. Why didn't the police try to get into June Brice's trunk either before or after her death?

Chapter 10

Judge Gilbert M. Keith
Fair Haven, Gloucester County, New Jersey
February 27, 1933

Justice of the Peace Gilbert M. Keith, a World War I veteran, was a strictly-by-the-book person. He didn't care for any illegal activities in the court system.

In July 1932, Judge Keith filed charges against Constables Henry Kruschka of Keyport, New Jersey, and Edward Hultner of Long Branch, New Jersey, for extracting illegal fees in the discharge of their duties.

In response to the charges, Constable Kruschka and Constable Abram Dixon filed charges of assault and battery on Judge Keith for an altercation in his office.

All of those charges were still pending in February 1933.

In the New Jersey Supreme Court, Judge Keith had accused nine justices of the peace and constables in the general physical area of his jurisdiction with false arrest, imprisonment, and malicious prosecution. That case was also pending in February 1933.

One Saturday in February, Gilbert Keith told his wife that he had received a threatening telephone message but didn't tell her the details.

On the morning of February 27, 1933, after leaving his home in Fair Haven, New Jersey, for his office in Red Bank, Judge Keith dropped from sight. County sheriff's deputies and state police conducted a massive search for Judge Keith.

When police interviewed Mrs. Keith, she stated that Judge Keith had been in constant pain since being involved in an accident five years earlier. He often had severe headaches. He had seemed depressed and despondent for some time.

Judge Keith's body was found on March 1, 1933, in the woods near the road in Lakewood. The location was a short distance from a hospital there. Workmen found Judge Keith's body with a cap covering his face.

The coroner, Herbert Le Compte, held a brief hearing and considered the evidence as follows:

1. Three bottles labeled "chloroform" were found near the body;
2. The cap was Judge Keith's;
3. Judge Keith allegedly purchased chloroform from pharmacies in Lakewood and Farmington, both of which are near where the body was found.

The coroner ruled that Judge Keith had committed suicide by inhaling chloroform that he put in a handkerchief in his cap and placing the cap over his own face. Mrs. Keith did not believe that such was the case but could not convince anyone otherwise. No other followup on the case was ever done.

Chapter 11

Judge Phillip R. Rabenau
Kirkwood, St. Louis County, Missouri
December 28, 1934

Raymond Batson, twenty-nine, an "unemployed 'negro' chauffeur and self-styled student of the law," was well known to the county courthouse crowd in Kirkwood, St. Louis County, Missouri. Those who were familiar with him described him as a notorious, quarrelsome character. He was a familiar client of the County Relief Association (county welfare). He had once protested because they wouldn't give him a pair of shoes to go with his Sunday clothes. He had also written to President Roosevelt to complain about the way he had been treated.

In the fall of 1934, Raymond Batson's wife and her aunt were arrested for disturbing the peace in an altercation with a juvenile girl. On December 13, 1934, Justice of the Peace Phillip Rabenau convicted Batson's wife and her aunt of disturbing the peace and sentenced them to thirty days in jail. Rabenau had allowed Batson to represent them, though Batson was no lawyer. On December 28, Christine Harris, fourteen, the juvenile who had been involved in the affray with Batson's wife and aunt, was found not guilty in the juvenile court at Clayton. Batson had been at that hearing. He interrupted the trial several times with loud and belligerent remarks. He pushed George L. Vaughn, Christine Harris's attorney, several times and attempted to punch him but then left the building.

This series of events set Batson off. Unhappy with the results of the juvenile proceeding and with a notion that Judge Rabenau had forged Batson's

name to a recognizance bond on December 24 so that his wife and her aunt could be released, Batson, described as husky and heavy-set, went home, armed himself, and headed over to 140 Kirkwood Road to Justice of the Peace Court.

Just after noon, Justice of the Peace Phillip R. Rabenau sat at his bench when Raymond Batson burst into the room and yelled, "You forged my name at Clayton." He raised a Luger automatic pistol and fired four times into Judge Rabenau's back. The judge died before he could get out of his chair.

Deputy Constable Jack Nece fired twice at Batson in the courtroom. The shootout continued; when Batson ran out into the street, the constable chased him. He shot twice more as Batson fled the scene. So many people began running when shots were fired that it was difficult to tell who the culprit was. Nece had received a superficial bullet wound before Batson escaped. He managed to shoot Batson in the left arm before he got away, but Raymond Batson kept on running. Nece stopped in a nearby restaurant to call police for assistance. Afterward, witnesses directed him toward Batson's destination.

Batson ran to the welfare office at 129 East Argonne Drive, at that time called the St. Louis County Relief Association, and ordered county employees to call the U.S. marshal. Five female employees in the office fled into the streets, except for one who locked herself inside a room on the second floor. Since the office was only a block and a half from the police station, Kirkwood police arrived when Nece did. They put up a ladder on which Orpha Kendrick climbed down as police shot tear gas bombs into the building.

Thirty minutes later, police captured Batson, who had sat down facing the door as if to engage in a shootout with his eventual captors. There was no further bloodshed. When Batson emerged with his uninjured arm raised in the air, police found not only the Luger but also a loaded .38 revolver in his pockets.

During the shooting in the courtroom, a stray bullet, which seemed intended for the constable, struck a dentist by the name of Dr. William E. Poole. Dr. Poole was dictating to the court stenographer. He fell and then managed to get up and walk to a table, where he instructed those around him to call for assistance. The following morning, Poole died.

Relatives of Batson's told authorities that Batson's brother was an inmate in an insane asylum. Dalton W. Schreiber, a Clayton attorney who represented a loan company, told authorities that he had recently sued Batson for eviction. Schreiber had foreclosed the mortgage, but Batson wouldn't leave the premises. He said that Batson told him several weeks earlier that he was "going to have to do something about Rabenau." Batson had still been angry at the time of the shooting because he had lost the case before Judge Rabenau involving his wife and her aunt. Schreiber also reported that Batson once used letterhead inscribed "Ray J. Batson, investment specialist and drawer of negotiary instruments." He said Batson was often in extensive justice of the peace litigation and always represented himself.

Judge Rabenau was forty-four at the time of his death. He had recently been re-elected to his second four-year term. He was a member of the Kirkwood Masonic Lodge, the Lions Club, and the American Legion. During World War I, he had served as a mechanic in the army Air Service overseas, spending eight months in France. Arthritis and sinus trouble caused him to be a patient for three and a half years in the Veterans' Bureau Hospital in Missouri. Rabenau's wife, Augusta, a son, Raymond, and a daughter, Ethel, as well as a sister and his foster mother, survived him. He was buried the following Monday at the National Cemetery at Jefferson Barracks after a funeral at the Bopp's mortuary. Rabenau was so well liked that the Bopp's funeral chapel overflowed with friends and relatives. The funeral procession to the cemetery extended over two miles.

Justice of the Peace Lewis issued a warrant charging Raymond Batson with the murder of Justice of the Peace Philip Rabenau on December 28 and on December 29 with the murder of Dr. Poole. A coroner's jury returned a verdict of murder on December 29 after an inquest into Justice of the Peace Rabenau's death. The witnesses were the court stenographer, Miss Irene Schmidt, Constable Nece, Justice of the Peace George Booth of Valley Park, and Marshal Richard James, all of whom were in the courtroom at the time of the shooting.

On the evening of December 28, Batson, who by then was a patient in the county hospital, made a statement in which he claimed that Judge Rabenau had mistreated him. Justice of the Peace Lewis did not have Batson brought to court for the coroner's jury because of threatened violence against Batson. He was afraid the man would be lynched. Batson remained in the county hospital under the armed guard of ten police officers and two deputy constables, but no mob violence erupted. His trial was scheduled for the following week.

(Note: This author has been unable to ascertain the outcome of the charges against Batson.)

Chapter 12

Justice and Mrs. William A. Pierson
Austin, Travis County, Texas
April 24, 1935

Associate Justice William A. Pierson of the Texas Supreme Court (the highest civil court in the state), sixty-four, and Mrs. Pierson were shot to death on Bull Creek Road about four miles west of Austin, Texas, on the evening of April 24, 1935. The couple's son, Howard Pierson, twenty, a University of Texas student, said two highwaymen killed his parents in a robbery. Howard was shot in the arm.

Howard Pierson took his parents, William and Lena Pierson, driving on the scenic road en route to a pecan experiment station on the Colorado River. About three miles beyond Bull Creek, two men stepped in front of the automobile and pointed guns at them, forcing them to stop the car.

Howard Pierson said, "One of the men had straight black hair, wore a white shirt, and gray pants while the other had curly hair. The black-haired man held the guns on us while the other man took our wallets, money, and my father's watch."

Howard said that Judge Pierson got real angry, grabbed at the guns, and said, "I'll see that you're punished for this!"

One of the men said, "Aw, go to hell."

Judge Pierson told Howard to go for the other man.

Howard jumped on the second man and started choking him. They fell to the ground, struggling. The man pulled out a gun and shot him in the arm. He heard the other man shooting, too, so he got up and ran, hiding in the brush for five or ten minutes.

After the men left, Howard drove back home and called the authorities. He took police to the scene of the shooting on the Bull Creek Road, where other police had already recovered the bodies of Judge and Mrs. Pierson.

65

After nine hours of the police questioning Howard Pierson about the murders, Howard broke down and admitted that he had made up the whole episode. He confessed to his parents' murders. He said that he had lured his parents to a quiet country road about fifteen miles from Austin, shot them several times, and shot himself. His motive was partly revenge. He wanted to be a scientist. His father wanted him to be an attorney. Howard wanted the $17,000 in insurance money on his father's life to continue his studies at the University of Texas. He had told a friend earlier that he had intended to kill his parents for the money. He wanted to kill his father. He would have to kill his mother as well, or the money would go to her. The friend didn't alert the authorities, because the story was just so unbelievable. He later made a written statement.

Howard admitted that he first shot his mother, then his father, and then, after they fell, he shot each of them in the head just to make sure they were dead. Lastly, he shot himself in the arm. He had bought the gun the previous Saturday in Galveston, Texas, driving fifty miles from Houston, where he had been working, to get it. After he killed his parents, he drove ten miles from where he left them and hid his father's watch and his mother's purse. Later, he took police to the hiding place, where they recovered the items.

Autopsies showed Judge Pierson had been shot four times. Mrs. Pierson had been shot three times.

The police detained Howard Pierson in the county jail pending an insanity hearing. Dr. Joe Wooten, a friend of the family who talked to Pierson in a jail cell, said Howard suffered from dementia praecox. The doctor described hallucinations that Howard had that his parents discriminated against him in favor of his brother and sister.

Dr. Wooten recommended that Pierson be placed in the state hospital for the insane for observation for a month or two. District Attorney James P. Hart said that in his study of the case he was trying to decide what route to take, charging him for (capital) murder or proving the young man was insane. Howard was indicted for two counts of murder.

Dr. Wooten said, "He held an imaginary resentment against his parents which was based on his mistaken impression they had discriminated against him." Howard believed he was adopted. "He believed his parents favored his brother and sister," Wooten said. When Howard was twelve, he and the rest of the family spent a year abroad. Howard attended a French school. He disliked Europe, France, and Paris, and wanted to go home to Texas with his father when his father returned earlier than the rest of the family. His father refused to take him with him.

Physically, Howard was rather small and dark. The year after their return to the states, when Howard re-entered Texas schools after being gone for a year, the other children teased him and called him "Frenchy." That teasing, coupled with an occasion years before when he and his parents had been stopped at the Mexican border and Howard was mistaken for a Mexican child, intensified his belief that he was adopted. Sometimes while he was in the Travis County jail, Howard would write compositions in which he called his parents Judge and Mrs. Pierson.

For a while, reporters interviewed Howard in jail until the judge put a stop to it. One reporter stated: "He also had an idea he could become a great scientist. His failures in school he blamed on his parents, felt they were standing in his way. He wanted to obtain his father's insurance money to re-sume his studies." He had the idea that as a scientist, he could save the world. He declared that he was a "special person like Jesus," destined to save the world by science. He claimed a great "board of scientists" directed his life. The board directed his actions and observed his thoughts and doings by agents and by a special machine, which they focused on him even if he was miles away from them. His greatest future invention, though, was going to be immortality. He talked about the endocrine glands and replenishing the chemicals secreted by them. If that didn't work, he would transplant the brains of old people into the bodies of young people, so that the knowledge of the older person would be operating with a young body. Howard's idea was that brains could live for hundreds of years. Eventually, he would incubate babies mechanically and operate on their brains when they were small, ren-dering them feeble-minded. When the baby matured into an adult, he would transplant the old brain into the body. There was later evidence that Howard thought that his parents were enemies to his plans and that it would be best for mankind for them to be destroyed.

Howard's insanity hearing was scheduled in the 53rd District Court before Judge C. A. Wheeler. He was examined at Austin State Hospital and found to be schizophrenic. Doctors testified that it was unlikely that he would ever re-cover from his mental illness. Dr. W. R. Houston testified that schizophrenia might be cured if it was discovered early enough but after it took hold of a per-son, it was extremely unlikely that the person would ever recover.

During observations of him at the jail, Howard showed no emotion and no remorse for the murders. He did not even request to go to his parents' fu-neral. And he didn't think he was insane. Experts said that he could distin-guish right from wrong in every instance except when it came to his own delusion.

Howard's brother, William H. Pierson, was a medical student at the University of Chicago. His sister, Mrs. Harvey (Alice Lenore) Thomas, lived in Salina, Kansas. William flew into Austin and made a statement in Howard's defense. He said the family had known for quite some time that Howard was mentally ill. They had nothing but sympathy for him.

The bodies of Judge and Mrs. Pierson were taken from the site of the murders to a funeral home. The funeral was later held at University Baptist Church. Both Judge and Mrs. Pierson were active members and volunteers in the church. The pallbearers and honorary pallbearers consisted of judges, justices, former law partners, doctors, the governor, former governor, lieutenant governor, and other distinguished members of the state. Burial was in the Texas State Cemetery.

Judge Pierson was born in Gilmer, Upshur County, March 12, 1871. He was a graduate of Baylor, having received his bachelor's degree in 1896. In 1898, he graduated from the University of Texas with a bachelor of laws degree and was admitted to the practice of law. In 1901, he married Miss Lena Haskell of Evansville, Illinois, and Liberty County, Texas.

Justice Pierson, a Democrat, served in the Texas legislature from 1901 to 1905. He passed a bill establishing the College of Industrial Arts at Denton (now University of North Texas). He also led a fight to secure passage of a bill remitting state taxes of Galveston County to the City of Galveston for the building of the seawall after the 1900 Storm disaster. From 1913 to 1921, he served as the judge of the 8th Judicial District Court.

Howard was finally committed to a hospital as criminally insane. He escaped twice, once on the evening of April 15, 1938, and on December 9, 1952. There were two basic problems recapturing him the first time. He had never been fingerprinted, the sheriff said, because he had been from a prominent family and some figured that fingerprinting wouldn't be necessary. Secondly, there was no money to conduct a search. After several years, the sheriff sent out letters and posters, determined that he would find Howard before the end of the year, when the sheriff would leave office. The first time Howard was recaptured in Minneapolis two and a half years after his escape. He worked as a collector for a magazine.

The second time he was recaptured in 1955 in Syracuse, New York, when he went for a consultation with a psychiatrist. An attorney he had consulted contacted Texas authorities. When he was captured, Howard listed his occupations as dishwasher, window washer, porter, and salesman. He had been living in Philadelphia until three months before, when he felt people were watching him. He said he worked in Rochester and Buffalo before going to Syracuse. When reporters took his picture, he said, "Please don't let them take my picture for use in the newspaper. I wish they wouldn't write about me in the newspaper. This publicity isn't good for me."

Finally, in June 1963, after Howard had been held in Rusk State Hospital for another eight years, doctors found that he was medically sane. He was, by then, forty-nine. Travis County Probate Judge Herman Jones received a letter from Dr. Charles W. Castner that said to contact the Travis County sheriff "to take Howard Pierson from this hospital and place him in the proper custody." Since the law didn't allow doctors to make a determination that Howard was legally sane, a trial on that issue would have to be held.

After transfer to the Travis County jail, a visiting judge from Hillsboro, District Judge Sam Johnson, sitting for the 147th District judge Mace Thurman, Jr., who disqualified himself because he had sat through the original sanity hearing when he was a law student, presided over the jury trial on September 12, 1963. Howard Pierson was found legally sane.

During Howard's whole ordeal over the years, his brother and sister, William (known as Bill) and Alice, had stuck by him. Howard's parents had left an estate of less than $50,000 that had been divided three ways. Howard's third had been invested for him and had grown considerably between 1935 and 1963. The sum approximated $800,000 when Howard came to trial. Bill and Alice found the best attorney they could to represent Howard in both the sanity trial and the murder trial. That man was University of Texas- and Harvard-educated Thomas Morrow Reavley. Reavley later said that Howard's siblings could have been greedy and set Howard up for a guilty plea, which is what the district attorney wanted, which included an offer that he would go free after the conviction. Had that happened, however, Howard would have lost all rights to the proceeds of his parents' estate. Instead, his brother and sister unselfishly wanted the best for him.

As soon as the sanity trial ended, Howard's murder trial was scheduled, again to be presided over by Judge Sam Johnson. It was tried in November 1963, before a jury. His defense was not guilty by reason of insanity. Three doctors testified for the defense that at the time of the killings, Howard did not know right from wrong. His diagnosis was paranoid schizophrenia. His delusions included the ability to save the world with his scientific inventions. Dr. D. B. Klein testified that over a year before the murders, he had examined Howard and recommended that he be treated for mental illness. Howard's parents never got him help. The superintendent at Rusk State Hospital testified that Howard had been sane at the time he killed his parents. The jury of seven men and five women found Howard not guilty of murdering his parents twenty-eight years earlier. He was set free.

Subsequent to his release, Howard had one more court hearing. It involved his estate, which had been managed by his brother as guardian. Dr. William Pierson had seen to it that Howard's money was put to work in real estate. He received substantial royalties over the years from the mineral rights. There were also cash accounts and bonds. Dr. Pierson petitioned the court to release him as guardian of Howard's estate so that he could hand over the estate to Howard, but Mr. Reavley didn't believe that Howard was capable of managing his money. After all, Howard had been locked up most of his adult life and was naive as to the ways of the world. Mr. Reavley managed to get Howard to agree that the money would remain invested and under others' control. Howard would receive the income, which was substantial. He made it so that Howard never wanted for anything. The arrangement was so liberal that Howard could purchase a new car every other year.

Mr. Reavley, in an oral history interview, stated that he advised Howard to move to another state and change his name. Howard followed his advice, moving to Seattle, Washington, and changing his name to Robert Hamilton. Howard corresponded with Mr. Reavley for a while until he became angry over the money situation. According to Mr. Reavley, a woman noticed that Howard was well off and convinced Howard that he needed to get control of his money. Howard demanded his money and when told that he couldn't get it, he angrily terminated all contact. Howard Pierson subsequently died in a drowning accident.

After Howard's death, his estate had grown to about a million dollars. Although his sister and brother had never been interested in his money, their heirs engaged in a huge fight over it.

Thomas Reavley went on to serve as county attorney of Nacogdoches, Texas secretary of state, Travis County district judge, Texas Supreme Court justice, and justice of the U.S. Court of Appeals.

Chapter 13

Judge N. J. Johnson
Rutledge, Grainger County, Tennessee
June 18, 1937

On June 18, 1937, Raymond Corum, twenty-nine, a Rutledge hardware and seed merchant, walked into County Judge N. J. Johnson's chambers at the Grainger County Courthouse just after noon, whipped out a pistol, and shot Judge Johnson three times. The judge lost consciousness and was rushed to the Howard-Henderson hospital. He died three hours later, at 3:10 P.M., of bullet wounds to the lungs and stomach. The fifty-six-year-old judge never regained consciousness.

Corum was as well known in the small country community as the judge. Immediately after the shooting, he dropped his gun and gave himself up to a deputy sheriff who had come running when he heard the shots. The sheriff, Robert H. Williams, happened to be driving by the Grainger County Courthouse when he heard the shooting. He thought some boys were playing with firecrackers. When he went inside, Deputy Miller already had Corum in custody and possession of Corum's pistol. The sheriff took Corum to the Knox County jail, which was in the next county, in Knoxville, Tennessee, to be held on a felonious assault charge until he could get the facts and swear out a warrant for murder. He worried that there might be some trouble in Rutledge. He wanted to be free to investigate further without worrying about a lynching.

In a public statement, Sheriff Williams said that he thought Raymond Corum and the county judge were on good terms. The sheriff didn't know of a motive at the time he took Corum in. Corum said that he did kill the judge but insisted, "I'll do my talking in court."

Later that night, when interviewed at the county jail after being told that the judge had died, Corum said, "I'm sorry for his family and his wife and also because of my wife and mother, but I'm not sorry it happened. I'll give testimony in the courtroom that will show my side of this thing."

The *Knoxville Journal* reported that Corum reportedly said he met his sister walking down a corridor from the judge's office when he entered the building. "She walked in front of me and I don't see how I missed her," Corum reportedly said.

The funeral took place the day after the killing, at the Bean Station Baptist Church. Judge Johnson was buried in the church cemetery. Over a thousand people attended the funeral. Judge Johnson left a widow and one son.

Raymond Corum waived the examining trial and returned to Grainger County for prosecution. The preliminary hearing was scheduled for the following Wednesday. Corum had conferred previously with former Tennessee governor Ben W. Hooper of Newport, who was a friend of the Corum family, and with Rutledge attorney J. C. Ward, who agreed to be co-counsel for his defense. He was true-billed by the grand jury on August 2, 1937.

Subsequent to him being charged with murder, Corum's defense team filed a motion with the circuit court challenging the jury array and requesting the jury panel be quashed. They claimed it was not properly constituted. They alleged that the jury box was stuffed with the decedent's political friends. The legally appointed jury commissioners (one of whom was a Corum) had not placed the names in the jury box and drawn them out as was required by law. Two of the three legally appointed and qualified commissioners had been replaced with two persons who had not been legally appointed by the current circuit judge. The original appointees' term had not expired. The two removed commissioners had been appointed by the previous circuit judge. They hadn't vacated their offices and hadn't been properly removed. The other (illegal) commissioners had no authority to do anything, much less, as alleged in the motion, remove all 400 jurors' names from the jury box and refill it with 400 names of their friends. The new array was composed entirely of Judge Johnson's political friends and adherents.

The prosecution never brought Raymond Corum to trial. Subsequent to his arrest, he was charged with weapons offenses and given six months in a workhouse, a fine, and cost of court, but the sentence was suspended until the next term of court. Corum never served a day more than he had served at the Knoxville jail.

Corum also never held another full-time job. Jack McGoldrick, who was eleven at the time of the killing, used to go fishing with Raymond Corum, whom he knew as "Snake." Snake became a reprobate, doing odd jobs, never having a steady job.

The story that Snake told Jack about the incident was that Judge Johnson needed killing. He had heard that the judge, who was a known womanizer, had seduced Raymond's sister (Mrs. Hugh Waller). Snake went to the courthouse to confront the judge about his sister, and when he did, he found his sister in the judge's chambers being compromised by the judge. It was then that he pulled out his pistol and shot the judge dead.

In order to save the embarrassment of a trial, and because popular belief by many was that the killing was justified, the county never brought Corum to justice.

Chapter 14

Judge Lewis Vernon Trueman
Ogden, Weber County, Utah
July 23, 1943

It was 1943. The United States was embroiled in World War II. General Patton, under the command of General Eisenhower, had quickly knocked the Germans out of Sicily. The Russians had just repelled the Nazis on the Eastern Front. In Ogden, Utah, a celebration of the Mormon founding was under way.

Austin Cox, thirty-eight, had recently been discharged from the military. Co-workers described Cox, a tall, thin man with a narrow face, as dull. A laborer, he never seemed alert enough to learn a trade. He often had imaginary grievances against other people and institutions. He had been on work relief several times and often had complaints about that. Once when he worked as a laborer on a school, he claimed to have injured his hand and fought a long time for compensation. It turned out later that he had actually injured his hand in a fistfight.

A few weeks after Cox was discharged from the military, his wife divorced him in a hearing before Judge Lewis Trueman. It was February 19, 1943. The marriage had been a short one; Cox was a wife beater. His wife wanted out. Wanda Cox received an interlocutory decree; the divorce would be final on August 19. Cox did not attend the hearing. His attorney appeared on his behalf. In the divorce proceedings, the parties stipulated and the judge ordered the payment of alimony to help defray the cost of their child, who was born in May, three months after the hearing. Cox had threatened Wanda several times since the divorce, but he had paid the money.

Wanda Carter had married Cox when he was a guard at the Clearfield Naval Depot. The marriage had been rocky almost from the start. She said he was jealous and just plain "mean." He had once tried to kill her by strangling her. He had also tried to pull her tongue out with a piece of wire. Cox had been fired for abusing his wife and remained unemployed when the summer began.

On a Friday night in July 1943, around 11:00 P.M., after spending hours drinking with a young friend, Austin Cox borrowed a .12 gauge shotgun and went gunning for everyone against whom he had an imagined grudge and anyone else who stood in his way.

When he was through, Cox had murdered five people and wounded three more. Shot to death were the following:

1. Mrs. Jane Stauffer, twenty-nine, at her home,
2. Mrs. Stauffer's mother, Mrs. Elizabeth W. Burton, sixty, visiting from Irwin, Idaho,
3. Samuel Nelson, forty-nine, a neighbor of the Stauffers,
4. Mrs. Bessie Brooks, twenty-nine, who was found dead on her front porch, where she ran after she witnessed her husband being shot, and
5. Lewis V. Trueman, fifty-one, judge of the Second District Court.

Cox started out looking for his ex-wife at the home of Jane Stauffer. Cox demanded to see his wife when he arrived. When they told him that she wasn't there, he began shooting.

Both Mrs. Stauffer and her mother were found dead on the floor inside Mrs. Stauffer's home. Mrs. Burton's body fell in front of the washing machine, under which her little four-year-old granddaughter, Beverly Jane, had crawled when she heard the shots and screams. When Police Lieutenant E. L. Shaw heard a child crying, he was unable to find anyone and thought it must be a neighbor baby. Fifteen minutes later, still hearing the sobs, the lieutenant returned to the back porch, crouched down next to the body of Mrs. Burton, and found the little girl, who screamed and held out her arms to the man. He had to move Mrs. Burton's dead body to get to the girl. She had been hiding there for over forty-five minutes.

Mr. Nelson, who had been sitting on his brother's front porch with his wife, mother, and sister, heard shots and thought someone was celebrating Pioneer Days. He said to Cox, "Why don't you do some of your celebrating over here?" Cox shot him at close range.

Police were at the scene at the Stauffer home when they received a phone call from Dr. Frank Bartlett, a neighbor of Judge and Mrs. Trueman's. He had heard shots, seen a lone man drive away in an old shabby car, and run to the

Trueman home to see whether he needed to render assistance. He found Judge Trueman on the floor, Mrs. Trueman holding her husband's hand.

Mrs. Trueman reported to the police that she and her husband had retired for the night and were asleep when they were awakened by a crashing noise downstairs in their home. Judge Trueman got up, turned on a light, and the two of them looked out the window. They saw a man outside the house. Judge Trueman called to the man and asked what he was doing. The man's answer was to blast the judge with his shotgun. The pellets struck the judge in the head; he fell and died immediately.

Wounded over the course of the evening were:

1. Bert Stauffer, husband of Jane Stauffer. Shot in the hand and the shoulder.
2. Dale Brooks, twenty-nine, husband of Bessie Brooks. Shot in the hand and arm.
3. Merlin Brown, state highway patrolman. Shot in the ear.

While authorities were setting up roadblocks and searching for the assailant, Austin Cox drove up behind the police station. He had other grudges to carry out. He wanted to "get" Deputy Sheriff George E. Weatherstone and one or two other officers who had arrested him once when he had been beating his wife. At the time of his arrest, he'd told the deputy, "I will get you for this." He also was after Justice of the Peace Alfred Gladwell of Burch Creek, who had found him guilty of an assault on his wife.

Carrying his shotgun, he walked inside, closed the heavy metal door behind himself, and headed through the desk sergeant's office toward the captain's office. The city auditor, the deputy city auditor, the building engineer, and several officers ran into the captain's anteroom. Police Radio Technician F. D. Thompson slammed the captain's office door when he saw the man with the shotgun. When they heard shots, others in the captain's office ran into the anteroom. The slamming of the door distracted Cox and caused his aim to be off. He had fired two shots at two state highway patrol officers headed his way, but the shots shattered the glass in the door, hit a door panel, and only grazed State Highway Patrolman C. Merlin Brown's ear. Two military policemen, who had been in the room next to the desk sergeant's office, tackled Cox, who put up quite a fight. The state patrol officers ran over and beat him over the head with the butts of their guns. According to reports, it took at least half a dozen blows to his head and face before he would finally let himself be subdued, but he continued to utter curse words at the police as he lay on the station floor.

The *Deseret News* reported that Cox struggled with the officers and said, "Why in the ———— don't you shoot me? Come on ————, get it over with."

When police completed their investigation, they were unable to explain why Cox had gone to the Stauffer home. Though Cox told Police Chief Rial C. Moore that he had received a telephone call that his ex-wife, Wanda May Carter Cox of Porterville, was at the Stauffers', Wanda said that she didn't know the Stauffers.

Judge Trueman was born in Roanoke, Virginia, October 10, 1891. He married Ora B. Johnson in Virginia on July 21, 1918. They had just celebrated their twenty-fifth wedding anniversary a few days before his death. In 1920, he graduated from Mercer College in Georgia. A Democrat, he served in the Florida legislature in 1925, 1926, and 1927. He practiced law in Florida, including two years as a prosecutor. He was vice president and charter member of the bar association of the Florida First Judicial District. He served as an aide on the staff of Florida Governor Doyle E. Carlton from 1928 to 1933 and moved to Ogden in 1933, where he began as an associate with Joseph Chez, who later became Utah attorney general. He was a member of the Ogden Chapter No. 2, Royal Arch Masons and Elks Lodge in Ogden.

Judge Trueman had been appointed to the bench in 1939 after his predecessor, Judge Eugene E. Pratt, became a Supreme Court justice. Trueman was elected in 1940. Before his appointment, he was an assistant county attorney since 1937.

Besides his wife, his father and two half-sisters of Roanoke, Virginia, survived him.

At a memorial service held in honor of Judge Trueman on July 29 in his courtroom, Judge Trueman was described as "a self-made man, affable, friendly, courteous, and independent." Members of the bar said, "He had administered the law honestly and without fear or favor. He lived among us a good fellowman."

Justice David W. Moffatt of the Supreme Court of Utah said, "I found him ever a genial, vigorous, interesting personality, with whom discussion or debate was stimulating and agreeable but never bitter."

When Austin Cox was asked after his arrest how he had found the judge's house at night, he said he looked up the address in the telephone book. He also admitted that he had been to the judge's house on another occasion before July 23.

As part of Cox's defense, his lawyers alleged that he was insane at the time of the murders. Two "alienists" were appointed by the court to examine him. They were Dr. Owen P. Heniger of the Utah State Hospital and Dr.

A.A. Robinson of Ogden. On August 31, the court held an insanity hearing. Cox was found sane.

The murder case was tried to a jury on September 2 and 3, 1943. John H. Stulce, a friend of Cox's, testified that on various occasions Cox had told him that he would find the judge, Sheriff Watson, two deputies, and his wife "and get them all." He said that on the afternoon of July 23, the defendant appeared to be more intoxicated than he had seen him in quite a while. Another witness, though, a seventeen-year-old boy whom Cox had spent a lot of time with that day at the Pioneer Days celebration, testified that they had been unable to get the alcohol they had wanted and had been reduced to sharing a large bottle of beer. He said that Cox was not drunk that day. The former Mrs. Cox testified that when she and Austin Cox discussed getting a divorce, he had told her that he would kill anyone who participated in taking her away from him. He said that he had worked for seven years around the State Mental Hospital of Arizona and that he could "beat a murder rap."

Austin Cox, killer of Judge Trueman. (Courtesy Utah State Archives)

Austin Cox had never met the judge he murdered. His attorney appeared for him in court and entered into a stipulation for the terms of the divorce.

After a trial that lasted six days, Cox was sentenced to death by firing squad on September 8. The execution was set for October 15.

Cox appealed on several technical grounds. He alleged that his former wife shouldn't have been allowed to testify, that the indictment was insufficient in that it didn't specifically set out the time and place of the murders, and that his requested insanity instruction wasn't given. On April 18, 1944, the Supreme Court of Utah ruled against him on all grounds.

Austin Cox, State Prison Number 7554, was executed by shooting at 5:40 A.M. on June 19, 1944, at the state prison. Utah was the last state to use a firing squad to execute prisoners.

To this day, according to a county law librarian, the court clerks at the courthouse in Weber County report that Judge Trueman's ghost frequently roams his fourth-floor courtroom.

Chapter 15

Judge Charles H. Jackson
Mountain Grove, Wright County, Missouri
March 29, 1948

Ernest Afton Scott, forty-eight, and his wife, Verla, forty, were farmers in Missouri. They were the parents of ten children ranging in age from two to twenty. Two of their children were married. In the spring of 1948, Verla Scott did something that was not commonly done in those days. She separated from her husband and filed for divorce. Judge Charles H. Jackson would have been the judge to hear the case. It was filed in Wright County, one of the six counties in Judge Jackson's district.

According to local legend, Mrs. Scott had consulted Judge Jackson as to what she should do to escape the frequent beatings administered by her husband. Judge Jackson had sent her home to try to make her marriage work because she had no job skills and a passel of children. Even though Verla went home and made the effort to keep the family together, Ernest had beaten her again. She escaped from her husband and saw Judge Jackson on the street, where she asked him again what she should do. Locals say that either Ernest Scott saw them talking or small town gossip got back to Scott that she and the judge were seen talking.

Judge Charles H. Jackson was distinguished by being physically handicapped. He only had one arm but never allowed that to restrict his activities. He was an active golfer, hunter, farmer, and sportsman. According to official news reports, on March 29, Judge Jackson, fifty-six, and his secretary, Mrs. Pauline Ball, went to Mrs. Ball's parents' home so the judge could look at some cattle he was interested in purchasing.

Her parents, Mr. and Mrs. Andrew Torkelson, owned a farm about seven miles away from Mountain Grove, Missouri, in Douglas County, contiguous to Wright County. Douglas County was not in the judge's district. At about

5:00 P.M., as Judge Jackson and Mr. Torkelson stood in the barnyard talking, they saw another farmer, Ernest Afton Scott, a neighbor of Torkelson's who lived just across the road, drive up in his car. He parked and got out, with a .32 Winchester rifle draped over his arm, and came into the yard. Scott said, "Torkelson, step aside."

Judge Jackson asked, "What are you going to do?"

Scott replied, "You broke up my home."

Judge Jackson stepped back and said, "I was only trying to help you."

Scott then shouldered his rifle. The judge ran, but Scott shot him in the back. The bullet hit the judge near his left shoulder, breaking his collarbone and lodging in his back. Scott ran to the judge's car, tore the wires loose under the hood, jumped into his own vehicle, and fled, driving into Mountain Grove.

At the home of Mr. and Mrs. James Raney, his parents-in-law, Ernest Scott asked to see his wife, Verla. He coaxed Verla outside, saying he only wanted to talk to her. Walking to his car, he pulled out his rifle and shot her. The bullet hit her in the right arm, traveled through her body, and came out through her left arm. She died instantly.

Both shootings took place within a span of forty-five minutes. Scott fled again, this time abandoning his car about a mile from his home.

Elmer Hold, a witness to the first murder, drove into town and told a deputy in the sheriff's office of the murder. The deputy notified the state highway patrol headquarters at Willow Springs. A manhunt began which lasted two days. Authorities searched the Scott home and found $4,000 but not Scott.

Scott hid in the wooded area near Mountain Grove, successfully evading capture until the next evening, when he went to the home of Jennings Tucker, who lived three miles south of Mountain Grove and spent the night. The next morning, Tucker took Scott to Scott's father's home and the elder Mr. Scott called Sergeant Earl Barkley of the state highway patrol, who took Ernest into custody.

On Wednesday morning, March 31, first-degree murder charges were filed in Magistrate E.L. Colton's court in Mountain Grove, Wright County, for the murder of Mrs. Scott. Later, charges were brought in Douglas County for the murder of Judge Jackson, Douglas County being where Scott killed the judge. The sheriff held Scott in the Wright County jail without bond. The court scheduled the preliminary hearing at Hartville on April 8.

Judge Jackson was born April 8, 1893, in Norwood, Wright County, Missouri. He graduated from the Norwood High School, Southwest Missouri State College, and, in 1914, from Kansas City School of Law with an LL.B.

degree. He began practicing law in 1914 also. He was elected and served as Wright County prosecuting attorney from January 1, 1915, to 1920. In 1922, he moved to Mountain Grove, where he bought stock in the First National Bank and became cashier. Later, he sold the stock and became a full-time attorney. He served as Republican state committeeman for several years. During his tenure, he was secretary of the Republican State Committee during the Harding campaign in 1920. In November 1940, he was elected judge of the 18th Circuit, which consisted of Wright, Webster, Polk, Dallas, Hickory, and Camden counties. Judge Jackson was very well known in Camden County, where he held his first court hearing in Camdenton on January 6, 1941. He was a member of the Executive Council of the State Judiciary at the time of his death as well as a member of the Masons, the Order of the Shrine, and Kiwanis. He actively worked for underprivileged children, served on the Mountain Grove School Board for several years, and supported local athletics both morally and financially. He was survived by a wife, Fay Jackson, who inherited their estate valued in the approximate amount of $50,000, including their farm and cattle, and by five brothers, G. J. Jackson, Otho Jackson, H. M. Jackson, all of Norwood, P. H. Jackson of Kansas City, and H. N. Jackson of Pawhuska, Oklahoma. Judge Jackson enjoyed boating on the Lake of the Ozarks.

According to news reports, the only motive for the killing of Judge Jackson was that the judge recently rendered a verdict against Ernest Scott in a civil suit in Wright County. The defendant, however, was quoted in the newspaper as saying, when asked why he'd shot the judge, "Oh, I don't know, I thought he'd broke up my home."

It was also supposedly well known that Judge Jackson was a "skirt chaser" and that on the day of his death, he was not discussing cows with the farmer but philandering with the farmer's daughter. Some folks thought that perhaps the judge and Mrs. Scott were involved with each other; she thought that the judge would help her get away from her husband. Still others said that the judge was the biological father of the tenth Scott child. At the trial, Scott's attorneys tried to raise the issue of the judge's womanizing, but the presiding judge kept it out of evidence. The official transcript of the trial is missing from the clerk's office.

On April 8, 1948, Scott waived the preliminary hearing in the case for the murder of his wife and continued to be jailed without bond. He was bound over to the June term of the court. At a hearing on May 22, 1948, Scott's defense attorneys, General W. and Clyde Rogers, of Gainesville, Missouri, appeared and requested that a Dr. Sartain examine Scott as to his mental condition. That motion was granted at defense's expense. On June

17, Scott and his attorneys appeared and filed a motion for change of venue. That was granted. The Missouri Supreme Court appointed Circuit Judge Fred H. Maughmer of Savannah, Missouri, to hear the case. The case was reset to June 28.

The trial began on July 1. Wright County Prosecutor Frank Collier asked the jury of twelve men for the death penalty. Roscoe Patterson and A. M. Curtis of Springfield assisted in the prosecution. Defense attorneys argued that Scott was insane at the time of the shootings and couldn't be held responsible. Prosecutors subpoenaed fifty-four witnesses, including the defendant's fifteen-year-old daughter, Willa Mae, who witnessed the shooting of her mother. After two days of testimony, the jury deliberated for only fifty-three minutes and cast three ballots before deciding that Ernest Afton Scott should die in the gas chamber at Jefferson City, Missouri, for the murder of his wife.

Ernest Scott was never tried for the murder of Judge Charles Jackson. Many locals believed that the "powers-that-be" did not want the judge's reputation besmirched by testimony of his "affairs."

Judge Maughmer instructed defense attorneys that they had until July 31 to file their motion for new trial and set the hearing on the motion, if one was filed, for August 7. Scott did file such a motion, alleging that two of the jurors were related to his deceased wife's family and that the jurors were allowed to visit Judge Jackson's grave during a recess in the trial. The attorneys also argued that the quick verdict showed prejudice on the part of the jury and that they did not properly consider the evidence. The judge overruled all motions and arguments.

On August 9, 1948, Scott was transferred from the county jail to the state penitentiary at Jefferson City, Missouri, where he was incarcerated on death row. His execution date was set for September 21, 1948, but was delayed due to the appeal of his conviction. He managed to delay his case for a year until his appeal was denied on September 23, 1949. The court set his execution date for November 4, 1949.

Ernest Afton Scott was taken to the death house. His attorneys appealed to the governor to no avail. The small stone house looked almost like a church with a white cross embossed on the entrance sidewalk. At 11:58 P.M., Scott entered the death chamber from a tiny adjoining cell. He was dressed all in black, including a black mask over his eyes. There were two chairs with straps. Over fifty witnesses, officials, guests, and reporters lined the five windows. Two guards strapped Scott into one of the chairs and left when a minister entered.

After Reverend Kelly spoke to Scott, Scott told the minister, "Goodbye. I'll see you in heaven."

"Goodbye," the minister said and stepped outside the chamber, the door clanging shut behind him.

Warden Eidson stepped forward, flipped a lever, and pellets of cyanide shot into a container of acid. Smoke-like fumes rose quickly and filled the room. Scott tensed; his head fell back, then slumped forward. Five minutes later, they started the blowers. A bit later a doctor went inside, examined Scott, and declared him dead. The doctor said that Ernest wore a half-smile on his face.

Chapter 16

Judge Allison D. Wade
Warren, Warren County, Pennsylvania
January 13, 1954

Norman Moon, twenty-nine, a World War II Air Force veteran with red hair but not with a temper to match, at least according to his family, stood 5'11" and weighed 175 pounds. When he returned from fighting the Nazis, he went into the construction business with his father and brothers. He was a foreman and managed the work crews well, running bulldozers, laying pipe, stringing power lines, and paving roads.

In the summer of 1949, Norman was on a construction job laying a power line through Tidioute, twenty-one miles east of Warren. There he met Janet Schwab, twenty-eight, the daughter of a car dealer. Janet was a blonde whom Norman often described as "the most beautiful girl in the world." It was love at first sight. The couple married on July 1 and went to live in Connellsville in southwestern Pennsylvania, near where Norman had been born. Three months later, the Moons moved to Leadville, Colorado, where Norman got a job selling trailers. He also started abusing his wife.

In 1951, the couple returned to Connellsville and stayed together until July 24, 1952, when Janet filed assault and battery charges against Norman in a Fayette County magistrate's office. She alleged that Norman had beaten her with his fists, knocked her to the floor, and called her vile names. She said that he threatened to kill her if she did not get out. There was also a notation of nonsupport and desertion on the complaint jacket, but nothing came up in court about that.

Norman was arrested and released on a $500 bond. Janet moved home with her parents. On September 8, 1952, Janet swore out a complaint of nonsupport in Warren County. Norman decided that he could defend himself. His well-to-do parents could have supplied him with counsel even if he couldn't have afforded an attorney himself. His earnings were about $100 per week, not a small sum in the early 1950s. Norman Moon's bail was set at $300 cash. He made bond and was released. Justice of the Peace Tracy M. Greenlund forwarded the criminal charges of nonsupport to the president judge of the 37th Judicial District Court, Allison D. Wade.

On September 26, 1952, Judge Wade conducted a hearing where Moon presented his defense, including cross-examining his wife himself. The case was continued from month to month until finally, after Moon did get an attorney and briefs were filed, Judge Wade made an order that read substantially as follows:

AND NOW, to-wit, December 29, 1952, the above case having come before this Court for hearing, and upon consideration of the testimony taken, it is hereby ordered, adjudged and decreed that the defendant, Norman W. Moon, shall pay to Lenor C. Jordan, one of the Probation Officers for the county of Warren, the sum of Thirty ($30.00) Dollars per week for the support and maintenance of his wife, Janet L. Moon, commencing January 5, 1953, and continuing each and every week thereafter until further order of the court, costs to be paid by the Defendant.

But Moon had no intention of paying and, in fact, never paid the support. On February 17, 1953, the prosecutor filed a petition for a bench warrant, which was granted by Judge Wade. A bench warrant directing the Sheriff to bring Norman Moon before the court was issued on March 6. On July 17, the bench warrant was returned. Moon had been arrested. There were more hearings, more testimony, and more legal argument. Moon's bail was increased to $500 cash to guarantee his appearance on September 9, 1953, or else forfeit the bond. On July 31, Moon and his attorney filed a petition to dismiss the nonsupport case. Moon posted the extra $200 bail on August 3. On September 9, another hearing was held. Moon and his attorney requested a dismissal or at least a reconsideration of the amount of support, which Judge Wade denied on September 30, 1953. Moon's attorney then appealed to the Superior Court in Pittsburg on the grounds of prior prosecution in Fayette County, which contained a nonsupport charge in addition to the assault and battery charge. The Superior Court affirmed Judge Wade's decision in December 1953, finding that there had never been a nonsupport charge filed in another county.

When Norman Moon appeared to collect a copy of the Superior Court's ruling at the Superior Court clerk's office in Pittsburgh, he asked a clerk for the names and addresses of all seven of the Superior Court judges who had ruled on his case. The clerk didn't like the look on his face, so she refused to give out the information. The only thing Moon would get from her would be written materials relevant to his case. He paid the $1.50 for the written opinion and left.

Upon receiving the Superior Court ruling, Judge Wade, anticipating finally concluding the Moon matter, set another hearing, this time for Norman Moon to show cause why he should not be incarcerated for failure to pay the support ordered more than a year before. He was over $1,500 behind. That hearing was scheduled to take place on January 13, 1954. In addition to Norman Moon, present in court that day were Janet Moon's attorney, Harold S. Hampson,

Judge Allison Wade

Warren County district attorney, Meyer Kornreich, a Dr. John Thompson, who was awaiting a hearing in another case, clerk of the courts, Ralph E. Sires, court reporter, Mrs. Bernice R. Seavy, and George Todd, courtcrier.

Harold Hampson testified later that when he arrived he talked to Norman Moon. He asked Moon if he knew what he wanted to do about this matter, "and he said we would be told in due course."

Before the proceedings started, Meyer A. Kornreich, the district attorney of Warren County for nine years, approached Moon and tried to shake hands with him, but Moon turned away. Kornreich told him that his attorney said he couldn't be there that morning so they could defer until the afternoon, but Kornreich later testified, "Moon said 'No, I want to get it over with now. Or words to that effect.'" It was 10:10 A.M. Kornreich left. He returned around 11:00 A.M.

Judge Allison D. Wade, fifty-one, had gone downstairs to handle a case involving a disabled lady who could not climb up to his courtroom. After that case was concluded, the judge returned shortly before 11:00 A.M. The judge always sat at the end of the bench closest to the jury box rather than in the middle. The judge called the case. Mr. Kornreich told the judge a little history of the case, for the record, and that the opinion from the Superior Court had recently come down. Mr. Hampson made a statement also, including some history of the case. All the proceedings were within Moon's hearing.

Courtcrier George Todd later testified, "The D.A. asked Mr. Moon if he understood him correctly in that he still refused to comply with the court order.

Moon replied, "Absolutely. That is correct."

Judge Wade said, "Will you come forward, please?"

Moon stood up where he was sitting behind the railing. He wore a jacket that zipped down from the middle. When he stood, he deliberately opened the right flap of his jacket. From where Kornreich sat he could see the outline of a gun stuck in Moon's belt. Kornreich saw Moon start to reach down for what he thought was a gun, so Kornreich jumped up from the chair and ran toward the door. He heard one shot when he got to the corner of Mr. Sires' desk. He ran downstairs to the sheriff's office and called the state police and the borough police.

Norman Moon, killer of Judge Wade

Moon fired first at Hampson and then at the fleeing Kornreich. Hampson said, "As soon as I heard that shot, I fell down to the floor and I crawled. I crawled on my stomach, expecting another shot, until I got in immediately behind the witness stand. Then I paused for just a moment to see whether there would be any more shooting. When I heard nothing, I crawled on my stomach through the door that goes into the judge's chamber over to my right." Hampson went in and called the local police. The line was busy. He had heard a second shot just before he got to the judge's chamber. While inside the judge's chamber, he heard other shots.

The courtcrier testified,

I heard a noise immediately back of the bench which indicated that the judge was scrambling along—

The judge said, looking at a position toward the platform, and addressing his remarks in that direction, "I will not sentence you. No, I will not sentence you."

... Moon said, "You will back down now, you bastard, you will back down now," and that was followed by additional shots, two, I believe.

87

The judge stood up and called, "I am shot. I am shot," and he then started and ran or limped very badly in a running gait past the front of my desk, that is, toward the courtroom from my position back of the desk, and around toward the chambers.

The judge collapsed in front of the witness stand and front part of the jury box.

Bernice R. Seavy, the official stenographer and secretary to the judge, felt a bullet whiz past her and crawled under her desk. She testified, "Judge Wade said, 'Don't shoot. Please don't shoot. I won't sentence you.'

"He said, 'You goddam fucking son of a bitch, you will never get the chance to.'

"As Moon said that he shot right toward the judge, and the judge's legs straightened out and he rolled over and I don't know anything after that."

The courtcrier thought he heard Moon changing the clip in the gun. He heard footsteps on the linoleum. He heard the lock of the door as it opened and then a woman screamed. He heard five or six shots all in the space of about a minute or a minute and a half.

Samuel F. Bonavita, a practicing attorney in Warren County, described the scene outside the courthouse. The sidewalk was clean leading from the Courthouse to the street, but there was snow shoveled and piled approximately two feet high on both sides of the sidewalk in front of the Courthouse. The walkway was clear down to Moon's car, a Dodge four-door sedan, where he had run.

Bonavita had seen Moon earlier in the morning inside the courthouse, heard shots, and seen Moon run down the stairs and outside, so he followed him. "He had the driver's door open. I yelled down to him and I said, 'You are not going any place, bud,'" and I raced down to his car and stopped at the right rear.

"He circled toward the back of his car. He had a jacket in his left arm and it was covering his right arm. When he got about three feet from me he removed the jacket and he had a .45 Colt automatic in his right hand and he pointed that at me directly and he said, 'Don't try to stop me or I will shoot you.'"

They saw two state police troopers crossing the street. Moon pointed the gun in their direction and said, "'It is all over, I may as well finish it now.'" The troopers didn't see him. They were on their way to the courthouse in response to the phone calls. They ran at right angles to his aim and entered the courthouse.

Moon backed around the car and told Bonavita, "'Don't grab me or I'll shoot you.'" Bonavita had some conversation with him—not knowing that he'd shot the judge, "... like it's not so bad." Moon got in the car and drove away as Bonavita said, "'You shouldn't get so excited over a small matter.'"

Dr. John E. Thompson was in court waiting on another case. When the shooting started, he got under a bench. When it stopped, he could hear Mrs. Seavy crying, "'Help, help, the judge has been shot.' After that I came over to where the judge was lying ... I examined him. He was breathing as though his lungs were full of moisture or blood and his color was ashen gray. His eyes were open, but there was no reaction to light and his pulse was almost imperceptible."

The district attorney asked Thompson at the later trial, "Did he die in your arms?"

Dr. Thompson said, "He did, right there as I had my hand on his wrist. He died right there."

It had been only three or four minutes from the time the last two shots were fired until Thompson got to Judge Wade.

Bonavita turned and ran back into the courthouse, where he met up with the two state policemen. He told them that he didn't know what the man had done, but that the guy with a gun had just driven away. The troopers took Bonavita with them, all of them running back outside and flagging down another trooper cruising by. They all climbed inside and, siren blaring, raced out west of town in the direction Moon had gone. It wasn't long before they caught up with Moon. When Moon wouldn't pull over in response to their demands, two of the officers started shooting at his tires. After many rounds, a carefully placed shot blew out Moon's left rear tire and he skidded into a snowbank.

Moon climbed out of his car before the state policemen could get to him. He put his .45 to his throat and fired a shot. As he fell to the ground, blood splattered the white blanket of snow around him. The officers immediately placed him in custody and drove him to Warren General Hospital. He did not die. Medical professionals wired his shattered jaw in three places and released him to the county jail two weeks later.

Janet Schwab and her family were devastated by the news that Norman had killed Judge Wade. Besides being well known in the community, the judge had been a personal friend of the Schwab family. Mrs. Schwab, Janet's mother, said, "He was a wonderful judge. I can't understand why this had to happen." She went on to say that Norman had always been incredibly jealous of Janet. "At her wedding when her father kissed her after the ceremony, Norman became very jealous and went into a tantrum." A year before the murder, on Halloween, Moon had come to the Schwab home armed with a shotgun and looking for Janet. Mrs. Schwab, who had been on the telephone, told him she was alone in the house. He pointed the shotgun at her and shouted, "Drop that!" She said she dropped the phone instantly and when he stormed upstairs looking for Janet, Mrs. Schwab ran out of the house.

William Lutz, deputy coroner for the county, conducted the autopsy on Judge Wade. He found that the judge had been shot twice. A bullet entered at almost the armpit on the left and came through at the floating rib on the right. It traveled diagonally down at almost a forty-five-degree angle. The second bullet didn't pass through—it entered from the left and was found just under the skin on the right.

In 1902, Judge Wade was born in Warren to H. Douglas Wade and Alice J. Wade. He had been a lifelong, active member of such organizations as the Kiwanis Club, the Warren County Historical Society, Shakespeare Club, Conewango Club, and Trinity Memorial Church. He had graduated from Warren High School in 1920. His B.S. in commerce was earned at the University of Virginia. He received his LL.B from the law school at the University of Buffalo. He had also attended Harvard.

After being licensed to practice law in 1930, Mr. Wade was first associated with the firm of Bordwell and Eldred for two years before opening his own partnership with Richard P. Lott in 1932. He had served as county solicitor for nine years and was active in the Republican Party, having served as county chairman and national committeeman. He was first elected president judge of Warren and Forest Counties for a ten-year term in 1942.

Judge Wade had been actively involved in public speaking and juvenile affairs. On a personal level, his main hobby had been art. He had won many awards for his oil paintings. His wife, Ruth Tillotson Wade, an invalid, predeceased him after a fall down some stairs two years earlier. They were the parents of a daughter, Noel, age nine at the time of his death. His sister, who lived in Harrisburg, Mrs. Lucille Wade Williams, also survived him.

On January 15, 1954, Chief of Police Michael Evan filed information with the justice of the peace, Tracy M. Greenlund, resulting in charges against Norman Moon for the murder of the judge.

Funeral services for Judge Wade were held on January 16, 1954. He was so well thought of that, besides relatives from out of town, hundreds of people attended the judge's funeral. Attorneys and local, state, and federal judges from all over Pennsylvania came to show their respect. U.S. Supreme Court Justice Robert H. Jackson, a close friend of Judge Wade's, sent a message that read in part, "Had a personal friendship and great respect for Wade and find his assassination almost too shocking to believe. Wish I could join fellow lawyers in attendance as a mark of respect to a good judge."

On January 18, 1954, a warrant charging Moon with the murder was served on the defendant at Warren General Hospital, where he was still recuperating from his self-inflicted gunshot wound.

On January 20, 1954, Governor John S. Fine named Alexander C. Flick, Jr., fifty, president of the Warren-Forest County Bar Association, as president judge of the 37th Judicial District. Also on that day, Pennsylvania Attorney General Robert E. Woodside appointed two special prosecutors, David S. Kohn and Harrington Adams, deputy attorneys general, to prosecute Moon.

Moon was released from the hospital on January 29 and arraigned before Justice of the Peace Tracy M. Greenlund, who remanded him to the Warren County Jail.

On March 3, 1954, the grand jury of Quarter Sessions Court returned a true bill and the trial was set for May 10 before newly appointed Judge Flick in the very courtroom and courthouse where the murder had been committed.

On May 10, Moon's trial opened with Moon being represented by Samuel D. Bramer, his family's corporate attorney, assisted by T. A. Waggoner, E. H. Beshlin, and J. B. Nathan. The judge ordered a photo blackout of the courthouse but assigned the first two rows of the courtroom to the press, to be accessible as soon as the jury venire roll call ended. Newspapers appealed the order, but the criminal justice system rolled on. one-hundred-four persons were summoned for the venire. Jury selection was completed by May 17 and the trial began.

The state brought in twenty-two witnesses, including District Attorney Kornreich, who was unable to prosecute the case, since he was a witness.

Another witness was William Kress, the operator of a general merchandise store. Moon had bought the gun from him on January 12, 1954, at 2:00 P.M. He had asked specifically for a .45 caliber Colt automatic. When he showed Moon a used one and quoted him $30, Moon said, "That is a hell of a price to ask for a gun in that condition."

Moon said he wanted to shoot target, that he had been in the army and knew the gun. He bought fifty shells. The new Colt .45 came with two clips. He made out an application on that date, left, and came back some ten to fifteen minutes later. He told Kress that he had gone across the street to a cafe to the restroom. He said he was sick and appeared very pale. He told Kress that he didn't want to wait the forty-eight hours the law required before taking the gun with him. Kress argued with Moon, but Moon talked him into letting him take the gun with him, in violation of the law. He said he had a cold in his bowels and was so far from home that it would be bad for his condition and out of his way to come back for the gun. Under Pennsylvania law at that time, only a uniformed officer could take a gun at the time of purchase. The forty-eight-hour waiting period was to give the police a chance to object to the applicant. (Mr. Kress was later prosecuted in Allegheny County for this sale.)

Another important witness for the prosecution was State Police Officer Charles C. Naddeo. He testified that at the hospital, "We asked him whether or not he intended to kill Judge Wade and Mr. Hampson? He replied, 'Yes.'"

Nurse Marion Freeborough, who had been present when state police were questioning Moon, testified as follows:

"You may state whether or not you heard Sergeant Mehallick ask this question:
"Question: How many people did you intend to kill?"
"Yes, I did."
"Do you recall how it was answered?"
"I think he used his fingers, put up two fingers."
"Who did?"
"Mr. Moon."
"Also asked did he intend to kill judge?"
"Yes."
"Hampson?"
"Yes."
"And did he intend it when he bought the gun?"
"Yes."
"Did he buy the gun for that purpose?"
"Yes."

The defense called six witnesses, most of whom were Moon's relatives. Norman's mother testified that Norman was the youngest of her four sons. He had always been a quiet boy and hadn't gotten out much. He stayed home evenings and read, usually had library books to read for school; would read the *Saturday Evening Post, Reader's Digest*. Played checkers with his father. Sometimes his friends would come in and they'd play Monopoly. Norman was manager of the football team in his junior and senior years at high school. Norman left for the service in February of his senior year of high school, 1944. His mother said they gave her his diploma. He discharged from the air force in November of 1945. He and two of his surviving brothers, including one who was married, lived with them and worked for their father doing telephone lines. (One brother had been killed in the war.) Another brother was married and had his own place. In 1949, Norman and his father, for whom he still worked, came up to the Warren area. Norman met Janet Schwab and, his mother testified, "She was very anxious to get married."

They went on a ten-day honeymoon and returned to Connellsville to an apartment. The marriage was a very unhappy one from the beginning. Janet was very nervous and emotional. Mrs. Moon said, "One time I was called out, called by their landlord who said she was carrying on in such a terrible way that she would have to call the police."

"I asked her to please not call the police. She says, 'Then can you do something about it?' She says, 'Will you come out and see if you can get her settled down. I cannot stand it. My husband is sick. She just screams, carries on. I cannot have it."

After Norman and Janet separated, Norman spoke of taking his life. His mother grew worried when he wasn't sleeping well. She searched his room and found a gun in the drawer of the chifforobe. A small gun, not a rifle. It wasn't the Colt .45; it was smaller. She hid it in a cupboard.

Moon himself also testified. He said he wore a dress shirt, gray pants, gray flannel sport shirt, and light jacket. He entered through the main entrance, having parked out front. The judge was sitting in the "center" of the bench.

Moon:

> I stood up and I got rather excited. I pulled the revolver out from my belt—I had it under my belt and I don't know, I knocked the safety off the gun and shuffled the sliding mechanism of the gun-that part on top-and a shell came out. I had anticipated killing myself but pretty much in the excitement I just started shooting. I got awfully mad. I was pretty much mad, extremely mad when the case hadn't even been called into court and I was sitting there and was just called before the bench for sentence. I started shooting and I have a faint idea of what I did but exactly what I done—I have ideas on that, on what I did since, but as far as exact actions I can't explain every one of them because I have a much different vision of what happened in the court that day than what I have heard so far.

He said he wasn't intending on shooting anyone, was going to kill himself, but he got so mad—the judge, after he fell, got up and started coming at him. (Some witnesses said it appeared that the judge tripped when he got up.) So he pointed the gun at the judge.

On Tuesday, May 25, four months after the murder of Judge Wade, the jury of ten men and two women brought in a first-degree murder verdict and fixed the penalty at death. Immediately, Moon's attorneys set about filing post-trial motions. On May 25, a motion for new trial was filed by the defense.

July 31, 1954, Sheriff L.E. Linder filed a petition praying the court to appoint a sanity commission to inquire into the prisoner's condition. Moon had engaged in some rather strange behaviors while in the custody of the sheriff at the county jail. The judge granted the petition. Moon was removed to Warren State Hospital, and the court appointed Dr. Robert H. Israel, Dr. William S. Walters, and Dr. Pierson Eaton to the commission.

On August 5, the commission examined Moon at Warren State Hospital. Their findings were reported to the court on October 13. On October 15, Moon was returned to Warren County Jail from state hospital. On October 21, the report of the sanity commission was filed with the court. Judge Flick, upon considering the findings of sanity commission, statements of the defendant's counsel, and consideration of the entire proceedings, found Norman W. Moon to be legally sane and ordered proceedings in the case to be continued.

On October 29, counsel for the defendant filed exceptions to the court's findings of October 21, 1954. On February 9, 1955, the court dismissed the exceptions filed to Court Order of October 29, 1954. On February 28, 1955, an appeal was taken to the Pennsylvania Supreme Court. On April 19, Moon was taken to Western Penitentiary. On October 4, the Pennsylvania Supreme Court reversed the order of the lower court and the record was remanded for procedures consonant with high court's opinion.

Two years after the murder, the legal maneuvering continued. On January 28, 1956, the court, after re-examining findings and recommendations of sanity commission, ordered proceedings in the case to continue and any additional reasons for a new trial be filed. On February 14, exceptions to the court opinion of January 28 were filed by the defense. On March 29, exceptions to the January 28 opinion were dismissed. On April 30, a second appeal to the Pennsylvania Supreme Court was filed. On November 7, Judge Flick heard final motions for a new trial and set January 9, 1957, as the date on which he would give his opinion. Finally, on January 10, 1957, Judge Flick denied all sixteen motions for a new trial. He proceeded to sentence Norman W. Moon as follows:

And Now, January 10, 1957, the sentence of the law is that you, Norman W. Moon, be taken hence by the Sheriff of Warren County to the jail of that County from whence you came, and from thence in due course to the State Penitentiary at Rockview in Centre County,

Pennsylvania, and that you there suffer death during the week fixed by the Governor of the Commonwealth, in a building erected for the purpose on land owned by the commonwealth, such punishment being inflicted by either the warden or deputy warden of the State Penitentiary at Rockview, or by such person as the warden shall designate, by causing to pass through your body a current of electricity of intensity sufficient to cause death and the application of such current to be continued until you are dead, and may God, in His infinite wisdom, have mercy on your soul.

On April 23, 1957, Moon asked the Pennsylvania Supreme Court to set aside death sentence on grounds he failed to receive a fair and impartial trial. The court upheld his sentence on May 27. On July 1, 1957, Governor Leader fixed the week of September 30, 1957, as the date for Moon's electrocution. Moon then applied for clemency to the State Pardons Board, who considered his appeal for life imprisonment on September 17, 1957.

Then, on November 15, 1957, Governor Leader granted an execution stay until December 2 and three Pittsburgh psychiatrists, Drs. Henry W. Brosin, James M. Henninger, and Robert J. Hidson examined Moon at the request of the Pardons Board.

In a move that surprised and angered local citizens of Warren, on November 21, 1957, the governor, acting upon the recommendation of the Pardon Board, commuted Moon's death sentence to life imprisonment and committed him to Farview Hospital for the Criminally Insane.

Norman Moon's legal maneuverings didn't stop there. During the next thirty-five years, he filed writs and appeals of every imaginable kind in both state and federal courts. In 1975, Moon was found to be mentally competent and was sent from the hospital to the state prison. At sixty-six, he was diagnosed with cancer in his neck. He applied to have his life sentence commuted. The Board of Pardons had actually recommended that his sentence be commuted in spite of protests by Judge Wade's daughter, the district attorney's office, and Attorney Hampson's son. In June 1992, Moon died from complications of a throat surgery before he could be released.

Chapter 17

Judge and Mrs. C.E. Chillingworth
West Palm Beach, Palm Beach County, Florida
June 14–15, 1955

Judge Joseph Peel, Jr., was a promising young attorney and politician who let impatience and avarice control his destiny. He was intelligent, attractive, and came from a good family. Almost from the beginning of his law practice, though, he'd been attracted to the dark side. He won the position of municipal court judge and began business dealings with the wrong element.

Peel soon became involved in protection, the numbers racket, moonshine, and Loteria Cubana, an illegal lottery based on a legal Cuban lottery. Peel had made friends with many disreputable people, but two of the main ones were Floyd "Lucky" Holzapfel, a white man, and Robert David "Bobby" Lincoln, a black man.

One of his duties as municipal judge was to sign search warrants for police officers. Inevitably, though, the targets of the police raids would find out about the warrants before the police could serve them. Peel also was in a position to draw up defective warrants or to acquit the defendants when they appeared before him. Sometimes he would convict some of his cohorts and fine them, merely for appearance' sake. He would take the amount of the fine from his protection money.

Peel also practiced law on the edge. The way complaints or grievances on lawyers were handled in Florida at that time was for a sitting circuit court judge to hear the matter against the member of the bar and, if action against the attorney was necessary, to refer the case to another circuit court judge. In 1953, Peel was charged with representing both parties to a divorce, clearly a conflict of interest. His case was forwarded to Judge C. E. Chillingworth for discipline after a hearing by another judge. Judge Chillingworth surprised everyone by issuing a public reprimand to Joe Peel "because of youth and inexperience of counsel."

After Peel's election as municipal court judge in 1954, a part-time position, in early 1955 he once again was brought up on charges that he had acted inappropriately in a divorce action. It seems that he told one of his female clients that her divorce had been finalized when, in fact, it had not. She had remarried and given birth to a child, and when she and her husband applied to adopt another child, the investigating authorities informed her that there was no record of her divorce. She was a bigamist, and an unhappy one. The new charges against Judge Peel were set before Judge White, who, if he found that Peel had violated the code of conduct, would again refer the case for action to Judge Chillingworth. The case was set for June 15, 1955.

Peel was anxious not to appear before Judge Chillingworth, who had made it known earlier that if Joe Peel was charged with violations of the code of ethics again and came before him, he would disbar him. Peel called his friend Lucky Holzapfel and told him, "We'll have to get rid of the judge." Holzapfel suggested their mutual friend Bobby Lincoln to assist him. Since all three of them were involved in the rackets together, if Peel lost his law license and his position as municipal judge, all three of them would lose thousands of dollars of income.

Peel, Holzapfel, and Lincoln met and devised a plan. A few days later, Holzapfel took Lincoln in his car and pointed out Judge Chillingworth. Peel took Holzapfel and showed him the Chillingworth beach cottage and explained the layout. Holzapfel cased the area.

Shortly thereafter, Peel told Holzapfel that Judge Chillingworth would be alone at his beach house in Manalapan on the evening of June 14, 1955. Mrs. Chillingworth would be visiting one of their daughters. But, Peel said, if any witnesses were around, they would need to be gotten rid of, too.

Judge Chillingworth and his wife, Majorie, had dinner at the home of the Palm Beach County tax assessor and then left to drive to their summer beach house in Manalapan. When they got home, they prepared for the following day and then got ready for and went to bed.

Lucky and Bobby rented a boat and traveled by water to the Chillingworth home. They had engine trouble, and it took over an hour to get there. It was after 1:00 A.M. when they arrived.

Lucky Holzapfel knocked on the door and woke up the judge. The judge appeared at the door in his pajamas. Lucky gave him a sob story and then pulled a gun on him. Lucky asked if anyone else was home, and the judge said yes, his wife, and called to her at Lucky's instruction. Mrs. Chillingworth came to the door. After they knocked out the floodlight, Bobby searched the premises to make sure no one else was around. The two men bound the couple with adhesive tape and made makeshift nooses around their necks. Mrs. Chillingworth screamed a long scream when she was led down the stairs toward the boat. Lucky hit her in the head with his gun. He picked her up and both fell again, down the stairs and the sand dunes, resulting in the trail of blood that was found the following day. They took Curtis and Majorie Chillingworth down to the boat, forced them to get in, and headed out to sea.

When they were about three miles out, the men weighted Majorie down with a spear fishing waistband. "Remember I love you," the judge called to her as Lucky and Bobby threw her over the side. "I love you, too," she said to her husband. She sank immediately.

The two approached the judge to wrap a spear fishing waistband and weights around him, but the judge fought with them and ended up overboard, his hands still bound behind his back with adhesive tape. He tried to swim away, but Lucky hollered to Bobby to hit him. Bobby grabbed the shotgun that Peel had loaned him to hunt squirrels with and hit the judge with it. Lucky took the shotgun away from Bobby and hit the judge in the head so hard that the stock broke and fell into the water. Bobby grabbed the judge by his pajamas and pulled him back toward the boat. Lucky wrapped the anchor rope around the judge's neck, tied it to the anchor, cut the end that was attached to the boat, and threw the anchor (a pipe in a concrete block) overboard. The weight of the anchor pulled the judge to the bottom of the ocean as Lucky and Bobby watched. After throwing their guns overboard, they headed to shore, where Lucky called Peel and told him the job was done.

The Chillingworths were never seen again. Early the following morning, a building contractor appeared at the Chillingworth home to receive some instructions for some repairs, but no one answered the door. Knowing the judge's penchant for punctuality, the contractor became concerned. He found an open door and called out to the judge and his wife; no one answered. Upon closer inspection of the premises, he found that the beds had been slept in, the bedclothes thrown back as if they had gotten out of bed. He telephoned the judge's office, but the judge had not appeared for court though hearings were set that required his presence. The builder immediately raised an alarm.

Police began an investigation. They discovered a trail of blood leading from the back door to the beach, as well as rolls of adhesive tape. The beach sand appeared disturbed, as if a struggle had taken place; a partial footprint remained apparent near the edge of the water. Additionally, the floodlight at the back of the house had been smashed. Inside the house, authorities found that the couples' clothing from the previous night had been hung neatly in the closet and their jewelry and money remained untouched on the bureau.

Although the judge and his wife often enjoyed a dip in the lagoon outside their home, neither was an avid swimmer and would not have gone out far. While the three grown Chillingworth daughters maintained a vigil at the beachfront cottage, searchers in planes and helicopters scanned the area. Small craft deployed to conduct a surface search. Skin-divers and deep-sea divers dove into the depths of the ocean near the parties' home but found nothing. Friends raised rewards amounting to over $100,000, quite a sum for the time, but no demands for ransom were ever made.

The day after the murders, Judge Peel missed his court date with Judge White, but White ordered additional action against Peel. Two weeks later, state's attorney Phil O'Connell filed disbarment proceedings against Peel. Judge Lamar Warren of Fort Lauderdale disbarred Peel for ninety days for "dishonest conduct and unprofessional acts." Two weeks after that, Peel resigned his municipal judgeship. Amazingly, the police raids that took place after Peel's resignation caught the targets unaware and were successful.

Two years later, on May 23, 1957, in a probate proceeding brought by their children so that the estate could be settled, the probate judge declared them dead. The probate court judge found that Judge and Mrs. Chillingworth had "disappeared under circumstances not consistent with continuation of life."

In 1960, the mystery began to unravel. Several prominent officials had never given up searching for a solution. Among them were Sheriff John Kirk, Chief of Police William Barnes, and State's Attorney Phil O'Connell, a longtime friend of Judge Chillingworth's. At some point in time in the years after the couple's disappearance, it seems that all three of these individuals had come to the same conclusion: former West Palm Beach City Judge Joseph A. Peel, Jr., was involved in the murders. The difficulty had always been in getting enough evidence to convict him.

Meanwhile, after Peel got his law license back, he took a young attorney named Harold Gray into his office. Shortly thereafter, he took out a $100,000 life insurance policy on Gray and tried to have Gray murdered several times. Lucky Holzapfel was involved yet again. Fortunately for Gray, the men were unsuccessful. Their plans unraveled, though, and Peel and Holzapfel as well as James Yenzer, the insurance agent, were charged with several felony offenses. Through a technicality, Peel won his case on a motion to quash. He resigned from the bar in 1959, making feeble excuses about the construction business.

Holzapfel, Yenzer, and Peel did not stop their criminal activities.

Eventually, Holzapfel was arrested for theft of some guns. Police leaned on Yenzer to get to Holzapfel. They soon found out that Peel had tried to get Yenzer to kill Holzapfel because Holzapfel knew too much. Yenzer was unwilling to go that far. He began to work with the authorities.

Another man, Jim Wilber, a former police officer and a bail bondsman, was also Peel's and Holzapfel's friend. He agreed to cooperate with the Chillingworth investigation.

Holzapfel made bond on his gun arrest and then jumped bond, running to Brazil because Brazil had no extradition treaty with the U.S. He stayed there a few months and then returned to Florida. His friends Yenzer and Wilber met with him in a motel room in Melbourne, Florida, and the three of them got very drunk. Unbeknownst to Holzapfel, the motel room was bugged.

During the two days of drinking, Holzapfel talked about the Chillingworth case. It was recorded on tape. He was arrested and, upon questioning, confessed to his part in the kidnapping and murders. Peel was now in the securities business. After the preliminary hearing, at which Holzapfel again confessed, Joseph Peel and his securities business partner, J. Donald Miles, decided that he would have to get rid of Holzapfel. Peel contacted Yenzer and asked him to do the job. Yenzer, of course, was already working for the police. Peel and Miles were arrested October 5, 1960, for planning the murder of Holzapfel. They were released on $25,000 bond. Peel disappeared.

The state's attorney wanted additional evidence on the Chillingworth murders other than just Holzapfel's testimony. He approached Bobby Lincoln, who was serving three years in the federal pen for moonshining. He offered Lincoln immunity. Lincoln and O'Connell cut a deal, with Lincoln agreeing to testify against both Peel and Holzapfel.

On November 4, 1960, Joseph A. Peel, Jr., was located in Chattanooga, Tennessee, and arrested on warrants charging him with the murders of Judge Curtis E. and Majorie Chillingworth.

A change of venue caused the murder trial to be held in Fort Pierce, Florida, at the St. Lucie County courthouse. Judge D. C. Smith of Vero Beach presided. State's attorney Phil O'Connell was Peel's chief prosecutor. Peel had tried to cut a deal just after being arrested and then later denied it. Peel was represented by Carlton L. Welch of Jacksonville, a college friend and fraternity brother. The family allegedly could not afford a criminal defense attorney, not that anyone could be found who was willing to defend Peel. Welch owed Peel a favor for something Peel had done for Welch during their college days.

During the trial, the evidence showed that Peel and various associates had planned several other murders. He and his friends were termed "the Murder Unlimited gang." The list of murders and planned murders were as follows:

Completed murders: Judge and Mrs. Chillingworth in 1955, and Lew Gene Harvey, 1958 (he and Holzapfel had murdered him by "mistake"); Attempted murders: Harold Gray; Planned murders: State's Attorney Phillip D. O'Connell and Lucky Holzapfel; and Prospective murder: James A. Yenzer.

In the end, Lincoln testified for the state. Afterward, he returned to federal prison to finish serving his time for moonshining. In November 1962, he was released and moved to Chicago. His wife divorced him and got custody of the children.

Holzapfel got the death penalty, but it was commuted to life in prison, where he had a release date of 2009.

Peel received life in prison, pled *nolo contendre* (no contest) to the murder of Mrs. Chillingworth, and received a second life sentence. He was paroled December 23, 1979. By the time of his release, his wife had divorced him, and the children had changed their names. He was immediately picked up and transferred to federal prison to serve eighteen years for stock fraud, though he was released early to die of cancer in 1982, nine days after his release. To his dying day, he denied responsibility for the murders.

Chapter 18

Judge William Lynn Parkinson
Chicago, Cook County, Illinois
October 26, 1959

William Lynn Parkinson was born on September 18, 1902, in Attica, Indiana. He attended Purdue University in Lafayette. He was a Republican. President Dwight D. Eisenhower appointed him to the United States Federal Court for the Northern District of Indiana in 1954 and then to the 7th Circuit Court of Appeals in 1957. Before serving on the federal bench, Judge Parkinson served on the Tippecanoe County Circuit Court in Lafayette, Indiana, from 1937 to 1954. He was admitted to the practice of law in 1923 and was a member of the firm Parkinson and Parkinson for sixteen years before taking the bench. He was married to Elsie Ruth Parkinson on June 17, 1927. They had two children, William Lynn Parkinson, Jr. and Ruth Ann Parkinson.

The 7th Circuit Court of Appeals is located in Chicago, Illinois, where the judge had to move to take office. On October 26, 1959, a blustery day, Judge Parkinson, fifty-seven, reportedly was not feeling well and left his office to go to his nearby apartment at the Drake Hotel. His route would take him along Lake Michigan, the beach being 1,000 feet from the hotel. When he never made it home, his family became alarmed.

According to his son, the judge suffered from low blood pressure. He could have fainted and fallen into the icy lake water, drowned, and been swept away by the current. His hat was found on the beach miles south of the hotel where he and his wife lived. His glasses were found in an underpass between the hotel and the Oak Street beach. His umbrella was found on the beach.

Investigators were told over the next few days that the judge ordinarily stopped at bars on the way to his hotel and had a few drinks, though his family refuted this. On the day of his disappearance, his bottle of Ritalin, which he took for his low blood pressure condition, was found empty. It was said that he should have taken two at a time but that he had taken four; the bottle should have been half full if he had taken the proper dosage.

Bartenders in two taverns told police that on October 26, the judge had stopped and had two drinks in each bar. It was believed that the alcohol and the medication might have had an adverse effect on him. At about 5:30 P.M. he was seen headed back toward the courthouse. Witnesses said he had fallen several times and broken his umbrella's handle. An elderly couple tried to assist him but was unable to, so they called two young men over to help. The two young men helped him into a cab so he could go to the Drake Hotel. The cab driver, Albert Swanson, forty, said the judge appeared ill. Judge Parkinson slumped down in the back seat over the few blocks to the hotel. When he got out, the judge had added a $5 tip to the $.65 fare. Mr. Walter P. Paepcke, chairman of the board of Container Corporation of America, saw the judge shortly before 7:00 P.M. in the Drake Hotel arcade. He was walking toward the hotel lobby. He was never seen again.

Mrs. Parkinson told authorities she believed her husband was a victim of amnesia. (There was a municipal judge, Judge Harry Peyser, in New Hampshire, who wandered away in 1938 and returned about a month later, a victim of amnesia.) People compared his disappearance to that of Judge Crater, who disappeared in 1930 in New York and was never seen again.

The Coast Guard dragged the deep water on the north side beach of Lake Michigan and didn't find anything. Although it was thought that his poor health caused the judge's disappearance, Chicago was a city of corruption and other problems in that era. The FBI entered the investigation two days after the judge disappeared. The search spread to Indiana. Reports of sightings came from as far away as Fort Wayne, Indiana. There, a woman reported that she saw the judge peering into a store window. Friends and relatives thought he might have wandered back to Valparaiso and South Bend, Indiana, where he had lived and practiced law for so many years.

On October 31, five days after the judge's disappearance, the chief detective ordered the search of Lake Michigan to stop. No reason being issued to the public, speculation was that the judge had not drowned. The Coast Guard, however, kept dragging the lake until November 2. On November 4, 150 skin divers were recruited for a mass search of a part of Lake Michigan on the following Saturday. The 150 divers showed up, but only 100 entered the cold water. During the six-hour diving expedition, four divers were stricken with cramps from the icy water conditions, but otherwise none were seriously injured. A police boat and a Coast Guard utility boat were deployed to assist the divers. Again, nothing was found.

Reports of sightings of the judge continued to come in from around the Chicago area as well as Indiana and other areas of the country. His colleagues discussed his recent concerns that he worried too much and felt despondent because he was slow in making his decisions. He had expressed to several friends that perhaps he should have never taken the 7th Circuit appointment, that he should have stayed in Indiana. They reassured him that perhaps he was slow, but he was always sure and deliberate about his rulings. He was well respected by his peers.

Six months after his disappearance, on April 24, 1960, Judge Parkinson's body was found within a half-mile of where he had disappeared. A man walking on a breakwater near Chicago's north side found the body wedged between some rocks under the water in a construction site. A driver's license and American Bar Association card found in his belongings helped identify the body.

After a hearing on May 2, 1960, an inquest jury ruled that Judge Parkinson died of drowning but left "elements of mystery" about exactly how he came to his death, fixing no time of death or responsibility for the drowning.

Chapter 19

Judge James N. Colasanto
Alexandria, Fairfax County, Virginia
November 24, 1970

Theobalt Magnini, forty-seven, was a Pentagon clerk. He had been with the Pentagon for twenty years. By 1970, his salary was $18,500. He was born in Italy and served in the U.S. Navy from 1942 to 1945. After the war, he worked first with the adjutant-general's office of the Army Signal Corps and then with the Army's Comptroller Department. In 1963, he worked for the Army office of the chief of research and development before moving to his current job in 1964. Neighbors described him as a quiet man. Neighborhood children liked him because he let them climb the apple tree in his back yard and eat his apples. He was married and had four children who he and his wife, Vera, raised as strict Catholics. Their oldest son had been killed five years earlier in an automobile accident. The two other grown sons had their own apartment. A neighbor reported that Mrs. Magnini and their teenage daughter had moved out of the Magnini home in mid-July 1970.

In 1966, Magnini filed a complaint against his neighbor for keeping vicious dogs. Every time Magnini would walk by, the dogs would bark at him and nip at his heels. After a while, it became too much for the man. He had asked the neighbors to control their dogs, but it didn't do any good, so he filed a complaint at city hall. At the hearing, the judge took evidence and listened to testimony. It turned out that the dogs were Chihuahuas. Judge James Colasanto dismissed the case.

Theobalt Magnini carried a grudge. Four years after the court hearing, Magnini, still upset with his neighbors, the dogs, and the judge, took his revenge.

At 6:50 A.M. on November 24, 1970, Municipal Judge James Colasanto, sixty-four, went to his front door after his wife heard a noise that she thought was their pet poodle. He intended to fetch the morning newspaper and, if the dog was indeed at the door, let him in. What he found, he told his brother later, was a man who looked vaguely familiar, though he couldn't place him.

In Alexandria, Virginia, in 1970, a municipal judge heard cases involving traffic offenses, general misdemeanors, and civil cases involving up to $3,000. Little cause would seem to exist for a judge to take security precautions even so minor as to unlist one's phone number. As a result, when Judge Colasanto opened his front door, he didn't expect to be met by a hail of gunfire. Shot six times, he fell in his doorway as his son, Pete, watched the assailant walk calmly to his car and drive away. Pete Colasanto described the shooter as a white male driving a dark, late-model Ford Galaxie. A neighbor boy confirmed that he'd seen a middle-aged white man in a dark overcoat flee the area.

The rescue squad rushed the judge to the emergency room at Duke Street Hospital. The judge was conscious for part of the morning and carried on conversations with family members and a priest but later went into shock. He received blood transfusions as the doctors removed the bullets, which were lodged in his right and left shoulders, his right and left sides, his arm, and his back. He was in surgery for over eight hours.

In the meantime, television newsman Joseph McCaffrey received a call from a man who claimed to be the assailant. His name was Theobalt J. Magnini. He lived in a subdivision of Alexandria called Arlandria. He said to McCaffrey, "I am the man who shot the judge." He asked McCaffrey to come to his home and hear his story, but McCaffrey went to the police, who didn't want him going to the man's residence alone.

Inspector Francis Johnson, Detective Captain Norman Grimm, and several uniformed police officers, as well as Sergeant Cecil Kessler and Smokey, a German Shepherd K-9 police dog, accompanied McCaffrey. The police called out to Magnini on a battery-powered bullhorn but got no response. An officer telephoned the Magnini residence from a neighbor's home, but no one answered. Police worked their way around to the back of the house and broke open the back door. They sent Smokey inside first. Shortly afterward, the dog bounded back out to his handler. The authorities knew then that something was not right. When they entered the brick duplex, police found the man face down on the living room floor. A .357 magnum lay by his side with one fired shell in the chamber. He was dead from a single gunshot wound to the head.

Police sent Magnini's gun to the FBI for ballistics testing. It was confirmed that it was the same gun as was used on the judge. Magnini had purchased it at a gun club at Fort Belvoir, a few miles from Alexandria. Police closed the case.

Joseph McCaffrey reported that the Magnini told him on the phone that he shot the judge due to a long-standing grudge. Judge Colasanto lay in the hospital for two days while his family kept vigil. He died on Thanksgiving Day, 1970, and was buried two days later at St. Mary's Cemetery, near his parents, after a High Mass.

Judge Colasanto had been appointed to fill an unexpired term on the bench in February 1953. He was admitted to the bar in 1929 and practiced law in Alexandria for forty years. He was the past president of the Alexandria Bar Association and of the Alexandria Kiwanis Club. He was also a member of the Fraternal Order of the Eagles and the Sportsman Club. He attended the Washington College in Chestertown, Maryland, and National Law School in Washington, D.C. Originally from Waterbury, Connecticut, James Colasanto was one of several sons of a prominent Italian family. The parents came to this country in 1940. Both of them had come from tiny towns near Naples, Italy. His brother, Nicholas, served as vice mayor and city councilman. His brother, Michael, served as a federal marshal. As a youngster, the judge played basketball. His high school team won national acclaim. His wife's name was Mary. They raised two sons, two stepsons, and a daughter.

Chapter 20

Judge Harold J. Haley
San Rafael, Marin County, California
August 7, 1970

It was a hot Friday morning, August 7, 1970, the fifth day of the jury trial of James David McClain, thirty-seven. McClain, a convicted felon serving time in San Quentin, was being retried in Marin County, California, his first trial having ended in a hung jury in June.

A native of El Paso, Texas, McClain had a long rap sheet extending back to his youth. Although he reportedly graduated from high school, his educational level tested out at around the fifth grade. The incident for which he was on trial that day was the March stabbing of a San Quentin guard with a fourteen-inch knife as the guard made an inquiry about an inmate fracas.

The judge on McClain's case was Harold J. Haley, a very personable, popular, and devout man. "God help me to be a good judge," Judge Haley said on the day of his induction into office and on every day thereafter.

Governor Pat Brown appointed Judge Haley on December 18, 1964. Previously Haley served as municipal court judge in Marin County in 1956–64, appointed by Governor Knight. Before that, Judge Haley served as San Rafael city attorney from 1949–56, district attorney of Marin County in 1943–45, and deputy district attorney 1932–43 and 1945–47. He was in the private practice of law from 1928 to 1943 and 1945 to 1956. He was admitted to the California Bar on October 4, 1928, after receiving his LL.B. that same year from the University of San Francisco Law School.

Born November 14, 1904, in San Rafael, California, Harold Haley married the former Gertrude Ursula Ahern on May 24, 1933. They had three children, Patricia, born in 1934, and twins Joan and Carol in 1937.

Judge Haley was a member of all bar-related organizations as well as the Elks, Rod and Gun Club, and Country Club. He had a long history of community service dating back to his youth. He was a Republican and had served as Republican county chairman. Deputy District Attorney Gary Thomas once described Haley as "a saint." A California state senator described him as "a kind and understanding person."

On that Friday morning, August 7, 1970, the court bailiff, James Layne, noticed that a young black man with bleached hair who entered the courtroom was the same person who had remained as a spectator the day before after asking whether it was the McClain trial in progress. But now, the bailiff noticed that the young man carried a leather briefcase, had a bulge under the left side of his coat, and kept his right hand in his pocket. It was 10:45 A.M. Testifying for the defense at that time was Ruchell Magee. McClain, who represented himself, had summoned San Quentin to bring a busload of convicts as witnesses. Just outside was another inmate, William A. Christmas. Both men were in chains.

Originally from Louisiana, Magee, twenty-three, arrived in California after his release from prison. He was first incarcerated as an adult at sixteen for attempted rape. It was only months before he turned to a life of crime in California. His sentence for kidnapping and robbery: life.

Christmas came to California in 1953 from Nebraska, where he was born. In and out of the California Youth Authority as an adolescent for such things as car theft, burglary, and possession of marijuana, Christmas was sentenced to San Quentin in 1964 for second-degree burglary. While there, he was a problem inmate and in 1966 had been found in possession of a weapon, which resulted in his term of years being lengthened.

Concerned at the large number of San Quentin inmates summoned for trial, police authorities had warned Judge Haley that it would be dangerous to unchain all of the witnesses, so only McClain was not in chains. The judge didn't want to prejudice the jury against him. Magee was on the witness stand when the young man from the previous day entered the courtroom.

In the lock-up down the hall were numerous other witness inmates who were to be called later as the trial progressed.

Deputy District Attorney Gary W. Thomas, Judge Haley's nephew by marriage, was prosecuting McClain.

The bailiff, concerned that the trenchcoated young spectator was dressed oddly for a summer day and acted strangely, crossed the courtroom toward the man when suddenly the man whipped out weapons and tossed them to McClain and Magee. As he turned toward the bailiff, the young man pulled a semi-automatic carbine from under his trenchcoat. "Freeze!" he yelled and ordered everyone down on the floor.

McClain cried, "For the love of God, take these handcuffs off."

109

The spectator and Magee sought out the San Quentin guards in the hallway for the keys to the handcuffs and to free Christmas. They forced the guards into the courtroom at gunpoint and made them remove all shackles and handcuffs from Magee and Christmas.

Magee told the captive audience, "I want to be a free man, so help me, God."

Shortly afterward, the four tried to free the inmates who were in the holding cell. The other convicts refused to join up with the escapees and stayed where they were.

Within minutes, the four men had taken several hostages, including Judge Haley, to whom they tied a shotgun around the neck with adhesive tape. Taken hostage in addition to Judge Haley were Deputy District Attorney Thomas, and Jurors Maria Graham, Joyce Rodoni, and Joyce Wittmer, who they wired together with piano wire. A court reporter had also been made a hostage but managed to slip out of the wire and lie face down on the floor with several people rounded up by the escapees, including bailiffs, guards, and other jurors.

McClain gave a speech to jurors about the injustice of accusations. The young man who brought the guns kept saying, "I want to kill somebody." As word spread, courthouse personnel locked the doors to their offices, called for help, and hid under their desks. Inside the courtroom, Judge Haley urged everyone to stay calm and tried to assure the convicts that everyone would cooperate. McClain and his cohorts proceeded to march Judge Haley and the other hostages down the Hall of Justice corridor. McClain held a gun to Judge Haley's head and led him by the handle of the shotgun aimed at his face.

McClain rapped on the door to the pressroom at the end of the hall to make demands for the release of the "Soledad Brothers," a group of prisoners awaiting trial for the killing of a guard at Soledad Prison. The newsmen had locked the door and refused to answer. It turned out later that the young accomplice's brother, George Jackson, was one of the defendants charged in the Soledad killing.

McClain had made Judge Haley telephone Sheriff Louis P. Mountanos before leaving the courtroom. The judge had told the sheriff that "lives are at stake." The inmates grabbed the phone and told the sheriff to call off his "pigs" or the hostages would be killed. They told them to come to the courtroom, where they could negotiate. When they met up in the hallway, the inmates made the sheriff and deputies put up their hands while they fled with the hostages. They also ran into a photographer, Jim Kean, forty-seven, who they ordered to take photographs and of whom they demanded the release of the "Soledad Brothers" in exchange for the hostages. One of the gunmen called out, "We are the revolutionaries!"

After the inmates and the hostages left the courtroom, Bailiff Layne and one of the San Quentin prison guards went for weapons. Next door, Deputy District Attorney J. Michael Anthony had heard the rattling of chains and after a while went to see about the noise. Anthony saw a man with a gun at Judge Haley's head, so he locked the main courtroom door. As word spread, a highway patrol officer burst into the sheriff's office above the courtroom and locked the door, reporting that a man had a machine gun downstairs.

Lieutenant Tom Lightfoot of the Sheriff's Department went to the north archway and saw the inmates ushering the hostages out of the building lobby. The convict with the M-1 semiautomatic disarmed several deputies and bailiffs who had been posted around the archway and fired three shots in the air to show that he meant business. The hostages were then herded around a corner of the building. Lightfoot radioed for help.

The hostages and inmates walked to a waiting yellow Hertz rental van. Dozens of sheriff's deputies and San Rafael police officers had rushed to the scene. The van began pulling away, but the east exit was blocked. Vehicles from the San Rafael Police, San Quentin Prison, California Highway Patrol, and Marin County Sheriff's Department circled the building like a wagon train.

There was a flash of light. Gunfire exploded inside the van. Witnesses said it lasted for about two minutes. When it was over, Judge Harold Haley was found in the rear of the van, where he had died from a shotgun blast that had blown off part of his face. He had also been shot in the chest. Deputy District Attorney Gary Thomas had grabbed a gun and shot three of the assailants, saying later, "I hoped I killed them." They shot him three times, one bullet severing his spine. Juror Maria Graham was wounded in the arm. The other two jurors were uninjured, except for the trauma of being kidnapped, and were treated for shock.

Although no one is sure who actually fired the first shot, the young accomplice had been driving the van. When he stopped at the roadblock, he fired a gun at San Quentin guard John Matthews, who opened fire, killing him.

The San Quentin guards never got the message to let the van pass. Their usual orders are "no escape, no hostage." An assistant warden later stated that it was clear that the judge and deputy district attorney were to be killed. He said that no one who intends to negotiate, to not kill someone, ties a gun to a hostage's neck. To do so would render it impossible for the party to put the firearms down and surrender.

At Magee's trial later, Thomas testified that Magee fired the shotgun, and one of the others shot the judge in the chest. Gary Thomas had grabbed the accomplice/driver's gun. Thomas got off several shots, probably shooting McClain, Christmas, and Magee. McClain and Christmas were killed. Magee was wounded in the chest. It's probable that Thomas was shot both inside the van as well as by the San Quentin guards outside. Six or more shots were fired into the van and at least four from it.

Authorities later learned that the young man who had entered the courtroom with the weapons was Jonathon Jackson, seventeen, a Pasadena high school graduate and brother of San Quentin inmate George Jackson. George, one of the "Soledad Trio," and Angela Davis had been lovers.

Angela Davis, the radical college teacher who had been fired from her teaching job at UCLA for inflammatory speeches since the Board of Regents couldn't get away with firing her for being a Communist, had been an outspoken defender of the "Soledad Trio," as the three defendants were officially called, along with actress Jane Fonda.

Davis left the area shortly after the shooting incident. "The Trio" had been affiliated with the violent, radical Black Panthers. The FBI charged Davis with unlawful interstate flight to avoid prosecution for leaving California and placed her on their Ten Most Wanted List, only the third woman ever to earn such a distinction. In California, she was indicted for murder, kidnapping, and conspiracy for aiding and abetting in the escape by supplying the firearms. She was extradited from New York, held in California for sixteen months, and bonded out.

At her trial, the jury consisted of eight white women and four white men. They acquitted her based on testimony that showed the following:

• The guns that were registered in her name were kept at the headquarters of the "Soledad Brothers" Defense Committee and Communist Che Lumumba Club in an apartment she shared with another woman.

• Jonathon Jackson had been alone in the apartment on the Saturday before the shooting with permission to "use the equipment."

• Other testimony refuted state's testimony that Davis had been at the prison shortly before the incident.

• There was testimony from witnesses who were present when Davis heard about the shooting that Davis was upset and distressed upon hearing about it.

The surviving convict, Ruchell Magee, was charged with kidnapping and the murder of Judge Haley. A psychologist testified that Magee was acting under "diminished capacity." Magee hadn't planned to escape, but being presented with the opportunity, he couldn't resist. The prosecutor, Gary Thomas, however, testified that Magee pulled the trigger on the shotgun that killed the judge. After the jury deliberated for sixty hours, the trial judge declared a mistrial.

Magee could be described as his own worst enemy. In both trials, his behavior in the courtroom was out of control. He mistrusted lawyers and wanted to defend himself. The judge refused his request and appointed attorneys to defend him, although he often acted in his own behalf during the trials, overruling the advice of his attorneys. In his first trial, Magee was chained to his chair but still managed to kick and spit on his court-appointed attorney. He also called the judge a "Ku Klux Klan member in disguise." He often shouted at the judge and had to be removed from the courtroom. In his second trial, he physically assaulted his attorney after climbing across counsel table to get at him. The jury convicted Magee in the second trial.

Deputy District Attorney Gary Thomas survived the shootout but was permanently disabled by a bullet in his spine. He also suffered damage to his heart. Governor Ronald Reagan appointed him in 1972 to the Marin County Municipal Court bench. Subsequently, he served as a superior court judge of Marin County.

Ironically, a year after the courthouse escape attempt, and before Angela Davis and Ruchell Magee came to trial, Jonathon Jackson's brother, George, was killed in an escape attempt at San Quentin.

After the incident at the Marin County Courthouse, the judiciary considered holding all trials of convicts at San Quentin, where proper security could be had. One thousand inmates staged a strike in protest, demanding if that were so, that the jurors be selected from the prison population. After much discussion, the Marin County Superior Court judges ruled that it would be illegal to hold court at the prison.

Increased security measures, however, were put in place in many areas, not just Marin County. In San Francisco, the first bullet-proof partition was installed for the "Soledad Brothers" trial and, as far away as the Cambridge Massachusetts Superior Court, bullet-proof partitions were also installed between spectators and the judge and the defendants.

In Marin County, after the County Board of Supervisors refused to spend $41,000 on a bullet-proof shield recommended by the sheriff's department, a judge took the law into his own hands, so to speak. In the court where San Quentin prisoners would be tried, a judge ordered the shield be installed and waived bidding requirements so that it could be installed immediately. Many people believe that the judge exceeded his authority, but none of them had to sit behind the bench.

Gertrude Haley, Judge Haley's widow, died in June 2002, thirty-two years after her husband was killed in the shootout. She was ninety-eight years old.

Chapter 21

Judge Pierce C. Kegley
Bland, Bland County, Virginia
April 1, 1970

On April 1, 1970, Charles Edward Jarrell, seventy, a divorced white male with a seventh-grade education, from the small town of Bastian, planted himself on a bench and waited in the Bland County Courthouse hallway for over an hour for Judge Pierce Kegley. No one knew what Jarrell wanted, as there was no regular court scheduled for that day. When asked whether someone else could help him, Jarrell said he would wait for the judge.

Eventually, Jarrell went up to the office of James V. Shockley, the USDA representative, and asked for the judge. A few minutes later, the judge appeared and told Mr. Shockley that he needed to speak to Mr. Jarrell. He asked Mr. Jarrell to accompany him downstairs to his office. The two men walked downstairs.

County Court Judge Pierce Kegley, sixty-three, was quite popular in the small communities of Wytheville and Bland in the Virginia hill country, where just about everybody knows everybody else. He enjoyed hunting and fishing. He and Mrs. Kegley liked to travel and often drove to the western United States, including Alaska, and Mexico, camping out in their pickup camper. He was an avid reader. He enjoyed membership in many community organizations such as Kiwanis, the Masons, and the Democratic party. At one time he had been a dairy farmer and later an attorney in the general practice of law, that is, wills and

(Courtesy Robert Kegley)

estates, misdemeanors, civil cases. He served as president of the Bank of Bland. After his appointment as county judge, Judge Kegley was still able to practice law. Judge Kegley was a father and grandfather.

Judge Kegley's grandson, Clinton Kegley, also an attorney, who was, unfortunately, not born at the time of his grandfather's death, tells a story of how his grandfather was so trusting of the people in his community that he would pick up his grandchildren from school without telling their mother; it never occurred to him that there might be call for her to worry.

On April 1, after the judge and Mr. Jarrell went downstairs into the judge's office and closed the door, courthouse employees heard several gunshots. It was approximately 11:45 A.M.

The commissioner of revenue, G.C. Havens, reportedly looked out into the hallway near the courtroom and saw Mr. Jarrell and Judge Kegley standing not far from each other.

"Arrest that man and call a doctor," Judge Kegley said before stepping into his office and crumpling onto the floor.

Mr. Jarrell staggered fifteen feet down the hallway, where someone found him a chair. Both men were shot. The judge was known to carry a .38 caliber revolver. One was found not far from where he lay. Jarrell set a .22 caliber weapon down when he took the proffered chair.

Although there were no signs of a struggle in the office, the courtroom benches had been pushed aside and a man's hat lay on one of them. The walls held several bullet holes. Though ambulance attendants came immediately and rushed Judge Kegley to the hospital at Bluefield, West Virginia, he died en route on East River Mountain. His brother, Dr. George Kegley, who held the office of Bland County medical examiner, said that the judge was shot directly in the heart and in his right lung. Later investigation showed that Judge Kegley had gotten off five shots, but two of them misfired. The judge had cleaned his weapon recently. It was thought that the substance he used caused the gun to jam.

Jarrell was taken to the Wytheville hospital with two clean gunshot wounds, one in his right arm and one in his lower abdomen. He was given blood transfusions in case of internal bleeding. While in the hospital, he refused to give any statement as to what precipitated his gunning for the judge.

Judge Kegley was survived by his wife, Ruth Brown Kegley, two sons, Fulton Brown Kegley of Staunton, Virginia, and Robert Pierce Kegley of Bland, an educator, and one brother, Dr. George B. Kegley, as well as several grandchildren. The funeral services were held at Bland Layburn Presbyterian Church, where Judge Kegley was an elder. He was buried in the family cemetery at the farm.

Charles Edward Jarrell was indicted by a grand jury during its June term in 1970. The regular sitting circuit court judge, Vincent L. Sexton, Jr., being a friend of Judge Kegley's, recused himself from the trial of the case. The Supreme Court assigned the Honorable Glyn R. Phillips of the 27th Judicial Circuit to preside over Jarrell's trial.

It being indicated from Jarrell's behavior that he might have a mental problem, on October 23, 1970, Judge Phillips committed Jarrell to Southwestern State Hospital for observation. He also appointed three doctors to examine him.

On January 14, 1971, the doctors made their report. Jarrell suffered from "Psychosis associated with other cerebral condition, Psychosis with cerebral arteriosclerosis." In other words, Jarrell was psychotic and unfit to stand trial. Judge Phillips was forced to commit Jarrell to the Department for the Criminally Insane at the Southwestern State Hospital in Marion, Virginia, for treatment.

Jarrell's case was reviewed from time to time to find out whether he was competent to stand trial. In 1978, there was a period of time when the doctors thought he could be returned to Bland County for trial, but the process took so long that Jarrell relapsed and by January 25, 1979, he was "no longer able to participate or cooperate in his trial." In the latter part of 1979, it again appeared that Jarrell would be able to stand trial. By December, it was again concluded that he could not.

In 1980, at eighty, Jarrell was transferred to the Geriatrics Unit at Southwestern State Hospital when the Forensic Unit of the hospital was closed.

In 1987, at eighty-seven, Jarrell was transferred one last time. This time it was to Heritage Hall Nursing Home in Tazewell, Virginia. He was described as being disori-

Bland County Courthouse. (Photo by author)

117

ented as to time and place, confused, hard of hearing, having poor vision, unable to ambulate, and requiring total assistance in his bathing, shaving, dressing, and generally taking care of his bodily functions.

Though a mystery remains as to the exact nature of Mr. Jarrell's complaint against Judge Kegley, it is generally believed that Jarrell was angry due to a dispute involving divorce and child custody.

There is still no security system at the entrances to the Bland County Courthouse.

Chapter 22

Judge William Johnson "Bill" Williams
Lake Anna, Louisa County, Virginia
May 30, 1974

Judge Bill Williams, forty-four, and his wife, Ann Hancock Williams, forty-two, liked to camp out. One of the places they enjoyed camping out was at Lake Anna in Louisa County, Virginia. Their tent site was down a small, two-lane dirt road not far from the water. In the middle of the night on May 30, 1974, the couple was in their tent on the banks of the lake when someone burst in and shot Bill Williams to death. The perpetrator dropped the gun inside the tent, fled, and was never apprehended. Mrs. Williams said that she was unable to identify the assailant.

Bill Williams was the municipal judge for the town of Chase City, Virginia. He was the former Louisa County attorney. Louisa County is in the 16th Judicial Circuit of Virginia. Circuit courts in Virginia, of which there are 31 circuits and 122 courts, have exclusive jurisdiction to try felonies as well as mental health cases.

Bill Williams was educated in Richmond public schools and after the war graduated from Randolph Macon College with a B.A. in psychology in 1955. He graduated from T. C. Williams Law School in Richmond, Virginia, in June 1964 with an LL.B. in law. He also passed the bar exam in 1964 and began the practice of law. He was in private practice until February 1967 in Louisa, Virginia. From there he went on to be a legislative assistant to Congressman William L. Scott in Washington, D.C., from February 1967 until August 1967. In August, Williams went back to private practice in Chase City, Virginia, citing in a 1972 bond application that he left for "money." He remained in private practice until November 1968, when he became judge of the town of Chase City.

Later, while still serving as municipal judge (at a salary of $1,800 annually), he obtained employment as a title attorney for Lawyers Title Insurance

Corporation at a starting salary of $850 a month, receiving a $200 a month raise in the first year. In his bond application, he listed ownership of $12,000 in life insurance with his wife as beneficiary, no real estate, and $6,000 in personal property as his only property.

As an applicant for the Academic Educational Program of Lawyers Title, he was described as "A 'slow starter' but maturing nicely." He was thought to have potential for advancement. In March of 1974, the couple purchased a house in Richmond on a V.A. thirty-year loan, but by no stretch of the imagination could they be thought of as wealthy.

Williams married Ann Hancock on March 25, 1970. Ann Hancock Williams was a legal secretary making $150 per month in 1972. This was not a first marriage for either of them. She had three children, Robert, Elisabeth, and Victoria. He had two children, William and Constance. Bill Williams stood 5'10" and weighed 155 pounds. He had brown hair and blue eyes. Ann Williams was 5'2" and 98 pounds. He served in the U.S. Navy from 1948 to 1952. He served as vice president and president of the Mecklenburg and Louisa Bar Associations.

On July 23, 1974, Ann H. Williams wrote a letter to Lawyers Title Insurance Corporation and applied for full payment of her deceased husband's life insurance. She stated as follows: "I would appreciate prompt and full payment of his life insurance policy to me as soon as possible inasmuch as my doctor will not let me work for some time to come and I have had no means of income since July 1st."

On August 26, 1974, Attorney W. W. Whitlock represented Mrs. Williams at a preliminary hearing; the case was referred to the grand jury for further investigation and possible indictment. On September 9, 1974, the grand jury indicted Mrs. Williams, saying that she "did feloniously kill and murder William J. Williams" in violation of Virginia Code Section 18.1-44. She pled not guilty and trial was set for February 6 and 7, 1975. The prosecutor was John B. Gilmer, attorney for the Commonwealth of Virginia. After a pretrial hearing on February 5, 1975, trial was held on the scheduled dates.

The evidence was as follows: Someone shot Judge Williams in the left temple in the middle of the night when he and his wife were camping out at Lake Anna. Police found the gun used to kill the judge under the judge's cot. It bore no fingerprints. The police dismantled the crime scene before daylight, including the tent, instead of preserving evidence. Judge Williams was often in ill health, an alcoholic, dissatisfied with his employment, unhappy with the direction his life had taken, felt criticized by his family members, had many financial problems, and frequently abused Mrs. Williams. Mrs. Williams nursed the judge and even saved his life several times by having

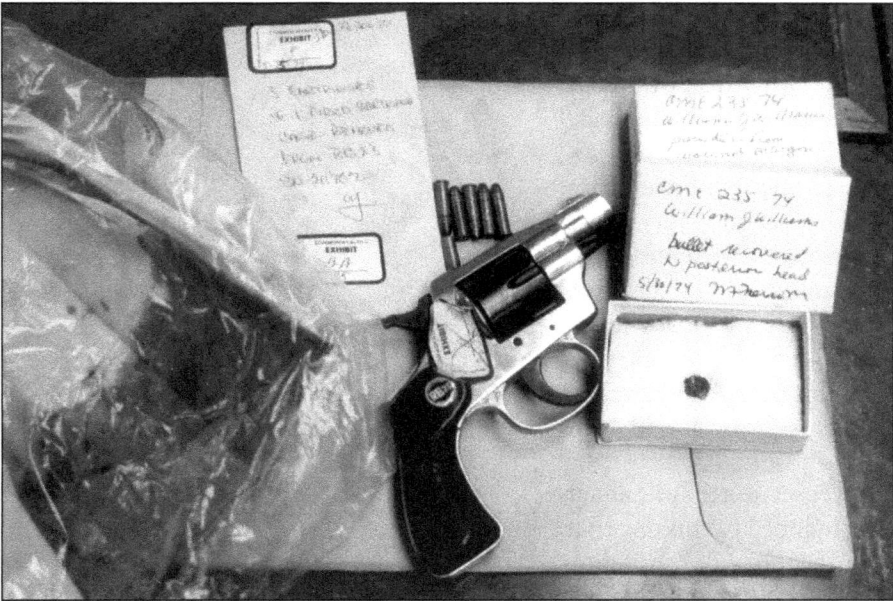

Contents of court file in Williams case. (Photo by author)

him rushed to the hospital when he was hemorrhaging. The judge had threatened suicide on more than one occasion. But for the lack of finger-prints on the gun, the case would have been ripe for a suicide presumption.

The state conceded that Mrs. Williams took good care of Judge Williams, that she was generally a kind and generous woman, but alleged that after being abused by Judge Williams time and time again, "something snapped" and she killed him.

The evidence from the defense showed that on the night in question Judge and Mrs. Williams were camping out in a tent alone. The pair was asleep when someone shot the judge. Mrs. Williams testified that she was partially awakened by a scratching noise, heard a gun blast, and abruptly rose up from her cot. She saw an object but could not describe what it was. She thought she saw someone running from the tent but didn't know any more than that. She left the scene, driving the truck to her parents' home where the authorities were summoned. She was always available to be questioned by the police and the police didn't even conduct a paraffin test on her.

On February 8, 1975, after three days of trial and deliberations, the jury could not reach a verdict and was discharged. Mr. Whitlock applied to the court to strike the Commonwealth's evidence and the court gave him two weeks to file a brief in that regard. In the meantime, the judge continued Mrs. Williams' bond and set a second trial for May 14, 1975 at 10:00 A.M. On March 26, 1975, the judge denied the defense motion.

On May 14, 1975, Judge Vance M. Fry empaneled a second jury. The same attorneys represented the state and the defense. Testimony was again taken over three days.

This time Ann Hancock Williams was found not guilty.

Prosecutor John Gilmer is convinced to this day that Ann Hancock Williams

The deceased Judge Williams inside tent at lake.

killed her husband and got away with it. Others in this small community have different ideas. Some people believe that Ann's mother killed Bill Williams. Ann's mother saw her daughter abused many times for several years. Perhaps she saw an opportunity to end the problem.

The consensus of several people in the community, including those who

know Ann's family, is that Ann's mother went out to the campsite, ran into the tent, shot Bill, and left. Ann said that she didn't see who did it in order to protect her mother. When her mother was on her deathbed, she was very insistent that she needed to see a priest before she died. She made a deathbed statement, the contents of which are unknown to all except her confessor. Ann later married a local doctor.

Louisa County Courthouse.
(Photo by author)

Chapter 23

Judge James J. Lawless
Pasco, Franklin County, Washington
June 3, 1974

Pasco, Washington, is in the southeastern part of the state, about 134 miles southwest of Spokane. It being a relatively small town, most people know one another, as well as those in the surrounding counties.

Ricky Anthony Young was one such well-known individual. Locals, especially police, described him as a tough, surly kid. He was a Prosser High School dropout who began his criminal career in 1971 with a burglary of a drug store. He was arrested and made his first appearance before Judge James J. Lawless. The judge found him guilty and sentenced Ricky to a year in the county jail, probated.

James Lawless had been appointed to the superior court for Benton and Franklin counties at thirty-three. He was one of the youngest superior court judges ever to serve in the state of Washington. By 1974, Judge Lawless had been a superior court judge for Benton and Franklin counties for seventeen years. At forty-three, in November 1967, he became the youngest judge ever to hear a state supreme court case, appointed justice *pro tem* to help clear a backlog of cases. He and his wife, Beth, were the parents of five children.

Ricky Young did not appear to benefit from his experience in the county jail and on probation. In the next three years, he got married. He and his wife lived in a house that they rented from her parents. When it caught fire, Ricky was arrested for arson. The authorities were able to connect Ricky to another fire. They alleged he set fire to the United Presbyterian Church of Prosser and charged him with second-degree arson. The two counts of arson were filed May 2, 1974, in Benton County Superior Court. The original trial date was in June 1974. Judge Lawless would have been the judge. Later, the charges were transferred to Pierce County on a change of venue.

Ricky also had pending charges for possession of explosives. He was alleged to have blown up a Benton County deputy sheriff's car. There were additional pending criminal cases by June of 1974. They included a probation revocation hearing from the October 5, 1971, burglary charge in Benton County and manufacturing controlled substance filed April 29, 1974 in Benton County Superior Court.

At about 3:10 P.M. Pacific Daylight Time on June 3, 1974, Judge James J. Lawless, by then fifty, received a box about the size of an envelope from his clerk. He sat down in chambers to open the package, which was addressed from the Benton County Superior Court and had an Expo '74 World's Fair sticker on it. Moments later, Judge Lawless was blown up by a pipe bomb. He died instantly.

Police quickly arrested Ricky Lynn Young, who by that time also had an alias of Anthony Mario Ragusin. He was twenty-two.

Young's attorneys filed for a bail bond, which was denied. Then Young's attorneys filed a change of venue in the case, which was granted. Another request for bail was denied again because of all of Young's pending criminal cases at the time of the bombing.

The cases that were transferred to Pierce County due to Judge Lawless' murder were tried on October 21, 1974. Ricky was sentenced to five years for the arsons. He was also sentenced to five years in federal prison for the bombing.

The first trial for murder was held in Spokane, Washington, on December 2, 1974. It ended in a hung jury. The judge discharged the jury on December 14, 1974. The second trial in the murder case was held in July 1975, also in Spokane. Ricky Young was convicted and sentenced to life in prison on January 12, 1976.

Young appealed his conviction, but the case was affirmed. He requested a rehearing by the Supreme Court of Washington, which was denied. He applied for a *writ of certiorari* to the Supreme Court of the United States, but that was denied October 2, 1978.

Chapter 24

Judge Joseph J. Crescente
Wanaque, Passaic County, New Jersey
November 4, 1974

Part-time Municipal Judge Joseph J. Crescente, seventy-one, held his court in the municipal building on Monday nights. According to his friends, he always behaved the same: donned his black robe, sat with his back to the window closest to the center of the room, and called his cases beginning around 8:30 P.M. His cases consisted mainly of traffic offenses, landlord-tenant disputes, family disturbances, minor civil cases, and misdemeanors.

Wanaque, New Jersey, was a town of about 11,000 people, mostly a working-class community in the rolling hills where many people owned arms with which to hunt. Judge Crescente had first been appointed by the city council right after World War II and had served ever since. He had been reappointed to the $2,500-a-year job the previous January.

On Monday, November 4, 1974, Judge Crescente had an unusually heavy docket of about forty cases, due to the previous Monday having been a holiday in observance of Veteran's Day. The gallery was full that evening, and one young man in particular didn't seem to want to settle down. Around the time the judge called the first case, police ejected the young man, who claimed to be there only to observe. A couple of his friends followed him out of the building.

Judge Crescente disposed of the first case and called the second one, when suddenly he heard glass shattering and felt something strike him in the back. He called out to Police Captain Joseph Cisco, "What was that?" and slumped forward. The courtroom was full of screaming people who ducked for cover.

Captain Cisco ran to the window and looked out upon the parking lot and street but saw no one. When he reached the judge, he saw blood under the judge's robe and realized the judge had been hit by something. Emergency personnel took Judge Crescente to Chilton Memorial Hospital in

Pompton Plains, where doctors immediately began surgery on his right shoulder. He died at approximately 10:30 P.M., just two hours after he'd been shot.

The police department of fifteen officers began searching immediately after the shooting. Authorities from several other towns in Passaic County assisted in a massive manhunt for the suspect seen by two young boys. The boys described a man shooting a .22 caliber rifle from a driveway across the street from the municipal building and gave chase, but the man ran through the Reverend Harry W. Schaumburg's back yard and disappeared between some houses. He was described as white, about twenty-five, six feet tall, 200 pounds, mustached, with shoulder-length brown hair, and wearing brown windbreaker and slacks.

On Tuesday, November 5, an unemployed laborer, David J. Vervaet, nineteen, was arrested and charged with Judge Crescente's murder. Vervaet was the young man who had been ejected from the courtroom for talking loudly and making noises. He was arraigned in county court in Paterson, New Jersey, and held without bond. Police said that Vervaet went outside and saw the judge's shadow through a closed Venetian blind on one of the four windows of the courtroom, which is on the second floor of the Wanaque Municipal Building. He later got the .22 and went across the street, stood in Reverend Schaumburg's driveway, and shot through the window, hitting the judge. Prosecutors reported that David Vervaet had appeared the previous summer before Judge Crescente on a disorderly conduct charge.

Also arrested were Robert "Bobby" Carroll, nineteen, a home repairman, and Michael Brady, nineteen, an employee of the Ford Motor Company assembly plant nearby, who were held as material witnesses on a $5,000 bond each until the authorities could investigate further. Carroll and Brady were the two friends who were with Vervaet in the courtroom.

By November 7, Robert Carroll was also charged with the murder and held on a $25,000 bond. Further investigation had revealed that there had been two shots fired, one hitting the municipal building and one hitting the judge. Robert Carroll had appeared before Judge Crescente on October 21, 1974, on charges of threatening to kill a seventeen-year-old high school student. Judge Crescente had referred the charges to the Passaic County grand jury.

Additionally, on November 7, Willard Bishoff, also nineteen, was charged as a material witness in the murder. His bail was set at $1,000.

After a grand jury investigation, findings were released that Judge Crescente's murder was part of a plot by four young men who didn't like law enforcement officials. The four had discussed burning a police car before they decided to shoot the judge, although some witnesses had stated that they talked of shooting through the window as a "prank" just to scare the judge. In addition to those already charged, the grand jury indicted another young man, John Martin, naming him as one of the youths ejected from the courtroom.

David Vervaet and Robert Carroll were tried together in Elizabeth, New Jersey after a change of venue. Although the defense alleged that the young men were just two crazy kids drinking beer with no intent to kill anyone, the prosecutor argued that Robert Carroll was the one who got down on one knee and took aim, killing the judge. Michael Brady testified that right after David Vervaet was kicked out of the courtroom, Robert Carroll said he was going to shoot the judge. Another man, George Merklin, testified that Robert Carroll had hated Judge Crescente since 1972, when the judge suspended Carroll's driver's license for four years. He said that Carroll screamed, "I did it. I did it," right after shooting the judge.

David Vervaet was convicted of manslaughter after thirteen hours of jury deliberations. The following day, Robert Carroll was convicted of second-degree murder. Both were found guilty of conspiracy to murder the judge.

Robert Carroll was sentenced on April 17, 1974, to the maximum penalty of twenty-eight to thirty years in state prison because he showed no remorse, according to Judge Thomas R. Rumana of the Passaic County Court. Rumana also sentenced Carroll to a concurrent term of two to three years for the conspiracy charge.

David Vervaet was sentenced to an indeterminate term at the Yardville Youth Correctional Facility. The judge described him as a follower who participated in the shooting "out of foolishness rather than malice." Judge Rumana imposed a maximum of ten years on Vervaet in case he should not be paroled due to rehabilitation.

Carroll and Vervaet both appealed their convictions but the appellate court upheld the sentences in 1977.

Joseph Crescente was one of the few lay magistrates remaining in New Jersey at the time of his death, having been appointed under an old state law that permitted governing bodies of cities to name laymen to the bench. Although he had attended law school, he had never graduated. Other young people who had appeared before him said he had always treated them fairly and with respect. He had previously been employed as a stationmaster on the Passaic County Line of the Erie-Lackawanna Railroad and had owned an independent insurance agency.

Crescente was so well known and popular that 400 people attended his funeral, where the minister described him as a man who "always came to church before presuming to sit in judgment before his fellow man." His wife, Marie, and seven children survived him. His murder was the first in Wanaque since 1913.

Chapter 25

Stewart Albert Cunningham
Louisa, Louisa County, Virginia
February 13, 1975

In the softly sloping hills of Virginia, in a smallish town where almost everybody knew everybody else, where one of the last self-educated men presided over his courtroom for more than twenty-nine years, much of his time devoted to helping troubled youth, shotgun blasts erupted one quiet afternoon. Those blasts shattered not only the dignity of the court but peaceable lives of the law-abiding citizens of Louisa County. When it was over, the judge lay dying; his bench and the statue of justice, which stood behind him, wounded with buckshot.

It was a bit after 2:00 P.M. on Thursday, February 13, 1975. An alleged arsonist had stood before the bench. She was being questioned as to whether she would qualify for a court-appointed attorney. A local woman walked into Judge Stewart Cunningham's courtroom. Behind her followed a young, burly black man wearing a long trenchcoat. Moments later, the young man flipped back his trenchcoat and pulled a sawed-off shotgun from under it. He fired, but it misfired. People—men and women alike—threw themselves on the floor. Judge Cunningham, being acquainted with the young man, stood up on his bench to address him. The young man then fired a second and a third time at the judge.

The buckshot flew into the left side of the judge's head, splattering blood on his glasses and the bench. The gunman ran down the hallway toward the door at the back of the small courthouse, about ninety feet from the double courtroom entrance doors. As he ran, the assailant found Sheriff Henry A. Kennon, who happened to be in the court clerk's office. He fired on Kennon, wounding him in the right arm. Mrs. Kennon, a secretary in the courthouse, hurried to her husband's side, and, after administering first aid, ran to assist the judge. Deputy Charles Rosensohn ran after the gunman and fired two shots at him in the hallway. As the man fled the courthouse, Rosensohn got off two additional shots, one of which struck the driver's side door of a red pickup truck, which the killer parked conveniently close to the courthouse so that he could make his getaway. The man drove south on State Route 208. Rosensohn and attorney Steve Harris jumped into the sheriff's car and followed him.

Dr. Evelyn Daniel, a physician at the nearby Louisa Medical Center, was present at the courthouse during the shooting and hurried to the judge's aid. She found his heart still beating. The rescue squad removed him to the medical center, 200 yards away, but his heart had stopped beating by then. Physicians and staff at the center attempted to resuscitate him for about twenty minutes before declaring Judge Cunningham dead.

Meanwhile, Rosensohn and Harris continued the chase. A red pickup truck, with a bullet hole on the driver's side door, was found abandoned on a logging trail. The suspect fled into an area several miles from the courthouse. Sheriff deputies and state troopers gave chase as well as attorney Steve Harris, twenty-six, who was in the courtroom at the time of the shooting. At one point in the afternoon, 200 officers engaged in the massive manhunt. The culprit and authorities exchanged gunfire. Trooper D.G. Hendley, who was a dog handler, and Trooper W. B. Walters of Louisa tracked the suspect with a German Shepherd police dog. State police said the perpetrator fired four shots at them with his .12 gauge sawed-off shotgun. Hendley fired at the man with his .38 caliber service revolver but wasn't sure whether he wounded him. Walters hit the man with a shotgun blast of his own.

About three hours after the judge's assassination, Curtis Darnell Poindexter was taken into custody. He had been wounded by gunfire in his chest and shoulder and by dog bites on the leg from the police dog, Fritz. The arrest took place about four miles southwest of the Louisa County Courthouse at the intersection of two dirt roads, State Routes 642 and 732. A State Police helicopter flew him fifty miles away to a hospital in Richmond.

Poindexter, twenty-two, and a local resident, was charged with the murder of Judge Cunningham, felonious assault in the wounding of Kennon and Rosensohn, and felonious assault in the attack on the two troopers, Hendley and Walters. He was also charged with possession of a sawed-off shotgun, which is illegal.

A background check was done on Poindexter, who had recently returned from living in Washington, D.C. Although he had been before Judge Cunningham shortly before the shooting for a traffic ticket and received a fine of $25, Poindexter had no other record. Louisa was a town of approximately

14,000 at the time of the shooting. Many of the townspeople were well acquainted with one another, including the Cunninghams and the Poindexters.

Poindexter had been working with his father, Alex Poindexter, as a pulpwood cutter on their farm since his return to the area. Although several people thought Curtis Poindexter had gotten involved with a radical group of Muslims while in Washington, D.C., there was no evidence of that. No motive for the violent episode was ever discovered.

Subsequent to the arrest and charges brought against Curtis Darnell Poindexter, Poindexter's attorney, JeRoyd X. Greene, of the firm of Greene and Poindexter, filed a motion for psychiatric examination and a motion for change of venue. In his motion for the psychiatric exam, Greene wrote that "at or near the time of the alleged offenses, defendant was reported by members of his immediate family as having suffered acute headaches and feeling of extreme depression and anxiety."

After a hearing on March 6, 1975, Poindexter was sent to the Southwestern State Hospital at Marion, Virginia, for psychological testing and psychiatric interviews. The doctors' task was to determine whether Poindexter knew right from wrong at the time of the murder and assaults and could understand the consequences of his acts. Additionally, the doctors and psychologists were to make a finding of whether or not Poindexter suffered from amnesia at the time he committed the offenses. Poindexter was admitted to the hospital on April 8, 1975.

There was a lengthy period of observation, examination, and evaluation lasting close to two months. Afterward, Dr. John F. Hacker, clinical director of the Maximum Security Division, in a letter dated June 11 to Judge D. B. Marshall of the Sixteenth Judicial District in Charlottesville, requested the judge to "send for this patient as soon as possible."

Dr. Hacker stated that Poindexter "is not psychotic," that he "is aware of his current legal situation and the charges against him," and that he "understands the legal defenses available in his behalf and understands the penalties possible." He went on to say that Poindexter knew right from wrong at the time of the offense and realized the consequences of his act and that "the offense appears to have been well planned and that he was not acting on an irresistible impulse." As far as the amnesia, the doctor responded as follows: "The report of the state investigators which indicated that the patient conversed in a rational and coherent manner on the flight to Richmond [after his arrest] is highly suggestive that his amnesia is spurious." Also, the doctor added, "the psychological testing ... indicates an attempt to simulate a mental disorder."

Authorities returned Poindexter to the State Prison Complex at

Goochland, Virginia, and held him there until his trial. The state moved for a change of venue, which was denied. Subsequently, Poindexter changed his plea from not guilty to not guilty by reason of insanity. Lawrence W. Wilder and Francis Chester represented him. Assistant Robert Horan represented the state. A jury of nine whites, three blacks, seven women, and five men was impaneled in the second week of December 1975. In spite of eyewitness accounts of the shooting death of the judge, the jury reported that they were hung up. The presiding judge declared a mistrial on December 16 after the jury reported for the second time that they were unable to reach a verdict.

In January 1976, the Commonwealth of Virginia again moved for a change of venue for the retrial of Curtis Darnell Poindexter. The evidence in favor of the transfer included an affidavit by an Albert M. Bazzanella, which stated in part, "there is a tremendous influence in Louisa County which flows from the Poindexter family and also from the feelings for Judge S.A. Cunningham and this has and will continue to have the effect of creating a heavy bias in these cases." In spite of strenuous protest by the defendant's counsel, on January 12, 1976, Judge David F. Berry, who had presided over Poindexter's first trial, granted the motion and transferred the case to the Circuit Court of Augusta County to be tried on May 17, 1976.

The retrial of Curtis Darnell Poindexter took place in Staunton, Virginia, in 1977. There, he was convicted of murder, for which he received a life sentence, two counts of attempted murder, for which he received twenty years each, and one count of possession of a sawed-off shotgun, for which he received two years.

Chapter 26

Judge Vincent A. Sullivan
Stonington, New London County, Connecticut
April 20, 1975

Probate Judge Vincent A. Sullivan, fifty-six, of Plainfield, Connecticut, and a woman by the name of Rose Marie Gaumond, forty-six, of Norwich, Connecticut, were found by his daughter, Susan Hall of Central Village, in a bedroom of the judge's summer cottage in Stonington one Saturday morning in the spring of 1975. The judge lay dead of a gunshot wound to the groin and one to the chest. According to a coroner's preliminary finding, Ms. Gaumond had committed suicide.

Judge Sullivan was divorced while Mrs. Gaumond was the wife of Elvear Gaumond, a Norwich painter. Police believed that Mrs. Gaumond killed the judge with an automatic handgun before killing herself. There was no sign of a struggle. Police said there were some indications of a motive for the deaths but did not say what they were.

For twenty years, Judge Sullivan had been a real estate broker and an insurance broker for twenty-five years. He became Democratic town committee chairman in Plainfield in 1954 and a Democratic state committeeman for the 29th District in 1960. He was a delegate to the three Democratic National Conventions immediately before his death, a delegate to the 1965 Connecticut Constitutional Convention, and a member of three Democratic state platform committees.

He was elected probate judge in 1962 and was re-elected for the fourth time in 1974. He had served as municipal court judge from 1960 to 1965.

He had served in the Army Air Corps in World War II.

Three daughters, Mrs. Susan Hall and Faye Sullivan of Plainfield, and Mrs. Vladimer Deyo of Massachusetts; a brother, John L. Sullivan of

Spencer, Massachusetts; and his mother, Mrs. Annette Potvin Sullivan of Spencer, survived Judge Sullivan.

Six months after the murder-suicide, police were still unable to explain what had happened and wondered whether the judge had connections to the "jai alai" scandal and organized crime. Judge Sullivan had been a political ally of John M. Bailey, who for many years was a powerful figure in eastern Connecticut Democratic politics. In November 1975, the Connecticut State Gaming Commission conducted hearings on charges that Bailey who, by the time of the hearings had died, had accepted more than $250,000 to help a Bridgeport "jai alai" developer obtain a state gaming license. Mr. Bailey's former law partner had testified that the law firm had done no legal work for Connecticut Sports Enterprises, Inc. or its president, David Friend, but also insisted that his former partner had never accepted legal fees outside the firm accounts.

Investigators said that Friend withdrew more than $235,000 from American Bank in Hollywood, Florida, packed it into a suitcase, and flew to Hartford on April 9, 1974, where he allegedly paid it to Bailey. Hartford bank officials reported that Friend rented a large safe deposit box that same day. The state's attorney had ledger sheets that showed a "late entry" of $250,000 in legal fees paid from stockholders to John Bailey in April 1974. The entry was for August 1, 1974, and was reported by Friend.

The gaming commission's hearings into the Connecticut "jai alai" scandal revolve around charges that Bailey and others accepted substantial payments or political favors. There was also a series of related charges involving asserted organized crime influence, tax evasion, and fraud.

Chapter 27

Judge Jack Prizzia
Union City, Hudson County, New Jersey
January 21, 1976

In the early days of 1976, former municipal judge Jack Prizzia, sixty-nine, testified before a federal grand jury in an investigation into illegal activities of the Union City police vice squad. The grand jury's focus was on the period of time when Judge Prizzia had been a sitting magistrate.

Several weeks after giving testimony, Judge Prizzia was due to be recalled before the grand jury and was waiting to be summoned. One day, as he walked through the lobby of his office building to his law office, he was accosted from behind and shot. A detective, who was in the Bergenline Avenue Professional Building for another matter, discovered him.

From all appearances, the assailant either had followed Judge Prizzia or had been waiting for him when Prizzia entered his office building. Judge Prizzia was shot with a .22 caliber pistol once to the head. Powder burns indicated the shot had been fired within inches of the judge's head. The evidence showed that the murderer intended to put a second bullet into the former judge's head, but the judge fell after the first shot. The second bullet went into his back. A third bullet hit him in the stomach. Doctors at the Jersey City Medical Center were able to remove the first bullet in pieces but didn't attempt to remove the other two, feeling that they were not an immediate risk to his life. Judge Prizzia stayed in poor condition until he finally died on February 17, three weeks after he was shot.

Investigators tried to communicate with Prizzia while he was conscious by using hand squeezing as signals but to no avail. Judge Prizzia tried to write, but it was illegible.

FBI and detectives from the Hudson County Prosecutor's Office investigated the shooting. The mayor's office announced that the attack appeared to have been made by someone with a personal grudge because the attack was "unprofessional." In other words, a professional wouldn't have missed the judge's head with that second bullet.

Police culled the judge's magistrate files, checked with personal and business associates to try to determine a motive, and looked at his private cases for any kind of grudge. As municipal judge and as a former prosecutor, Judge Prizzia handled both criminal and civil cases, including family law. At least one defendant in a criminal case he'd heard had threatened him.

Robbery was ruled out because Judge Prizzia's wallet, personal effects, and briefcase were all intact.

The case was never solved.

Chapter 28

Judge Edwin H. Helfant
Atlantic City, Atlantic County, New Jersey
February 15, 1978

It was just after 9:00 P.M. Darkness enveloped the snow-covered land-scape outside the Flamingo Motel. Someone driving a tan car dropped off a man approximately 5'7" to 5'8" in height, weighing between 150 and 170 pounds, wearing a black overcoat, black ski mask, and black gloves, and carrying a long-handled, curve-bladed snow shovel. The masked man went directly inside the bar.

It was the day after Valentine's Day in 1978. Former municipal court judge Edwin H. Helfant, fifty-one, sat at his usual table in the Flamingo Motel cocktail lounge with his wife, Marcine, and Leon Stricks. As was his custom most every night, Helfant, a part owner of the Flamingo with Stricks and Archie Grenner of Philadelphia, had arrived at the motel, gone to the office to use the telephone and made several calls, and told the desk clerk he would be in the cocktail lounge if anyone returned his calls.

Minutes later, a masked man walked directly to the booth where Helfant always sat. He walked up behind Stricks, placed a hand on Stricks' shoulder for balance, shot Helfant once in the head, and then pumped four more rounds into his chest. Mrs. Helfant screamed hysterically as her husband fell forward onto the table. Another man in the bar wrestled with the assassin, but the killer broke free and ran outside. Still another customer chased the man through the courtyard tunnel, across Chelsea Avenue, but lost him behind the Martinique Motel. Footprints later found in the snow led to tire tracks at the Algiers Motel. The police believed the tracks were from the getaway vehicle, which was waiting for him.

Two blocks from the Flamingo Motel, in an open area, police found more footprints and a .38 caliber Smith and Wesson snub-nosed revolver in a snowdrift. Police cordoned off the lounge and the courtyard and interviewed witnesses It was believed that the man carried the snow shovel as part of a disguise, hoping to fool people into thinking he was a maintenance man.

Inside the bar, emergency medical technicians put Helfant into an ambulance and took him to Atlantic City Medical Center. He died fifteen minutes after being shot.

Helfant had been in Trenton, New Jersey, for a trial in Mercer County Court in which he was charged with obstructing criminal charges approximately ten years prior thereto in an Egg Harbor City assault case. He had been a municipal judge for Somers Point and Galloway Township before being indicted January 17, 1973. The points raised on appeal to the United States Supreme Court included an argument that the New Jersey Supreme Court coerced him into testifying against himself. The case was dismissed and remanded to New Jersey for trial.

Helfant allegedly took $700 to quash assault and battery charges against a Mays Landing man involved in a 1968 brawl in a barroom. Prosecutors also charged that Helfant tried to prevent the Atlantic County prosecutor and grand jury from investigating him. Additionally, he was said to have forged the assault victim's signature on papers requesting that the charges against the Mays Landing perpetrator be dismissed. The case had not been proved at the time of Helfant's death.

Authorities also investigated whether or not the killing was mob connected. The summer before his death, Helfant broke up a fight between the nephew of an alleged mobster and a tailor. The tailor was later shot to death in Egg Harbor Township.

Helfant was a former president of the Atlantic County Municipal Judges Association. He had previously served as municipal judge in Somers Point in 1960–69 but was not reappointed by the mayor, George F. Roberts. A veteran, Helfant served in the Army Air Corps in World War II. He was a member of the Atlantic County Bar Association, and vice president of his Synagogue where he was said to have often worshiped twice a day. Born in Scranton, Pennsylvania, he graduated from Temple University and Rutgers School of Law.

Helfant had as many friends as he did enemies. Some people said he had a "heart of gold," while others said his heart was as "cold as ice." He was bald, stocky, and brash—known for coarse language even with strangers but also described as colorful, flamboyant, and dynamic. He lived near the beach with his second wife and children. He had a close, devoted relationship with his mother, who also outlived him.

There was speculation that former judge Helfant was possibly involved in a state investigation into Atlantic City corruption. His defense attorney said, "We alleged in the case that the attorney general had wanted to use Helfant to get to Herman 'Stumpy' Orman and Senator Frank 'Hap' Farley, and that when he couldn't give them anything, they socked him with this case. But that was just part of the advocacy process." Stumpy Orman was the former owner of the Flamingo Motel and had shared offices with Helfant in the 1960s for several years in the Guarantee Trust Building, which Orman owned. Shortly after Helfant's death, he claimed the two of them had been friends but not "good" friends. Orman, a retired real estate man, had been identified as Atlantic City's "crime czar" in the Senate Estes Kefauver rackets hearings in the 1950s. Orman and Helfant had been associates in several dealings. It was speculated that if Helfant went down with his case, he would take other crime figures with him. When authorities were asked whether Helfant had been an informant, they denied it but added that the public wouldn't be told even if it were true.

Many of Helfant's associates lived and died violent lives. Two of the potential witnesses against him were killed after his indictment in 1973. The owner of the Egg Harbor City bar that was the scene of the 1968 brawl died in a robbery. One of the brawlers, Sonny Parisi, was killed in a shootout in New York City. Two other men were convicted of dealing drugs and were to have their sentences reduced if they testified against Helfant.

A few days after the murder, rumors raged that Helfant was executed to silence him because he had been an informer for federal and state law enforcement for at least a year. Local, state, and FBI investigators joined forces to search for the killer, who allegedly would also be an assassination target because of the pressure Helfant's murder brought on Atlantic City.

Sources said the murder was a professional hit but not mob connected. The mob underworld wanted to keep a low profile in Atlantic City and would not have brought to bear such adverse publicity. The hit man was believed to be one of two involved in the February 1976 killing of a Philadelphia man at the Ensign Motel and the killer of a Pomona tailor in Egg Harbor during the summer of 1977. A mob hit would not have taken place on the target's own property. Sources said that the killing of Helfant at his own motel lounge would give the mob an excuse to hit the hit man.

Ten years passed before the murder of Judge Helfant was solved and the perpetrator convicted. All the suppositions surrounding the circumstances of his death were wrong. It turned out to be a revenge killing. His past had caught up with him.

In 1972, Helfant had agreed to fix a case for Nicholas "Nick the Blade" Virgilio, who had been convicted of murder but not yet sentenced. His possible sentence: twelve to fifteen years. The "fix" was arranged by Nicodemo "Little Nicky" Scarfo, who knew Judge Helfant. Helfant asked for $12,000 to get Virgilio a lighter sentence from the superior court judge but instead kept the money. Nick went to the pen with a twelve-to-fifteen-year sentence anyway and vowed revenge. When he got out of prison, he went back to Atlantic City and got a job in a restaurant as a maitre d'. First chance he got, Nick the Blade donned a ski mask and, with his friend Little Nicky driving, paid the fatal visit to the Flamingo Motel. Helfant had the unlucky distinction of being the first of Scafo's two dozen or more hits. It would take eight years to solve and ten years to convict.

On November 19, 1988, Scarfo, Virgilia, and sixteen other Mafia members received convictions for everything from loan sharking to murder. Nicky the Blade got forty years.

Chapter 29

Judge Martin K. Travers
St. Thomas, United States Virgin Islands
June 8, 1978

Judge Martin K. Travers, fifty-one, arrived on St. Thomas in the Virgin Islands on or about June 5, 1978. He held the position of Immigration Circuit Judge.

Travers lived in Nutley, New Jersey, with his wife but was assigned to hear deportation hearings in the Virgin Islands. The Virgin Islands and Puerto Rico had no immigration judges of their own. Judges from around the United States, including New York, Buffalo, Newark, and Los Angeles conducted all immigration hearings.

Judge Travers had heard cases for part of the day in St. Croix before traveling to St. Thomas, where he was to preside over deportation hearings the following day.

The judge was accustomed to walking or jogging for exercise every morning before he went in to work. The morning of June 8 was no exception. Judge Travers was out jogging when at approximately 8:25 A.M. three men accosted him in the vicinity of the St. Thomas Hotel. The area was near the cruise ship docks and the Sheraton Hotel, where the judge was staying. Two witnesses in a nearby automobile saw the altercation and called the police.

The three men stabbed the judge in the chest. An ambulance took the judge to the Knud Hansen Memorial Hospital, where he was pronounced dead on arrival. He was dressed in tennis shorts and tennis shoes. His wallet was missing, but there was no way of knowing how much money it contained.

Over seventy persons were rounded up the next morning, but the two witnesses were unable to identify the perpetrators. Authorities said that the slaying was the work of hard-core youths who had been robbing and assaulting people the whole week.

Judge Travers' body was shipped back to New Jersey for burial.

This case was never solved.

Chapter 30

Judge John Howland Wood, Jr.
San Antonio, Bexar County, Texas
May 29, 1979

Lee Chagra, the oldest of three brothers of Lebanese descent, born to a hard-working carpet dealer and his wife, was considered one of the most brilliant law students at the University of Texas. About twenty years later, he found himself on the wrong side of the law. It hadn't taken long for him to go from criminal defense attorney to criminal. He and his brother Jimmy (Jamiel), a drug dealer, threw away hundreds of thousands of dollars on gambling, drug and alcohol abuse, women, and high living. It was not unusual for either of them to lose $50,000 a night at the tables in Las Vegas. Their line of credit seemed to have no limit.

"Maximum John" Wood, sixty-three, hated drug offenders. His nickname and reputation came about because the majority of the time he assessed the maximum sentence under the law, even for first offenders. While that might not sound significant to the average person, at the time, the practice was to go light on the first sentence, perhaps probation, sentence a bit harsher the second time around, and throw the book at them on the third. There were no federal sentencing guidelines to follow in the 1970s. There was no hard-and-fast rule against probation. And Judge John Wood's sentences were considered harsh not only by the defendants and their lawyers but by Wood's brethren, as well. That's why federal prosecutors liked him so much. That's why defense counsel and defendants hated him so much. That's what led to his murder.

The legal profession is guided in its conduct by a code of ethics; the judiciary, by a code of judicial conduct. As well as being sworn to preserve, protect, and defend the constitution, a judge is supposed to be fair and impartial. Judge Wood was known to be a friend of the prosecution. He often ate with the federal attorneys and attended social functions with them. Rather than being respected by the bar, Wood was intensely disliked by many. There was a sense that he was not honoring the rules of the game. Higher courts often reversed him not only for his ignorance of the rules of evidence but also for his intentional disregard. It didn't matter to Wood. He seemed to think that as long as he kept the defendants off the street for any length of time that the way he went about it was all right.

U.S. Senator John Tower recommended Wood for the judgeship in 1970 when four additional federal judgeships were created in Texas. President Richard Nixon accepted the recommendation and appointed Wood to the Western District (San Antonio), which was presided over by U.S. Judge Adrian Spears. Though he was originally supposed to sit in San Antonio, because of the seniority of another judge, Wood was assigned to other divisions. Later, he would move back to San Antonio.

Before his appointment, Judge Wood had a busy civil law practice, including an active trial docket in the San Antonio firm of Beckmann, Standard, Wood & Keene. He had been with the firm practically since graduation from the University of Texas Law School in 1938. In 1941, Wood applied for a position as a special agent with the FBI and had a background check but was never employed there.

Mr. Wood, the attorney, served his country during World War II. He was appointed an ensign in the U.S. Navy Reserve on June 7, 1944, and entered active duty on July 27, 1944, at San Antonio. He was discharged from active duty effective December 25, 1945, as an ensign at Camp Wallace, Texas. He remained in the reserves until 1954, when he resigned and was discharged as a lieutenant, junior grade. He saw active duty on board the USS *Delphinus*. He was awarded the American Theater Medal, the Asiatic Pacific Theater Medal, and the World War II Victory Medal.

Although he began as a Democrat, Wood switched parties to support Dwight Eisenhower for president. He became a staunch Republican, devoting time and money to the party. For over twenty years, he and his wife, Kathryn Wynter Holmes of Nixon, led Republican campaign fund-raising drives. Wood had served as GOP committeeman for four years. Wood also participated in activities with the State Bar of Texas and the American Bar Association. He and his wife were the parents of two daughters. Born in

Rockport, Aransas County, Texas, Judge Wood and his wife kept a summer home there in Key Allegro, a restricted subdivision.

The well-to-do Judge Wood led a lifestyle that was conservative and social. His social activities included memberships in many organizations from the time he was young, such as the Alpha Tau Omega Social Fraternity while at the University of Texas and the San Antonio German Club (a social and dancing club) in the 1940s. Later, he was a member of the San Antonio Chamber of Commerce, San Antonio Research and Planning Council, Greater San Antonio Development Commission, Citizens' Committee of San Antonio, Sons of the Republic of Texas, Sons of the American Revolution, Texas Cavaliers and The Order of the Alamo, San Antonio Club, St. Anthony Club, University Club, San Antonio Country Club, and San Antonio Gun Club. He also served as an instructor in real estate law at Trinity University in San Antonio.

One Judge Wood and three Chagras made for an explosive situation. By the late 1970s, Lee Chagra had fallen on hard times. He was involved in gambling and drugs as well as drug dealing. Judge Wood had publicly embarrassed him in court, leading to further hard feelings. The feds had Lee Chagra indicted on a charge they had known wouldn't stick. The federal indictment had ruined Lee's reputation as an attorney, although he was already known as one who represented hardened drug dealers and other criminal defendants. His business was down; he couldn't win a case. He barely ever got retained. Finally, Lee had a stroke of luck. He was hired and won a major drug case.

He returned home the victor. His spirits were up. He was building a new suite of offices. He was wheeling and dealing. He was loaded. One Sunday afternoon in December of 1978, he was at his office alone when he received two male visitors. Lee thought they were there for a drug sale. They were there for robbery and murder. Lee had a steel floor safe full of money. They killed him and got what they came for, $450,000. According to Texas author Gary Cartwright, who conducted a lengthy and exhaustive investigation into this case and wrote a book and several articles about it (see bibliography), the money belonged to mobster Joe Bonanno, Sr. (now deceased).

Joseph "Joe" Chagra was the baby of the family. He was young, handsome, well educated, and easily influenced by his brother Lee. Later, Joe's brother Jimmy bullied him. Joe went into partnership in Lee's law firm, which was probably one of his biggest mistakes. Following in his brother's footsteps, he, too, became involved in fast living, including drugs.

Jimmy Chagra was the real bad actor in the family. For years, Jimmy had been heavily involved in gambling and later in selling and smuggling drugs. He dragged first Lee and later Joe down with him. Had Lee not been murdered himself (which was totally unrelated to the Wood murder), there probably would never have been a Wood assassination. As angry as Lee had been at Judge Wood, he was, after all, an officer of the court and had a much cooler head than his brother Jimmy. After Lee's death, and after Wood's assassination, Jimmy implicated his baby brother in the assassination, though it seems questionable now whether Joe had any part in it.

Jamie Boyd, U.S. attorney, and his assistant, James Kerr, were after the Chagras. They were friends with Judge Wood, often socializing with him. They took every drug case they could into Wood's court, and Wood almost unfailingly gave the maximum sentence allowable under the law to every defendant. Boyd and Kerr were conservative, very straight-arrow attorneys and despised the Chagra lifestyle. The defense bar disliked Boyd and Kerr in turn. Boyd and Kerr led an investigation into Lee and Jimmy's operations that lasted for years.

In 1978, James Kerr was driving his car when he was blocked in and it was riddled with bullets. There were two or three assailants, though Kerr couldn't identify any of them. He had crawled under the dashboard and wasn't seriously injured. Lucky for him, his assailants didn't check the interior of his car to be sure he was dead. That assassination attempt remains unsolved.

What happened in the Wood case was this: After Lee died, the federal government turned all its attention on Jimmy. Boyd and Kerr made it their business to put Jimmy out of business. Jimmy had been indicted, by design, in Midland, Texas, so that Judge Wood would be the presiding judge on his case. This practice is generally known as "forum shopping" (trying to get one's case filed in the court that will treat one the most favorably), a practice in which all lawyers would like to engage and a practice that is generally frowned upon by the bench. Still, it happened in the Chagra case. Jimmy Chagra knew he would never have a chance in Judge Wood's court. His brother was dead, and he was going down, probably for the rest of his life. Before his case could be heard, Jimmy hired a hit man. On May 29, 1979, Judge John Wood was on his way to work at the federal courthouse in San Antonio, Texas, when a sniper shot him. The bullet exploded inside his body. He died shortly thereafter. It was the first assassination of a federal judge in the twentieth century.

Three years later, and after an intensive investigation by federal authorities that rivaled the one into the disappearance of Jimmy Hoffa or the assassination of President John F. Kennedy, the first trial of the alleged murderers took place in the very courthouse where Judge Wood would have heard the drug case of Jimmy Chagra. After the assassination, it had been renamed the John H. Wood, Jr. Courthouse.

The defendants in the first trial were Charles Harrelson, the hit man, who had allegedly been paid $250,000; Jo Ann Harrelson, Charles's wife, who purchased the weapon used in the assassination; and Elizabeth "Liz" Chagra, Jimmy Chagra's second wife, who was involved in the payoff. The judge was William S. Sessions, a friend of Judge John Wood's. After forty days of testimony, all three were convicted of the crimes with which they were charged. Harrelson was sentenced to two consecutive life terms for murder and conspiracy. Jo Ann Harrelson was sentenced to twenty-five years. Liz Chagra was sentenced to thirty years on conspiracy and two more five-year sentences for obstruction and income tax evasion.

Jimmy Chagra was tried separately in Jacksonville, Florida, on four charges, including murder, conspiracy, and marijuana possession. He was found not guilty on the first two and guilty on the second two, and he was sentenced to fifteen years stacked on top of the thirty he was already doing for, among other things, "continuing criminal enterprise" (in the case Judge Sessions presided over after Judge Wood's murder), plus a fine of $220,000. He will be eligible for parole in 2007.

Joe Chagra, the youngest of the three Chagra brothers, pled guilty to conspiracy of murder and received ten years in exchange for his testimony in the San Antonio trial. He refused, however, to testify in the Florida trial of his brother, which is considered directly responsible for there being no conviction on the murder and conspiracy charges. He later said that he had falsified his testimony in order to get the feds off his back.

Charles Harrelson, father of Hollywood actor Woody Harrelson, had already served time for a previous contract killing. Additionally, he had been charged with another murder but had never been convicted.

After Harrelson had been arrested and was being transported from Van Horn to Houston, Harrelson made a telling comment to one of the agents. He said that because of the harshness of the sentences Judge Wood meted out, the judge had actually committed suicide.

Joe Chagra once said, "Judge Wood wasn't murdered; he began committing suicide years ago."

Postscript: Joe Chagra, who was released from prison after doing six and a half years, obtained employment as a paralegal at Hill and Ramos, an El Paso criminal defense firm. By 1992, he had also set up a business called "The Legal Edge," conducting legal research and writing briefs for criminal defense lawyers, generally in El Paso.

In 1994, Joe Chagra had applied to be readmitted to the practice of law. He underwent an eight-day bench trial against the State Bar of Texas in the 205th District Court in El Paso. (This was actually tried by Judge Peter

Lowry of the 261st District Court of Travis County, who was assigned. There is a rule that an out-of-county sitting judge must hear this type of case.) Part of his testimony was that he had lied twelve years earlier when he had testified against Harrelson and others in the Wood murder case in order to get a shorter sentence. He lost.

In July of 1995, Charles Harrelson, in the company of two bank robbers, used a makeshift rope in an attempt to escape from the Atlanta Federal Penitentiary. Prison guards in the guard tower fired a warning shot over the heads of the three men who were attempting to scale a wall. Harrelson, in the 1990s more famous for being the father of Hollywood actor Woody Harrelson than for being a hit man, was in the company of two bank robbers. Prison officials transferred him to Supermax, a maximum security prison in Colorado.

In December of 1996, Joe Chagra was driving with two passengers in his Toyota Land Cruiser in El Paso, Texas, when he lost control and the vehicle flipped. His two passengers were killed immediately. Chagra suffered a severed spinal cord, broken ribs, a collapsed lung, and a damaged heart. He died after several days in the hospital.

On September 11, 1997, Liz Chagra, Jimmy's wife who had been sentenced to thirty years in prison, died of cancer.

As late as 1998, Charles Harrelson was trying to get a new trial. U.S. District Judge Fred Biery heard the evidence in Denver. Harrelson, who was being financed by his actor son Woody, seems never to give up. He testified that prosecutors conspired with his defense attorney to make him a scapegoat in the assassination. He claimed that the people in Washington had to have a solution so they hung the case on him. Woody Harrelson attended the three-day hearing, at times applauding after the testimony. Along with Woody, Charles Harrelson's other two sons, Brent and Jordan, also attended, as well as Charles Harrelson's latest wife, Gina. It is ironic, because Charles Harrelson abandoned the family when the boys were small children. Their mother raised them alone in Ohio.

One evening during the course of the hearing, Judge Biery engaged in a game of pick-up basketball with Woody Harrelson at the hotel where they were staying. Such a hue and cry arose from the prosecution and the public that Biery ended up recusing himself from the Harrelson case. Subsequently, the case was assigned to another federal judge.

On March 14, 2003, the court denied the motion for new trial.

Chapter 31

Judge Frederick Fishman
Silver Spring, Montgomery County, Maryland
November 28, 1980

Silver Spring, Maryland, normally a relatively peaceful suburb of Washington, D.C., is home to thousands who commute each day. Among them was Judge Frederick Fishman, an administrative judge in the Department of Interior, Board of Land Appeals since 1972. Judge Fishman previously worked with the Bureau of Land Management in Denver and Washington and had served as special assistant to a number of assistant secretaries in the Department of the Interior. He was licensed to practice law in Massachusetts and Colorado. He graduated from Boston Latin School and Harvard, both of which were a great source of pride to him.

Judge Fishman and his wife, Evelyn, met in Baltimore, Maryland, and married in Boston in 1945. They were both sixty on the morning of November 28, 1980, and were the parents of two living children, Lawrence and Ruth. Ruth lived in California at the time of her father's death. Lawrence, born in 1951, followed in his father's footsteps. He graduated from the University of California Law School after having received his undergraduate degree from the University of California, where he was Phi Beta Kappa. A third child, Richard, who was three years older than Lawrence, was killed in 1978 in Israel, where he had gone to study, when a bomb exploded on a bus.

Friends of Judge Fishman described him as a political conservative, an intellectual with a biting sense of humor. Others said he had a great legal mind. They also said he liked to be "the king of his house."

The judge had great ambitions for his three children, but none of the children seemed able to settle down and start careers. Friends advised the couple to quit doing so much for their children and let them be responsible for themselves, but the advice was not taken.

Richard, the oldest son, attended the University of Pennsylvania, grew organic food in New England, decided to become a doctor and took the required courses, but then decided to study Orthodox Judaism first. After his second year of medical school, he took a year off to research medical ethics in the Talmud, the Jewish book of law, and then went to Israel and was killed. Richard had the role of family peacemaker. His death devastated each of the four surviving family members.

Lawrence played chess with his father when he was as young as six, often winning the matches, and won the Washington regional spelling bee in junior high, placing eleventh in nationals. He worked on the high school newspaper and founded an organization called the Student Alliance, which brought in speakers for controversial topics such as the Vietnam War and student conflict. He attended colleges in Florida, London, and Berkeley.

In law school, Lawrence Fishman worked as an advocate for mental patients. He also liked the punk rock scene, especially a group called "The Mutants." His friends remember that before he left California, Larry had a fear that the members of The Mutants were conspiring to take over his mind. After graduating from law school in California, he took and failed the California bar exam twice. Eventually, Lawrence took the Pennsylvania bar and passed it.

Lawrence held a temporary job in Philadelphia. He was a law clerk for Philadelphia Court of Common Pleas Judge Murray C. Goldman. Goldman had been looking for someone to do some writing. In order to explain away the time between law school and his application, Lawrence said during the interview that he'd been working on a novel since law school (two years). During the time he was employed there, Lawrence never told Judge Goldman that his father was a judge. Judge Goldman remembers Larry Fishman as a troubled young man.

Ruth changed majors several times as well, having focused on everything from languages to dance.

Lawrence and his mother were quite close, but his father and he never got on well, though the father recognized that the son had a brilliant mind. While living in California, Lawrence told a friend that he thought Judge Fishman was bad for the family and that he was a hypocrite. Lawrence frequently criticized his father, but he spent every dime his father ever sent him. About a month before Lawrence left for Philadelphia, he and his father had a major falling-out. The relationship remained strained.

After he'd moved, Lawrence called and told his mother that he wanted to enroll in Yale for a doctorate program in sociology. He also told her that he wanted to go to Brazil to visit people. His mother told him during that call that they didn't have that kind of money. They couldn't afford to send him everywhere he wanted to go. Larry replied in an unpleasant tone of voice, "You're very wealthy." He also asked her in that conversation whether she knew how the police department worked. That comment left her with an uneasy feeling.

In November of 1980, Larry telephoned his parents and said he was coming to see them. He wanted them to give him $100 to see a psychiatrist. His mother was elated that he had decided to get some help for his mental state. She had suggested it several times.

When Larry arrived on November 28, it was dinner time. The $100 lay on the table. Within a few minutes, he had killed one parent and wounded the other. It was about 7:00 P.M. when Lawrence Fishman shot his father numerous times in the upper body with a 9mm pistol. The judge and his wife ran outside, Frederick Fishman collapsing on the lawn. Mrs. Fishman ran to the neighbor's house two doors down. Other neighbors both heard the shots and saw the judge in front of his house. They called the police. Both Judge and Mrs. Fishman were taken to Suburban Hospital, where Judge Fishman died on the operating room table at 8:58 P.M. His autopsy revealed twelve gunshot wounds to his body, though some of the wounds were caused by the same bullet. Mrs. Fishman survived.

Judge Fishman had been in government service for almost forty years and had plans to retire in two months. More than 300 people attended his funeral. He was buried at King David Memorial Garden in Falls Church, Virginia.

Lawrence fled in a silver-blue Oldsmobile Cutlass with a Massachusetts license plate that he had rented from an agency in Peabody, Massachusetts. It was recovered in a city lot near the Trailways bus terminal in Richmond, Virginia, on December 3, after having sat in the lot for two days, been ticketed, and finally impounded. There was nothing in the car.

Authorities were unable to ascertain whether Larry had taken a bus. If he had, he'd paid cash. They weren't convinced one way or the other. He could have remained in Richmond. In Philadelphia, police investigated Lawrence's hangouts to see whether he'd returned. He had not.

Lawrence Fishman was indicted as follows: Count One: Murder; Count Two: Use of a Handgun in a Crime of Violence; Count Three: Assault with Intent to Murder; and Count Four: Use of a Handgun in a Crime of Violence. At the time of the killing, Lawrence William Fishman was a white male, five feet eleven inches tall with brown hair. He was born August 29, 1951.

Mrs. Fishman and Ruth were so afraid of Larry that they hired an armed guard to stand by while they packed up the house. They put everything in storage, sold the house, and took a long trip before settling in an undisclosed location.

Lawrence Fishman is still at large.

Chapter 32

Judge Gary Partridge
Ashland, Greene County, New York
September 28, 1982

In the tiny town of Ashland in the picturesque Catskill Mountains, residents don't ordinarily have to worry about serious crime. That wasn't true on the evening of Tuesday, September 28, 1982.

Daniel Rion had an appointment with Town Judge Josiah "Jay" Truesdell. On his way into town, Rion passed a man walking a bicycle toward Ashland. He didn't think anything of it and drove into town. Since he was early, he stopped to see his friend Raymond Myers. Later he walked across the street to the town hall for his appointment with the justice of the town of Ashland, Greene County, New York. He saw Judge Jay Truesdell pull into the parking lot and waited for him. Judge Truesdell got out of his car and greeted Daniel.

"You're early. That's good. We can get our business done first thing," the judge said with a smile and walked toward the town hall door.

Daniel was walking alongside the judge when suddenly a man wearing a dark brown cap, and a blue and white scarf at the neck of his jacket, approached them. The man's name was Edward R. Meyers. He pulled a hatchet from under his jacket and said something to the judge about $40 bail (for a charge of criminal trespass). He waved the hatchet around and ran at the judge. Judge Truesdell ran from Meyers and screamed, "Oh, my God! Oh, my God!"

Daniel Rion dropped the notebook he carried and took off after Meyers. Meyers was described as a white male with a long beard. He had a dark complexion. Daniel took a swing at him to slow him down so that the judge could escape. Meyers swung at Daniel with the hatchet and nicked him under the chin, then pushed Daniel back and hit him in the back of the head

150

with the hatchet. Daniel fell in the road, and Meyers started chasing the judge again. Judge Truesdell ran into a nearby house. Meyers followed Truesdell into the house through the screen door and then came right back out. When he came out, he ran after Daniel Rion again, but Rion ran into his friend Raymond Myers' house, where he had been before his appointment with Judge Truesdell (*Myers* not to be confused with *Meyers*).

Edward Meyers headed toward the Town building. Gary Partridge came out of his house, which was next to the Town building. Partridge, the former town judge, was in the company of his two daughters. Daniel Rion went back outside and Partridge said, "What the hell is going on?"

Daniel told him about the crazy man with the hatchet. Gary Partridge took his daughters back into the house and returned outside. Meyers was nearby, and Partridge said something to him. Partridge had a four-by-four board in his hand. Meyers went after Gary Partridge with the hatchet. Partridge struck out with the board but missed him. Meyers dropped the hatchet. The two started fighting on the ground, and Meyers produced a knife in his other hand. They wrestled on the ground with Daniel Rion trying to assist Partridge. Rion poked Meyers with his fists in the ribs, but it didn't have any effect. Then Robert Tompkins arrived. Tompkins told Rion to go to the firehouse and blow the siren for more help. Rion went into the firehouse, and Robert Tompkins went in after him. Rion remembers going back outside and falling in the street. That was the last thing he remembered before waking up in the hospital.

Robert Tompkins' brother, Larry Tompkins, was sleeping on the couch at his house half a mile away when his wife woke him up and told him the fire phone had rung; the rescue squad needed him at the firehouse. Tompkins jumped into his truck and drove to the firehouse. When he arrived, he saw Daniel Rion staggering down the right-hand side of the road. As Tompkins got out of his truck, Rion grabbed his head and fell into the road. Tompkins started for the ambulance when Meyers came from behind two cars next to the court and hollered, "You'd better get back or I'll get you, too!"

Tompkins thought Meyers was talking to him and stepped over to his truck to get a wrench to defend himself. He looked back and saw Meyers running diagonally across the parking lot toward the Partridge house, which was about fifty to seventy-five feet away. As he stood watching, Gary Partridge came down the steps around the corner onto the front lawn and Meyers jumped on him and started punching him. He had a hatchet in his right hand. Partridge only had time to grab a board to defend himself, but he never really got to use it. Partridge was able to knock the hatchet away, but he didn't see the knife. It looked like Meyers hit Partridge several times with his left hand. Larry Tompkins ran over to help Partridge and saw Meyers hit Partridge by the neck and realized that Meyers had a knife. Meyers went to stab Tompkins, but Tompkins got him by the wrist and stopped him. Then Robert showed up, their father arrived, and though Larry had Meyers down, he couldn't get the knife away from him. He hollered at his father to step on the knife. His father stepped on Meyers' hand and got the knife. They held Meyers there until the police came.

After they had Meyers subdued, Larry Tompkins glanced over at Partridge and heard him gagging, making a gurgling noise. He was on his hands and knees, holding his hand to his neck. Blood gushed onto the ground. As soon as the police arrived, Tompkins helped Partridge to the ambulance.

Judge Partridge (who at the time was a councilman) died from the neck wound. The state police charged Meyers with second-degree murder and incarcerated him in the Catskill jail. Attorney Greg D. Lubow, the public defender, was appointed to represent Edward Meyers even though Meyers had a bit of property.

The town justice, the Honorable Glenn Vanvalkenburgh, presided over a preliminary hearing in Greene County on October 4–5, 1982. Meyers was arraigned on November 23, 1982 in the County Court of the County of Greene before the Honorable John J. Fromer and entered a plea of not guilty to the five counts of the indictment, which were:

1. Murder in the Second Degree, a Class A-I Felony, in that the defendant, on or about the 28th day of September, 1982, at approximately 7:00 P.M., at Route 23, in the Town of Ashland, County of Greene, and State of New York, did with intent to cause the death of another person cause the death of such person or of a third person, to-wit: at the aforesaid date, time and place, the defendant did cause the death of one Gary Partridge by means of cutting the said Gary Partridge's throat with a knife;

2. Assault in the Second Degree, a Class D Felony, to-wit: with intent to cause serious physical injury to another person, cause such injury to such person or to a third person, to-wit: at the aforesaid date, time and place the defendant did cause serious physical injury to one Daniel Rion consisting of a huge laceration of the scalp and such injury was inflicted by means of a hatchet;

3. Attempted Assault in the First Degree, a Class C Felony, to-wit: with intent to cause serious physical injury to one Josiah Truesdell, the defendant attempted to strike the said Josiah Truesdell with a hatchet;

4. Criminal Possession of a Weapon in the Fourth Degree, a Class A Misdemeanor, to-wit: a hatchet, with intent to use the same unlawfully against one Daniel Rion; and

5. Criminal Possession of a Weapon in the Fourth Degree, a Class A Misdemeanor, to-wit: a knife, with intent to use the same unlawfully against one Gary Partridge.

Subsequently, in December 1982, the defendant, through his attorney, was evaluated for a determination of whether or not he could plead not guilty by reason of mental disease or defect. He was found competent.

On May 25, 1983, in response to a motion to withdraw filed by the public defender in which he stated that he had an inability to represent the interests of the defendant and to obtain the cooperation of the defendant, Judge Fromer allowed the public defender to withdraw. Dennis B. Schlenker of Albany was appointed in his place.

Finally, after a trial lasting six days, in August 1983, Meyers was found guilty of first degree manslaughter and first degree attempted assault. Sentencing took place on September 13, 1983, just fifteen days shy of the anniversary date of the murder. He was given an indeterminate sentence of eight and one-third years to twenty-five years on the manslaughter. On the attempted assault, he received a minimum of two and one-third years to seven years. Although in many jurisdictions it is common to run sentences concurrently, in this case Judge John J. Fromer ordered that the sentences run consecutively.

Edward R. Meyers was delivered to the Downstate Correctional Facility at Fishkill, New York.

On September 23, 1982, the defendant gave notice of appeal. He was still represented by Dennis B. Schlenker of Albany. He failed to prevail on appeal and remained imprisoned.

Chapter 33

Judge Henry A. Gentile
Chicago, Cook County, Illinois
October 20, 1983

Hutchie T. Moore became a police officer in 1962. He failed, however, to establish a distinguished record. He was fired in 1973 after a citizen complained of abuse but sued the department and was reinstated by the courts in 1977. Moore's son, Michael, shot and disabled Hutchie Moore in 1979. He was confined to a wheelchair thereafter. The department kept him on light duty until 1982. At that time, he was forced to go on disability. Moore's neighbors described him as a bitter man even before his son disabled him. Afterward, he grew worse, if that was possible.

Hutchie's personal life was no better than his professional one. His wife was miserable in the marriage. They got a divorce in Judge Henry Gentile's court, but the litigation did not stop. They continued litigating their property settlement. The case continued to fall in Judge Gentile's court for cleanup. On Friday, October 20, 1983, another hearing was scheduled for 11:30 A.M. At 11:20 A.M., wheelchair-bound ex-police officer Hutchie T. Moore, now fifty-five, arrived at the sixteenth-floor Daley Center Plaza courtroom for his hearing. Anyone not knowing the man would have felt sympathy for him as he sat in that wheelchair with a blanket over his lap and requested that Judge Gentile allow his attorney to withdraw.

After hearing the arguments on the motion, Judge Gentile denied it and began the motion for post-divorce division of property. An enraged Moore stood up from his wheelchair, pulled a .38 caliber revolver from under a blanket on his lap, and shot twice at the judge from ten feet away. One bullet hit the judge in the forehead.

Someone in the courtroom yelled, "Go for cover!" Everyone hit the floor. Moore then turned the gun on his ex-wife's attorney, James A. Piszczor, thirty-four, who had crawled under a table. Moore talked Mr. Piszczor out from under the table with reassurances that he would not harm him, then shot him in the chest and abdomen several times. Piszczor stumbled to the men's room, where he stayed until paramedics arrived. Laying the gun in his lap, Moore waited for authorities to arrive and arrest him. Emergency personnel transported Judge Gentile, sixty-three, to the Henrotin Hospital, where he died at 12:23 P.M.

Judge Henry Gentile was first elected circuit judge in 1978 and began serving in the Domestic Relations Division the following year. He graduated from Northwestern University School of Law and was admitted to the bar in 1947. He was a former police magistrate for Blue Island and village attorney for other suburban towns in the area. He belonged to the American Trial Lawyers Association and the Justinian Society of Lawyers, as well as the Blue Island, South Suburban, Chicago, and Illinois bar associations.

Attorney James Piszczor died at Northwestern Memorial Hospital after surgery. His wife and two children, ages six and two, survived him. An educational trust fund was established for the children at a local bank. Mrs. Piszczor began speaking out for gun control.

After the shootings, the police arrested Hutchie T. Moore and held him without bond. The grand jury handed down indictments in open court a few days later, during which Moore made rumblings about the justice system and about the courts being corrupt. Nine deputy sheriffs surrounded his wheelchair. The indictments were for two counts of murder and armed violence. He reportedly said, "The judges and these courts are not owned by the people of the state. The courts have just aided and abetted and denied me of all my constitutional rights. They made it impossible to save myself and my family." When he wouldn't reply to the question posed about court-appointed counsel, the judge appointed an experienced attorney with the public defender's office. Moore's crimes made him eligible for the death penalty.

There was no security at that time in the Daley Center, but this incident prompted discussion about security for the civil courts.

Though there was some question as to Hutchie Moore's mental capacity, Moore was found "fit for trial" by one jury. In another jury trial, he was tried on both murder cases and found guilty by unanimous verdict on August 1, 1984. However, the jury made the following finding: "We are unable to conclude unanimously that there is no mitigating factor or factors sufficient to preclude the imposition of the death sentence upon the defendant Hutchie Moore. We cannot unanimously find that the court shall sentence the defendant to death." Judge Harry D. Strouse sentenced Moore to life in prison with no possibility of parole on September 4, 1984.

Assistant State's Attorney Brian F. Telander filed an official statement of facts post-trial as follows:

> Mr. Moore is an arrogant, egotistical, anti-social personality who cares nothing of the law or the rights of others. Throughout the course of the pendency of the case and the trial, he was an obstructionist who constantly disobeyed the orders of the court and the Sheriff's personnel. He is a manipulative, chronic complainer who uses his wheelchair for sympathy. He should be carefully watched in prison and be granted no special privileges. He has a violent temper and should be considered extremely dangerous.

Both prior and subsequent to his convictions, Moore spent as much spare time as he could becoming a "jailhouse lawyer" in the jail library. He constantly made demands of the librarian, and if he didn't get his way, he would write to the judge demanding that the judge order the librarian to give him access to the library, even alleging quotes of the librarian in denying him access. Of course, there has always been the question of whether he was mentally unstable, and this behavior confirmed it, at least in the minds of some. He filed such documents as "Petition the Government for a Redress of Grievances," in which he stated that he was helpless, subjected to illegal trials without regard to the rules of court or the constitution. In March 1984, before his trial, he instructed his public defender to ask the judge to remove the public defender's office and appoint a law school professor with student assistants to defend him, as he believed the public defender's office, being funded by tax dollars like the court, was tainted. Subsequent to trial, he wrote the clerk requesting free copies of the transcript of his case so he could continue his barrage, saying,

> ... may I engage the services of your good office as my Servius Sulpicius Rufus: ("He aimed rather at enabling men to be rid of litigation than at encouraging them to engage in it." "[sic] laying out his whole subject and distributing it into its constituent parts, by definition and interpretation making clear what seemed obscure, and distinguishing the false from the true in legal principle.").

Thus making it clear that he either still suffered from mental difficulties or he was extremely good at the pretense.

Chapter 34

Judge Wilson L. Bailey
Port St. Joe, Gulf County, Florida
July 28, 1987

It was not a first marriage for either of them. Eleanor owned her home and sold it so that she and Clyde Melvin could build their dream home. Clyde didn't bring much into the marriage other than his personal effects and his know-how. They were married on December 22, 1970, in Donalsonville, Georgia.

They built their home. She supplied funds in excess of $34,000. He supplied most of the labor. Eventually their relationship broke down. One day they headed for divorce court.

Eleanor was nearly fifty-eight. She had never finished high school and had spent the previous twenty years of her life as a housewife. She suffered from hypertension and high blood pressure, back trouble, sciatica, and her left carotid was 100 percent occluded. She could not support herself.

Clyde, who was sixty-one and held a good job, had a bad temper and often became enraged and verbally abusive to Eleanor. He thought he should get everything, the house included.

The judge didn't see it Clyde's way. The judge awarded Eleanor the temporary use of the homestead, ordered Clyde out, and ordered him to pay alimony of $150 every two weeks. Later, after a final hearing, on October 17, 1986, the judge awarded Eleanor full ownership of the home, the Volkswagen, and $350 per month alimony. He also restored her name to Eleanor Inez Huckeba.

Clyde had no respect for the law. He didn't pay the alimony. There were no kids, just the house, what was inside of it, two vehicles, a boat, and his paycheck.

Judge Bailey, well known for doing what was fair, gave Clyde Melvin many chances. But Clyde still didn't pay. He wasn't going to pay no matter what the judge did. Months passed. Eleanor had to go on food stamps when Clyde didn't pay. On July 21, 1987, Eleanor Huckeba (nee Melvin) filed contempt charges on her ex-husband for failure to pay alimony. One week later there was a contempt hearing set on the second floor of the courthouse in the judge's chambers down the hall from the courtroom. "It should just take ten minutes," the judge told his bailiff when he'd phoned him at home and told him not to come in to work that day.

The judge's chambers—the hearing room, as it were—was a long, narrow one with a long brown Formica conference table centered therein. Deep-cushioned folding chairs lined each side of the table with one on the end closest to the judge's office for the judge. There were three doors leading into the judge's chambers: one from a public hallway, a private one leading past the judge's small restroom and into the judge's office, and one into the judge's office via a shared hallway with the bailiff, the secretary, and others.

Conference room where Judge Bailey conducted meeting before Clyde Melvin drew a gun. (Photo by author)

The judge sat nearest the two doors that led into his office. Ms. Huckeba sat on the judge's right with her attorney to her right. Mr. Melvin and his attorney, Robert M. Moore, sat to the judge's left.

It was a beautiful, sunny day in Port Saint Joe, Florida, a tiny hamlet on the Gulf Coast. Wilson Lamar Bailey, sixty-four, circuit judge for the 14th Judicial Circuit, had nothing scheduled except the Melvin hearing. Judge

Gulf County Courthouse. (Photo by author)

Bailey had told Bailiff A. C. (Claudius) Lanier that as soon as the hearing was over, he was going out to play golf. Lanier took advantage of the time off and went out to mow his lawn.

The five players in this courthouse drama were in the middle of discussions when Clyde Melvin stood up, walked over to the door leading to the public hallway, locked it, and walked back to his chair as he pulled out a .357 magnum. Ms. Huckeba jumped behind her attorney, Thomas B. Ingles, who fell on her when Melvin shot him dead. Mr. Moore, Melvin's attorney, fled the room when Melvin pulled out the gun. Judge Bailey ran out the side door that led to his chambers and ducked inside his private restroom. He pushed on the door, holding it closed. Melvin chased him and shot at the door, the bullet penetrating through the door. The bullet went into Wilson Bailey's mouth and exited through the back of his head.

Eleanor extricated herself from under her attorney and ran for the door to the hall. Melvin got off a shot at her but missed. (The door, with the hole plugged, is still there.) She unlocked it, threw it open, and ran to her left down the hall. Not knowing her way around the courthouse, instead of turning down the stairs at the end of the hall which would have taken her into the sheriff's office, she ran down the hall and into an enclosed catwalk.

Meanwhile, Ms. Huckeba's sister, Peggy White Paulk, climbed another set of stairs. She achieved the top step and the landing just as Clyde reached the doorway through which his wife had bolted. They came face to face and were well known to each other. Clyde raised his .357, shot her dead, and took off in pursuit of his former wife.

Catwalk where Clyde chased Eleanor / roof where sheriff shot Melvin. (Photo by author)

Ms. Huckeba had fled to the enclosed crossover. It had narrow windows perpendicular to the floor and no way out until one got to the other side. It was either turn back and face Clyde and his .357 behind her, or run across the catwalk and hope he didn't shoot her in the back as she ran. It was the stuff of bad dreams.

Sheriff Al Harrison heard the shots being fired inside his courthouse. He quickly ran to the parking lot, where he retrieved his rifle. He was an expert marksman.

Melvin caught his ex-wife, for she had no place to go except through the door leading to the roof. He had previously discarded the .357 for a smaller pocket-sized .22 caliber Freedom Arms Derringer and shot at her, but the bullet grazed her forehead like a wrinkle on a furrowed brow. Out on the roof, he grabbed her and put the Derringer to her as he dragged her to the north side of the annex in search of a means of escape.

Sheriff Harrison saw his chance—he quickly took aim and got off a shot at Clyde, bringing him down so fast with a gunshot wound to the neck that Melvin's other pursuers were able to overcome him before he could murder his ex-wife. The sheriff remarked later that Melvin accused his ex-wife of running around on him.

Clyde Melvin, a security guard at the St. Joe Paper Company since 1957, was charged with three counts of first-degree murder and one count of attempted first-degree murder. The public defender's office requested and was granted disqualification for conflict of interest. Not only did all members regularly practice law before the murdered judge, but they were well acquainted with the decedent attorney, Thomas Ingles, who had served as an assistant public defender from September 1, 1975, through September 15, 1986. Ironically, this was just before the Melvin divorce. Also, Robert M. Moore, Mr. Melvin's divorce attorney, was employed as a member of the staff of the public defender's office and would be a witness in the murder trial.

On August 21, 1987, the assigned judge, Carl H. Harper, retired, found that Melvin was indigent for trial purposes and appointed private counsel to represent him. The attorney appointed was Henry R. Barksdale of Pensacola, Florida. On August 31, 1987, Melvin entered a plea of not guilty and demanded a jury trial. Later, all four cases were consolidated so that they could be tried together.

The trial was continued several times for investigation and examination of the defendant as well as depositions of witnesses. On May 5, 1988, the defendant filed a notice of intent to rely upon the defense of temporary insanity. His attorney named thirteen persons, including five doctors, who would testify as to the nature of Melvin's insanity or mental defect or disorder. The motion stated that the defendant suffered from paranoid schizophrenic and/or paranoia delusional disorder, jealous and persecutory type, psychogenic amnesia localized type.

On May 27, 1988, Judge Harper granted a motion for change of venue and transferred the case to the First Judicial Circuit in and for Escambia County, Florida, in Pensacola. After the jury trial, Melvin was convicted and sentenced to life in prison.

Judge Bailey, who had been on the bench for fourteen years, had planned to retire the following July. His wife, Jeanette H. Bailey, two children, and two grandchildren survived him. He was buried at Boggs Cemetery in Blountstown, Florida.

Mr. Melvin's divorce attorney, Robert M. Moore, later became the county judge.

Chapter 35

Judge and Mrs. Vincent Sherry, Jr.
Biloxi, Harrison County, Mississippi
September 14, 1987

Biloxi, the second largest city in Mississippi, on the shores of the Gulf Coast, was in a state of transition. A large portion of the population wanted legalized gambling to revitalize their little city, which had historically flourished through vice and illegal gambling. The old guard wanted everything to stay the same, preferring to pretend Biloxi was a sleepy little tourist town.

Margaret Sherry, fifty-seven, formerly held a position on the city council from 1981 to 1985. She ran as a Republican candidate for Biloxi mayor in 1985 but lost. She was expected to run again in 1989. Described as a firebrand politician, she was opposed to gambling and anything else that current mayor Gerald Blessey was for.

Margaret Sherry's husband, Vincent Sherry, fifty-eight, had been appointed circuit judge in 1986. He was born in Brooklyn, New York, and served in the air force, where he retired as a lieutenant colonel, judge advocate general corps. In 1965, he lectured in military law at Vanderbilt University. His experience also included five years as a special master for the U.S. District Court, Southern District, 1975-1980.

Though Margaret was a Republican, Vincent Sherry was a staunch Democrat. They had been married for thirty-seven years. Sherry and his partner, Peter Halat, practiced law as criminal defense lawyers for many years. While they hadn't become filthy rich, they and their families had lived quite comfortably.

Halat had helped Margaret with her unsuccessful campaign for mayor. It was assumed that he would have helped her again in 1989. Halat graduated from Millsaps College with a history degree and from Jackson School of Law. In 1972, he was appointed to the Harrison County court bench by the gov-

Sherry home today. (Photo by author)

ernor, the youngest person in Mississippi ever to be a judge. In 1975, the Jaycees named him their Outstanding Young Man. In 1977, he resigned from the bench.

The Sherrys had raised four children to adulthood. They were Eric Sherry of Fort Walton Beach, Florida, Vincent J. Sherry III of San Francisco, California, Lynne Sherry Sposito of Raleigh, North Carolina, and Leslie Anne Sherry, nineteen, a student at LSU. The Halat children were a bit younger.

When, one morning, Pete Halat found the bodies of Vincent and Margaret Sherry in their home at 203 Hickory Hill Circle in a very secure neighborhood that backed up to the Sunkist Country Club golf course, many locals believed that the forces who wanted legalized gambling were behind the murders. Others believed it was the work of current mayor Gerald Blessey, who was a Democrat and knew Margaret intended to run against him again in 1989. It would be more than a decade before the whole truth became known.

The funeral brought out more than 500 people, including Governor Bill Allain, who had appointed Vincent Sherry to the bench. All four Sherry children came home to bury their parents, bringing the grandchildren to say their last goodbyes to Grandma and Grandpa Sherry. Pete Halat gave an al-legedly impromptu eulogy at the Blessed Virgin Mary Cathedral. At the cemetery, each of the four children placed a rose on each of their parents' coffins.

From all appearances, the murders were a contract killing, both decedents having been shot several times with a .22 caliber pistol. Judge Sherry had been found lying on the floor in the den–dining area of the house, shot three times in the face. Mrs. Sherry was found in their bedroom, clad only in a bra and panties, her glasses lying nearby. She had been shot four times in the head after an apparent struggle. Two slugs were also located in the bedroom wall.

It was Mississippi's crime of the century. A joint task force of city, county, state, and federal authorities began investigating, including the FBI Behavioral Science Unit of Quantico, Virginia. The first suspect was Mayor Gerald Blessey. Though a political enemy of Margaret's who defeated her in the mayoral race, he had expressed his sadness at her demise. He was out of town at the time of the murders.

It wasn't long before many others had the eye of suspicion focused upon them, among them the couple's son Eric, because he had told people that he had planned on being in Biloxi on September 14. Police didn't think he was emotional enough on the day the bodies were found. Former criminal clients of Judge Sherry's were also under suspicion, as well as local officials who were enemies of Margaret's. The authorities and the family thought that perhaps she had been the target, not the judge.

After months, Lynne Sposito, the oldest daughter, who lived in Raleigh, North Carolina, with her husband and children, grew disgusted with investigators. Her father's briefcase had been lost. His appointment book, which he was never without, had never been located. Authorities seemed to be bungling the investigation. People told her on the quiet that she had better conduct her own investigation or else the matter would never be solved, because some at city hall didn't want it to be. A year after the murders, police weren't even near solving the case and the joint task force disbanded. The children thought their mother's political activity had led to the murders, and police still thought some of Judge Sherry's former clients were to blame.

Pete Halat decided to run for mayor of Biloxi after Gerald Blessey announced he would not seek re-election. Halat gave the impression that a vote for him would be a vote for Margaret Sherry, but Lynne Sposito made it clear that the family had not endorsed Halat.

Gerald Blessey didn't like it that he had been blamed for Margaret Sherry's murder, even though he and Margaret had been political enemies. She had alleged that he was crooked. Though he had been cleared of the murder, he was targeted by the FBI in an investigation of the misuse of federal funds in the development of a waterfront project. Rumor had it that Margaret had been assisting the feds in their investigation before her death. In 1988, Blessey was indicted by a federal grand jury on conspiracy, extortion, and mail fraud charges. None of the charges involved the murder of Vincent and Margaret Sherry.

Everyone told Lynne Sposito to hire her own investigator, a former deputy sheriff named Rex P. Armistead. Armistead had also worked as an investigator for the Mississippi highway patrol and later the Mississippi attorney general's office. Armistead had reputedly killed nine people in the line of duty over the years. He had recently opened a business as a Memphis private investigator.

Lynne Sposito contacted Armistead, wanting to hire him. The trouble was, she had no money. Armistead wanted $50,000 to start the investigation. Eventually Lynn worked out a deal with Edward Hume to write the story of her parents' murder. She would give him access to everything they learned first, in exchange for sharing the royalties on the book. With the agreement in her pocket, Lynne could finance the investigation. Hume eventually published *Mississippi Mud,* a nonfiction book that is as fascinating a read as any novel ever produced (see bibliography).

Because of his knowledge and experience, Armistead immediately ruled out certain individuals as the contract killers. He also talked about the necessity of clearing Lynne's brother, Eric Sherry. Pete Halat, who had found the bodies, would also need to be cleared, since people who discovered bodies were often highly suspect. But, Armistead told Lynne after he got started in the investigation, Halat's name kept coming up.

Armistead focused on a man by the name of Kirksey McCord Nix, Jr., forty-six, nicknamed "Master" or "Godfather," who had been the recognized leader of the Dixie Mafia in 1971 when he was arrested for the murder of a wealthy New Orleans businessman. His criminal history showed arrests for such offenses as drug possession and sale, extortion, grand larceny, hot checks, possession of burglary tools, car theft, murder, armed robbery, and pimping. Armistead recognized Nix as a killer who was doing life without parole in the Louisiana State Prison at Angola for the 1971 New Orleans murder.

Nix was the son of an Oklahoma judge and an attorney mother who had never disciplined him as a child. Records show that from 1962 to 1968, every time Nix was arrested, his father intervened. No charges were ever filed. (His father is now deceased). Nix had gotten involved in the Dixie Mafia during his stint in the army. He'd been stationed in Biloxi. Nix had returned to Biloxi after his enlistment to go on to be involved in crime for the remainder of his life, even during his time in prison.

Nix was the mastermind of the ambush of (*Walking Tall*) Sheriff Buford Pusser and his wife in McNairy County, Tennessee, in which Mrs. Pusser was killed. At the time of the Sherry murders, Nix was being investigated for a telephone scam inside Angola. Pete Halat just happened to be not only Nix's attorney but also his friend.

In 1989, upon beginning his investigation, Armistead's contacts on the street told him that a man named Bobby Joe Fabian, a convict doing life without parole for the murders of a state trooper and a town marshal, might be involved in the Sherry murders. Armistead immediately went to Angola, where Fabian was doing time. Fabian, known in the Dixie Mafia as "Satin," had last seen Armistead almost seventeen years before, when Armistead had arrested him for the murder of a millionaire horse breeder in Tennessee. After talking with Armistead, Fabian agreed to cooperate. In April 1989, Armistead returned to Angola with a stenographer, a Biloxi police officer, and a Harrison County investigator. They had cut a deal with Fabian. In exchange for Fabian's cooperation, he could do his time in the Mississippi State Penitentiary at Parchman instead of doing life without parole in Angola in Louisiana. In Mississippi prison, he would be able to have contact visits with his wife and he might even make parole. Angola prison was something out of anyone's worst nightmare.

The story that Fabian told was of a homosexual scam that had gone on for several years and involved Kirksey McCord Nix, Jr. It eventually led to the murder-for-hire deaths of Vincent and Margaret Sherry and included Pete Halat, the judge's former law partner, who was currently running for mayor of Biloxi.

The mail-order scam was aimed at gay men. Inmates and someone working with them on the outside ran advertisements in the personal columns of magazines and newspapers and described themselves as young, small, cute, cuddly, and seeking a partner. They would establish a relationship by mail. After the relationship was established, the inmate would request money for various reasons. All the return mail would go to an address on the outside, thus the need for an associate in the free world who would forward the inmate's mail to him on the inside.

In one case, a reporter in California mailed over $17,200 before finally figuring out that he was being scammed. In another case, a Canadian man sent $43,000. Fabian bragged that one "sucker" had lost about $200,000 trying to arrange a liaison with "Eddie."

Kirksey McCord Nix, Jr., had plans for his share of the money. He figured that if he could save several hundred thousand dollars, he could bribe his way out of Angola prison. The drop that Nix, Fabian, and the others had used was in Biloxi, Mississippi, and Pete Halat was Nix's attorney. $500,000 had turned up missing, though, and Halat blamed Judge Sherry for the theft, though Fabian claimed he always thought Halat had stolen the money. In March 1987, Halat allegedly attended a meeting at Angola with Fabian, Nix, and another inmate, named Pete Mule. It was at that meeting that the plot to kill Judge Vincent Sherry unfolded. Fabian told Armistead that the hit would pay $10,000 plus $25,000 in "crank," an amphetamine.

The nominee for triggerman was a one-legged man named John Elbert Ransom, Fabian said. He had lived in Smyrna, Georgia, since he got out of prison in 1983 for a firearms charge. His criminal history dated back to 1943 for weapons offenses. He was sixty-two, a grandfather, and by all accounts, a crack shot.

In July 1989, Peter Halat, attorney, became Mayor Peter Halat of Biloxi, Mississippi. His platform was the war on drugs and drug-related crime. Of course, no mention had yet been made of his connection to the Sherry murders.

Later in July 1989, Fabian feared for his life and telephoned Lynne Sposito, telling her that he'd heard rumors that the information on the murders was coming from an Angola inmate. That meant his life was in danger. Lynne persuaded him that if his statement were videotaped there would be no point in his enemies killing him. He immediately agreed. On July 30, Ed Bryson at WLBT-TV of Jackson, Mississippi, went to Angola with a camera and recorded the whole plot as told by Fabian. When Bryson asked whether Judge Sherry was involved in the scam, Fabian said not in any way, shape, or form. There was talk that he had held the money, but Fabian didn't believe that. It was just Halat talking. They had never given any money to Sherry to hold. The group of inmates and Pete Halat just decided that someone had to "bite the dust," so it would be the judge. Margaret Sherry had to die because she was there; it was standard procedure for the killer to leave no witnesses.

Bryson went back and confronted Mayor Halat with Fabian's story. Halat flatly denied that he had any involvement in the murders. After WLBT broadcast the story with Fabian's image scrambled, Pete Halat held a press conference on August 2 in which he said that any allegations that he was involved was an outright lie. He admitted that he had a long-term lawyer-client relationship with Kirksey McCord Nix, Jr., but that their relationship had ended when he learned that Nix was involved in a prison extortion scam. He stated that Nix had hired him in 1979 to help him get parole for the 1971 murder of a New Orleans grocer. Also, Pete Halat had arranged a telephone marriage for Nix to Nix's stepdaughter, Kellye Dawn Newman, in 1983. Earlier, Halat's wife, Sandra, had been the real estate agent who had assisted in the purchase of an Ocean Springs home for Nix with an inheritance from his father.

The TV station refused to retract their story, so on August 7, Halat read a seventeen-page chronology of events that he said led up to the TV broadcast. Halat had ordered police officials to obtain prison records from Angola to show that he had not met with any inmates during March 1987 when the murder of Vincent Sherry had been discussed with Nix. Halat handed out copies of the visitor log, which showed no such meeting. Halat cried foul because Fabian could suffer no consequences from his statements. He claimed Fabian lied. He threatened to sue the TV station if it did not publish a retraction. Fabian was transferred to federal custody in New Orleans.

In September 1989, the judge declared a mistrial in the federal case against former Mayor Blessey in the waterfront development scheme. He and his cohorts were tried later for extortion. He was found not guilty in that trial.

Pete Halat avoided reporters as much as possible, going to extremes such as climbing fire escapes. A grand jury indicted Kirksey McCord Nix, Jr., on thirty-seven counts of conspiracy to commit felony theft. Also indicted were his wife, Kellye Dawn Nix, New Orleans attorney Joseph A. Rome, and two other Angola inmates. The scam had netted over a million dollars.

In December 1989, John Elbert Ransom, who had been arrested and charged with a Coweta County, Georgia, killing with similarities to the Sherry killings (for which he was later convicted and sentenced to twelve years in prison), was interviewed by the *Inside Report* TV program and denied killing the Sherrys.

In December 1990, a grand jury investigating the Sherry case indicted Kirksey McCord Nix, Jr., Mike Gillich, Jr., and Leonard Francis Swetman of Harrison County, Mississippi, with conspiracy to possess marijuana. The charges were not related to the Sherry investigation.

Sheri LaRa Sharpe pled guilty in 1990 to one count of felony theft in Louisiana in connection with the prison mail-order scam. She served ten months in a Louisiana jail. Nix and fifteen others were indicted in Louisiana, also. Nix was indicted on seventy-four theft charges.

In January 1991, a federal grand jury handed down an indictment in which Kirksey McCord Nix, Jr., and Mike Gillich, Jr., owner of The Golden Nugget, a Biloxi strip club and a former client of Vince Sherry's, were charged with conspiracy to possess marijuana. The charges were not related to the Sherry investigation.

In May 1991, Kirksey McCord Nix, Jr., John Elbert Ransom, Mike Gillich, Jr., and Sherry LaRa Sharpe, who had once worked in Pete Halat's law office and had several prior convictions, were charged in a sealed federal grand jury indictment handed down May 15, 1991, with conspiracy and wire fraud in connection with the scams. The indictment listed payments made by victims for the years 1986 to 1988. Nix, Gillich, Ransom, and Sharpe were also indicted in a conspiracy to commit murder in Vincent Sherry's death.

Subsequently, a six-week trial was held in which the four were convicted in November of 1991 in federal court in Hattiesburg, Mississippi. Mike

Gillich, then sixty-one, and Kirksey McCord Nix, Jr., then forty-eight, were found guilty of conspiring to kill Judge Sherry. They were each sentenced to fifteen years in prison. Sheri LaRa Sharpe was convicted of conspiracy and using interstate commerce to commit wire fraud. John Ransom was also convicted of lesser charges.

Biloxi Mayor Peter Halat continued to assert his innocence even though testimony in the trial linked him with the murders of the Sherrys. Federal prosecutors made statements that the murder cases were far from over. They continued their investigations regardless of the convictions. Evidence showed that Halat and Mike Gillich helped stash the profits from scamming gay men. When the money came up missing, they concocted a story about Judge Sherry skimming so that Kirksey Nix would not kill them.

In October 1996, nine years after the murders of Vincent and Margaret Sherry, a federal grand jury handed down a fifty-two-count indictment of Peter Halat (and others), Judge Vincent Sherry's former law partner and "best friend," for conspiracy to participate in a criminal racketeering organization. Halat, fifty-four by then, persisted in asserting his innocence, but the indictments showed that Halat was one of Nix's pawns in the homosexual scam. Halat's trust account relationship with Nix included Halat depositing and withdrawing money from the account as well as Halat renting safe deposit boxes for Nix and driving a 1977 Mercedes Benz automobile registered to Mike Gillich and owned by Nix.

The indictment said the facts were as follows:

- December 8, 1986, Peter Halat and an associate (Mike Gillich, who was not allowed inside the prison and so waited outside in the car) went to Angola prison, where Halat told Nix that Sherry had stolen a large portion of the money that Halat had been holding for Nix. Nix said that if Sherry didn't return the money, he would have him killed.
- January and March 1987, Halat met with John Elbert Ransom, a contract killer from Georgia (who was convicted of conspiracy in the first trial) and another person (established at the first trial to be William O. Rhodes, a convicted bank robber) about who would drive the getaway car.
- Spring or summer of 1987, Sheri LaRa Sharpe delivered a .22 caliber pistol with silencer to Glenn Joseph Cook, Sr., who test-fired the gun into the floor of his house.
- Summer 1987, Nix and "an associate" agreed to pay $20,000 to Thomas Leslie Holcomb of Texas to kill Judge and Mrs. Sherry.

- August 9, 1987, Ransom (with Gillich and Robert Hallal, who testified previously) discussed ways to kill Judge Sherry.
- Late August or early September 1987, Halat offered to pay half of the $20,000 fee to kill Vince Sherry.
- Early August and early September, Cook agreed to help kill the Sherrys. Nix approved the contract. Holcomb received a $4,000–$5,000 down payment to kill Vincent Sherry.
- September 11–12, 1987, Holcomb came to Biloxi to carry out the contract.
- September 14, 1987, Cook helped steal a yellow Ford Fairmont from Dees' Chevrolet in Biloxi, helped put an altered license plate on the car, drove Holcomb around the subdivision where the Sherrys lived, and pointed out the house. Halat and Nix talk by phone. Holcomb returned and killed the Sherrys.
- September 15, 1987, Nix and Halat talked by phone.
- September 16, 1987, Halat "found" the bodies. Halat and Nix talked by phone.
- In the latter part of September, Cook delivered the $10,000 balance of the contract fee to Holcomb in Texas.
- In 1989, Cook repaired the floor where he had test-fired the gun.
- In October 1989, two of Nix's associates removed the bullets from the floor of Cook's house and had it covered with carpet.

Thomas Leslie Holcomb, convicted armed robber, forty-four, of Evadale, Texas, was arrested by U.S. marshals and placed in the Harris County Jail, Houston, Texas, on October 11, 1996, charged with murder and conspiracy to commit murder, obstruction of justice, money laundering, wire fraud, and drug trafficking. The conspiracy to commit murder charge was brought under the federal Racketeer Influenced and Corrupt Organizations Act (RICO), a statute designed to prosecute organized crime. FBI Special Agent Gerald Peralta of the Gulfport, Mississippi, field office swore out a statement that said Holcomb, on or about August 26, 1987, was promised $20,000 for the killings. It stated that on September 14, 1987, after traveling from Texas to Biloxi, Holcomb murdered Vincent and Margaret Sherry.

Later in September, a co-conspirator, traveled to Texas and gave Holcomb the balance due on the contract. In 1991, Holcomb threatened an unnamed person to withhold testimony in the conspiracy case. In 1994, another co-conspirator threatened an unnamed person to withhold testimony. Thomas Holcomb was a carnival worker, a truck driver, and a Dixie Mafia wannabe.

On October 15, 1997, Sheri LaRa Sharpe was arrested in Colorado for eight counts of obstruction of justice, which included destroying crucial documents.

Also indicted were Kirksey McCord Nix, Jr., and Mike Gillich, Jr., who had been indicted and tried in the previous case.

Additionally named in the indictment, Glenn Joseph Cook, Sr., fifty-five, who in the 1950s had been a police officer and in the 1970s went to work for Gillich as manager of Gillich's strip lounges. He lost his beer license in 1974. He bought a $160,000 home in Biloxi with $50,000 down in 1988 though he had no apparent income. In Florida, in 1990, he was arrested for armed cocaine trafficking when he was stopped for speeding and found to have $20,000 cash, three kilograms of cocaine, and a .38 caliber Smith and Wesson on him. In 1989, he was charged in a cocaine importation and distribution ring operating out of Georgia and sentenced to nineteen years in prison.

The trial of Peter Halat and cohorts divided the Gulf Coast community of Biloxi. Just about everyone in town knew Pete Halat or had a relationship with Vincent or Margaret Sherry. Some folks thought that Pete Halat was a warm, honest, hard-working individual, while others thought he was a smooth talker, a manipulator, someone who would do whatever it took to get what he wanted. Everyone agreed, however, that the case needed to be resolved so that the town could heal and people could get on with their lives.

The case was tried in federal court in Hattiesburg, Mississippi. Federal prosecutors were led by James Tucker, fifty-seven, a twenty-seven-year veteran of the U.S. Justice Department who mostly demonstrated a laid-back demeanor, which served him well, especially in high-profile cases. He had tied together the prior Sherry case in 1991. Also prosecuting was John Dowdy, thirty, who began working for the Justice Department while still in law school, Richard Starrett, forty, and Peter Barrett, forty-nine, who lived in Biloxi and worked in the U.S. Attorney's Office in Biloxi.

Defending Peter Halat was David Chesnoff of Las Vegas. He had first made friends with Peter Halat when they both represented five defendants charged with cheating the President Casino in 1995. Chesnoff told the press that he admired Halat because Halat came from a working-class family in a poor section of Biloxi. Jeff Hall of Hattiesburg was appointed to represent Holcomb. Michael Adelman of Hattiesburg was appointed to represent Sharpe. Thomas Royals of Jackson was appointed to represent Nix. Robin L. Roberts of Hattiesburg was appointed for Cook.

Before the trial began, Cook was found mentally incompetent based on his paranoid behavior and his disorganized thinking. Dr. Emily Fallis, a Fort

Worth, Texas, psychologist, examined Cook, who informed her that he intended to call expert witnesses to testify about Judge Pickering's sexual preferences, among other things. The judge ruled that Cook needed treatment including counseling and medication and would be tried separately.

Halat's attorney filed several pretrial motions on Halat's behalf. He requested that Halat be tried separately from his co-conspirators because Halat had a clean record while the others did not. He also requested that Judge Charles W. Pickering, who had set the trial for May 20, 1997, recuse himself, because Pickering had presided over the previous trial. Some of his comments in the previous trial indicated that he had formed an opinion on the existence of a conspiracy. Additionally, Halat's attorneys requested that the trial be conducted somewhere other than south Mississippi because of all the publicity over the years. All motions were denied.

Opening statements began on Friday, June 6, 1997, after selection of twelve jurors and five alternates from a ten-county area of south central Mississippi.

The indictment showed that victims were only scammed out of $151,211. At the trial, however, prosecutors proved that one man alone was scammed out of almost $100,000, while another testified that he was out $20,000. In all, though the total would never be known, it is thought that victims turned over close to $1 million to Nix and his cohorts.

Perhaps the most incredible testimony came from Mike Gillich. He not only testified that he accompanied Halat to Angola prison to vouch that Sherry had taken Nix's money (even though he wasn't on the list of people who could get inside the prison and had to sit outside), but he admitted that he had wanted Vincent Sherry dead. He testified that Vince Sherry was "bad-rapping" him, his family, and his friends. Gillich said that he told Halat to tell Sherry to quit talking bad about them or he was going to hurt him. He said that after Halat came out of the prison and said that Nix was going to have to do somebody in if he didn't get his money back, that he, Gillich, helped arrange the hits on the Sherrys, offering money to several hit men. Finally, Thomas Holcomb, who he called "The Thumb," came to town and, after some persuading, accepted the hit. His testimony pretty much tracked the indictments after that, including details such as his arranging a place for Holcomb to stay in Biloxi.

Prosecutors also put on testimony from a career convict who had shared a cell with Holcomb. Michael Baylis testified that Holcomb told him he had murdered the Sherrys. He said he was so scared by the conversation that he told investigators. Another convict testified that Holcomb told him that Ransom had tried twice to kill Vince Sherry but had failed. The last time was two weeks before Holcomb actually did the murders. A young associate in the law office confirmed James Putnam's testimony. He had seen and had a conversation with Ransom behind the Halat and Sherry Law Office when Ransom had asked him where Vincent Sherry was approximately two weeks before the murders.

After four weeks of testimony, hundreds of exhibits, and sixty-five witnesses, the prosecution rested. The judge dismissed five of the fifty-two counts in the indictment. The defense put on their case, which consisted mostly of people who cast doubt on the credibility of the prosecution witnesses including a county sheriff, a former assistant district attorney, Sharpe's mother, a longtime friend of John Elbert Ransom, some previously recorded testimony from the prior trial, and two friends of Pete Halat. Former mayor Peter Halat did not testify.

The jury deliberated six days before reaching a verdict on all but seven counts, those being against Peter Halat. The judge ordered them to keep deliberating on the last seven. On Wednesday, July 16, 1997, Peter Halat was found guilty of one count of obstruction of justice for lying in the related 1991 trial when he denied that his office had received the money in the illegal scam and one count of conspiracy to obstruct justice for trying to get rid of scam records. Kirksey McCord Nix, Jr. was found guilty of one count of RICO (Racketeering Influenced and Corrupt Organization) conspiracy, one count RICO, one count conspiracy to escape, twenty-eight counts wire fraud, and one count conspiracy to commit wire fraud. Thomas Leslie Holcomb was found guilty of one count RICO conspiracy and one count conspiracy to obstruct justice. Sheri LaRa Sharpe was found guilty of eight counts of obstruction of justice and one count conspiracy to obstruct justice.

On Thursday, July 17, 1997, the jury returned the remaining verdicts. Peter Halat was found guilty of one count RICO conspiracy from as early as 1980 to October 1996 to engage in murder, fraud, money laundering, obstruction of justice, and drug trafficking, and one count conspiracy to commit wire fraud from as early as 1985 to October 1996 to bilk money from homosexuals over the phone and through Western Union.

On Friday, July 25, 1997, Judge Charles Pickering ruled that Kirksey McCord Nix, Jr., would have to give up $550,000 in proceeds from the scam he ran. As soon as the judge entered the judgment on September 23, 1997, prosecutors would begin searching out all Nix's bank deposits and attaching them.

On September 23, 1997, Judge Charles Pickering sentenced Peter Halat to eighteen years in prison. He sentenced the hit man, Thomas Holcomb, and Kirksey McCord Nix, Jr., to life in prison. Sheri LaRa Sharpe received five years.

Subsequent to the sentencing, federal prosecutors asked Judge Pickering to reduce Mike Gillich, Jr.'s twenty-year sentence received in the prior trial because he testified for the prosecution in the recent trial. Judge Pickering was not happy about the request and didn't reduce the sentence as much as the feds requested. He did change the sentence to release on five years' probation after Gillich served three more years. Gillich would be seventy-two at his release. Pickering also added several conditions:

- twenty hours a week of community service work for the hungry,
- a 10:00 P.M. curfew,
- and a restriction from "girlie" clubs, nightclubs, and casinos.

In January of 1998, a federal judge ordered Peter Halat and Kirksey McCord Nix, Jr., to pay $236,767 to each of the murder-conspiracy victims including the Sherrys' estate.

In July of 1998, Judge Pickering ruled that former Biloxi police officer Glen Joseph Cook, Sr., was now mentally competent to stand trial. Cook wanted the judge to let him claim insanity during the period of the murder-conspiracy, but that didn't happen. Rather than going through a complete trial, Cook pled guilty to obstruction of justice and waived his right to appeal before Judge Pickering in November of 1998, admitting under oath that he plotted with others to kill the Sherrys, paid Holcomb, and tried to intimidate a witness into silence. Judge Pickering sentenced Cook to nine years, three months, and twenty-one days in prison.

In October of 1999, the Fifth Circuit Court of Appeals upheld the convictions of Peter Halat, Kirksey McCord Nix, Jr., Thomas Holcomb, and Sheri LaRa Sharpe.

In June 2000, the United States Supreme Court refused to hear the appeals of the defendants in the Sherry murder-conspiracy case, thus ending a thirteen-year Mississippi saga.

Chapter 36

Judge Richard J. Daronco
Pelham, Westchester County, New York
May 21, 1988

Carolee Koster was twenty-nine when she began her affair with her boss at Chase Manhattan Bank in February 1979. She had started out at Chase in 1973 as coordinator of the learning center, a place where employees took night classes. In 1976, she was promoted to a position as a training analyst and became an assistant treasurer. In 1977, she transferred to personnel to write policies for clerical employees. In 1978, she became a second vice-president.

Allan Ross came from ABC to Chase Manhattan Bank as vice-president hired to reorganize the personnel department and save money. Carolee quickly worked her way up to "special assistant" to Allan Ross and talked him into getting her a raise. Ross, forty, was blond and well built. He'd wanted to be an actor and had engaged in amateur theater, but his parents influenced him to become a teacher. Later, he moved into personnel work. He had a wife and a little boy. Carolee was dark, attractive, and single. One wintry night they began a love affair.

Although the affair quickly grew hot and heavy, the couple meeting each other at least three times a week, it was relatively short-lived. For a while, Allan Ross stayed in town, spending the night at Carolee's apartment on a cot. Her mother knew of the affair. She often came and went while Allan was there. He talked about divorcing his wife. In May, he bought Carolee a small ring on Fifth Avenue, although he took it back a short time later when it turned her finger green.

Allan and Carolee began arguing and not getting along. Carolee made threats that she would tell his wife or his boss of the affair. In June, Allan recommended Carolee for a promotion and she got it. In August, Allan's wife and son went out of town for two weeks and Carolee spent those two weekends with Allan. By Thanksgiving, Allan and his wife were separated, but he began to date other women. Carolee wouldn't leave him alone. He managed to get her another raise in pay in February 1980. In March 1980, Allan Ross's boss decided that Carolee should report to another vice-president, but when Allan Ross informed Carolee, she protested and went to his boss. Alan Lafley told Carolee that she wasn't qualified for the position she was demanding, that he'd try to get her a job elsewhere. He said that if she wouldn't report to the vice-president he'd designated, then he would have no choice but to terminate her. He offered her a severance package, though it was not what she had originally demanded. Carolee Koster quit Chase on August 13, 1980.

Shortly thereafter, a well-known employment attorney made a demand on Carolee's behalf for a larger severance package. Chase offered a settlement, but Carolee refused, so the attorney got out of the case at that point. Carolee then filed a complaint with the New York City Commission on Human Rights and the (U.S.) Equal Employment Opportunity Commission (EEOC).

Allan Ross left Chase four months after Carolee. On February 23, 1981, Allan quietly married a woman who had come over to Chase from ABC. In May, Allan and his wife sent out wedding announcements. On June 5, 1981, Carolee requested a "right to sue" letter from the EEOC.

Although the affair only lasted six months and Carolee left the bank a year after the affair was already over, it was still another year before Carolee Koster filed her wage and sex discrimination suit against Chase Manhattan and Allan Ross. She claimed that Allan had coerced her into having the affair and then had her fired after the affair broke off. She filed the $2.5 million lawsuit on August 12, 1981, with glaring tabloid headlines and television interviews.

The second attorney for Carolee, the one who filed the lawsuit, received $8,000 in attorney's fees over a two-year period. After she fired him, he explained that Carolee simply didn't understand legal concepts and why certain things that had happened wouldn't matter in the lawsuit.

Carolee, her mother, Mary, and her father, Charlie, allowed the lawsuit to consume their lives. Charlie Koster quit his security job at Chase Manhattan Bank after the suit was filed, bought a mobile home, and moved to the Pennsylvania countryside. He and her mother began financially supporting Carolee while she actively participated in prosecuting her lawsuit.

The third employee-discrimination specialist advised Carolee to get a job, but other than a temporary part-time job and a bit of consulting work, she spent all her time on the case. At the end of their relationship, she owed this attorney $10,000.

In 1983 and 1984, Chase attorneys deposed Carolee Koster and discovered that her version of events differed greatly from that of Allan Ross. She claimed that he threatened her from the beginning to make her life on the job miserable if she didn't submit to his advances.

In 1984, Allan Ross and Chase filed to have the federal equal-pay part of the lawsuit dismissed unless Carolee could prove that she was paid less than a male in an equivalent job. Her attorney filed an affidavit for her, but then Carolee filed her own affidavit comparing herself to the man Lafley had wanted her to report to, Neil Owen.

In May 1985, a federal judge named Peter Leisure ruled in favor of Ross and the bank. This ruling cut off Carolee Koster's right to a jury trial and her right to seek punitive and compensatory damages, leaving damages for lost wages due to the termination and alleged wage and sex discrimination as the only thing she could receive.

Additionally, in May 1985, Carolee and her third attorney started preparing for trial. Carolee could not understand what the legal claims meant. She had an idea that she should have been paid her supervisor's salary and her subordinate's salary if she did their work. She also couldn't get her eyewitnesses together. Lastly, she failed to understand that Chase would be entitled to an offset for what she could have earned after she left Chase, but she hadn't really tried to earn anything and thought Chase should pay her forever. Ultimately, in July 1985, when Carolee wrote a letter to the court complaining about her third attorney, he, in turn, requested leave of the court to withdraw from her case. Carolee had decided to represent herself.

The Chase and Ross attorneys struggled along with their *pro se* opponent, who filed voluminous documents with long lists of witnesses she intended to call. They tried again to get the case dismissed and lost. A year and a half later, the case was ready for trial. It had been transferred to new federal district judge Richard Daronco.

Richard J. Daronco, fifty-six, wanted to be a judge from the day he entered the Albany Law School of Union University. After he graduated, he practiced law for a few years. He got involved in the Republican Party before being appointed judge of the family court in Westchester County in 1971 at thirty-nine. Three years later, he moved to Westchester County Court, where he served for another three years. After that stint, he served as an administrative judge for a year. He served as a justice of the New York Supreme Court from 1979 until 1985. From 1983 until 1987, he served as deputy chief administrative judge of the courts outside New York City, responsible for the administration of 450 upstate New York courts. In January 1987, President Ronald Reagan nominated Judge Daronco to the federal bench. He was confirmed by the Senate in May 1987 and sworn in on June 8, 1987. He was on the federal bench in Manhattan, one of twenty-seven judges of the United States District Court for the Southern District of New York, which included Manhattan, the Bronx, and six upstate counties.

Richard Daronco and his wife, Joan, lived in the tiny village of Pelham, New York, where the affluent population of 6,800 citizens was unused to violence of any type. Judge Daronco was described as a great family man, a churchgoer, and a wonderful neighbor who spent his time working on his house. The Daroncos were the parents of five grown children.

Carolee Koster continued to be her own attorney. In December 1987, before the pretrial conference, Judge Daronco advised both sides that they should be ready to discuss settlement of the case. At the conference, he talked to the attorneys, then he talked to Carolee Koster, and finally Chase offered Carolee $300,000 in full settlement of the case. After two days, Carolee refused the settlement. In February 1988, Carolee and the Chase counsel met again to try to settle, but Carolee wasn't having any.

The trial began March 23, 1988, with Carolee Koster representing herself. Her mother, Mary, served as her paralegal. When Carolee announced to the judge that her mother would be called as a witness, the judge excluded Mary Koster from the courtroom on the motion of the Chase attorneys. The Kosters didn't care for that bit of maneuvering and more than likely didn't understand it, either.

Charlie and Mary Koster had recently separated, though no one on the other side of Carolee's case knew about it. Charlie Koster sat in the courtroom the entire trial and ran errands for Carolee as needed. Charlie Koster acted out in the courtroom as the testimony unfolded, visibly and physically reacting with bodily movements. Near the end of the trial, Judge Daronco gently requested the man not to behave that way. Mr. Koster left the courtroom in anger though he had not been requested to leave. Judge Daronco also gave Carolee Koster great leeway in presenting her case and in examining witnesses, having made it clear to the other side that she would be allowed to ask questions her way. She took a good deal more time in her presentation than anyone had anticipated but was unable to make her case. During a three-week break midtrial, her people approached Chase's attorneys about reopening settlement negotiations but were rejected. The Chase attorneys knew they were winning.

Allan Ross was one of the witnesses Carolee called to testify. Allan had had a heart attack in 1985 and was waiting to see whether he would qualify for a heart transplant. He attended as much of the trial as his health would permit, together with his wife, Marilyn.

Twenty days after the trial ended, Judge Richard Daronco signed a judgment dismissing Carolee Koster's claims as to both defendants, finding that she had failed to prove the merits of her case, that she was responsible for her own termination from Chase Manhattan Bank. It was Thursday, May 19, 1988. Daronco's law clerk mailed the opinion to both sides that morning.

The judge and his staff discussed security precautions at the courthouse, expecting an adverse reaction from Carolee Koster. Although there was a security camera and intercom, the judge had never had it hooked up. He was a trusting soul, even leaving his home address listed in the phone book and mentioning in trial that he lived in Pelham. They decided to have the camera and intercom hooked up on the following Monday, thinking that Carolee would react with a verbal attack.

On May 20, even though Carolee hadn't received the decision yet, her father, Charlie, who had gone back to his house trailer in Bath, Pennsylvania, after the trial (her mother had flown to Naples, Florida, to her condo) drove to Pelham, New York, to locate Judge Daronco's home. Charlie Koster had told his wife that everyone had mistreated Carolee. He said that the judge was arrogant and had allowed Allan Ross to portray his daughter as the aggressive one in the affair.

On Saturday, May 21, 1988, Judge Richard Daronco slept until about 10:30 A.M., walked to town, took care of some errands, returned home, and began working in his yard on a red maple tree that needed trimming.

Charlie Koster spent the night in Pelham, though no one knows where. Around 2:00 P.M., Koster parked his car at a cemetery five blocks from the street on which the Daroncos lived. Tucking his .38 police revolver in his belt, he left most of his personal belongings, including his retired police officer badge, in his vehicle and walked toward the judge's home. The judge was busy trimming the Japanese maple in his front yard when Koster walked up. Before the judge could run, Koster pulled out his .38 caliber Smith and Wesson revolver and shot him four times.

It was about 2:10 P.M. Family members, hearing shots, watched from the window, horrified, as a white man shot their husband and father. Koster hit him in the chest, the back, buttocks, and struck a femoral artery in his thigh, causing profuse bleeding. Judge Daronco fled his assassin, screamed, "I need help!" and staggered into the house through the kitchen door. His killer followed. When Mrs. Daronco tried to close the door on him, Koster pushed through yelling, "I'm going to get him!" The judge managed to run through the foyer to the first-floor study, where he tried to barricade himself. He died behind a door from the wounds inflicted while outside. One shot was fired in the house.

When authorities arrived, they found Joan Daronco, daughter, Rosemary (called Murphy), and her boyfriend in the front of the house. Upon entering the home a few minutes later, they found the body of the murderer lying on the stairs with a single gunshot wound to the head. Judge Daronco, clad in sweats, which were blood-soaked, was found in the study, dead from loss of blood.

Upon investigation, authorities found that the killer was Charlie Koster, sixty-seven, a retired mounted policeman and security guard who had taken revenge on behalf of his daughter, who had lost her civil lawsuit in Judge Daronco's court just two days before.

Judge Daronco was the second federal judge killed in the twentieth century. Judge John H. Wood, Jr., was the first in 1979. (See chapter 30.)

Chapter 37

Judge Carol S. Irons
Grand Rapids, Kent County, Michigan
October 19, 1988

District Judge Carol S. Irons, forty, was the first woman judge to serve in Kent County, Michigan, where judges are elected to six-year terms. She was born in 1948 in Detroit, Michigan, to a mother who was a violin teacher and father who was a production engineer for Michigan Bell. She had two older brothers and was especially close to her brother Peter, who was her roommate for a while. She majored in philosophy at Olivet College and was married to a music professor for five years after she graduated.

After her divorce, Carol Irons decided to go to law school. She graduated from Wayne State University Law School in 1977. She worked in the Kent County Prosecutor's Office shortly after law school graduation and rose to become the chief of the appellate section. In 1982, at thirty-four, Carol Irons ran against six men and was elected to a district court bench, which in Michigan is the court that handles civil suits to $10,000, small claims, felonies, misdemeanors, DWIs, and preliminary hearings. She was an outspoken advocate against family violence and sensitized the county's male judges to issues involving women. She served as a positive role model for the county's female population, especially those in the legal field.

In 1988, Judge Carol Irons decided to make some changes in her life. She was happy to be running unopposed for re-election on the November 8 ballot. On June 21, she filed for divorce from her (second) husband of four years, police officer Clarence Ratliff. She enrolled in piano lessons and Bible study, lost weight, and changed her hairstyle.

Judge Irons' husband was a very different person from the judge. Their marriage surprised many people, because the judge was stern and tough on the bench but considered a liberal off the bench, being an advocate for

181

women and gays. Clarence Don Ratliff was considered by many to be a "redneck." He had served in the U.S. Marines, was still in the reserves, and was a career police officer. He was considered very "macho," rode a Harley Davidson motorcycle, and was even a member of a local motorcycle club. He also had been married once before.

On October 19, "Rat," as his friends knew Clarence Ratliff, finished a ten-hour shift. Afterward, he went to several bars and drank beer and whiskey with friends. One place was Kale's Korner Bar, where he spent time with longtime friends Police Sergeant George Pepper and Robert Kale, a former roommate from the 1970s and owner of Kale's. At about 11:00 A.M., Ratliff left the bar. His whereabouts are unknown for twenty to thirty minutes. He arrived at the county courthouse around lunchtime. Judge Carol Irons was in her chambers, working through lunch. County courthouse employees knew Ratliff as a twenty-one-year veteran of the police force as well as the judge's husband.

Danielle Smith, a deputy district court clerk who was working over the lunch hour, let Ratliff in the security door to the court office and hallway leading to Irons' chambers. Smith said later that Ratliff smiled and waved at her through the window and asked if Irons was in. She let him inside the corridor leading from the Hall of Justice lobby to court offices. She watched until Irons came out of her office. He followed Irons into her chambers. Smith did not know about the pending divorce.

Ratliff wore plain clothes and was armed with his 9mm semi-automatic pistol, but that was not unusual. He often carried a gun while off-duty, as most police officers do. While no one witnessed the actual events in Judge Irons' chambers, it is known that Ratliff put the gun to Judge Iron's head. She called dispatch and said, "My husband is pointing a gun at my head." Shots were heard moments later.

County sheriff's deputies and city police officers ran to the judges' office after the dispatcher received the alarm from the judge's chambers. Judge Irons staggered from her chambers and clutched her throat as blood poured from a wound in her neck. She cried, "Please help me."

Ratliff followed Judge Irons into the hall and began firing. Officer Wells pulled the judge into the court jury room; two officers took cover in doorways; and one officer, John DenBoer, who had been sworn into the police department in the same class as Ratliff, remained in the corridor and exchanged fire. A friend of the judge's, Mary Harrison, tried to stem the flow of blood as Judge Irons lay dying on the jury room floor, but to no avail.

DenBoer reported that when he took Ratliff into custody, Ratliff asked, "'How is she?'" and "kind of sagged and sobbed" when told that she was dead. Officer Hugh Roberts said he could smell alcohol on Ratliff's breath when he handcuffed him. DenBoer said he couldn't tell whether Ratliff was drunk or not. Sheriff's Deputy Robert Maier stated that Ratliff said, "I just couldn't take the bitch anymore."

When Ratliff was booked into the county jail, the security clerk said that Ratliff seemed "sad and dejected"; his speech was slow; he sobbed a few times; but he didn't appear to be intoxicated. Ratliff's blood alcohol level tested out at .14. (The legal intoxication limit is usually .10, though late in the twentieth century it was lowered to .08 in many areas.)

A month after he murdered his wife, Ratliff, a veteran of the Grand Rapids Police Department, resigned his commission. He would have been eligible for retirement in two more years. In February 1989, Ratliff began collecting his pension and used it, among other things, to pay for a mortgage on his home on the Muskegon River.

Kent County Prosecutor William Forsyth, who knew both Judge Irons and her husband, removed himself from the murder case, saying that he could not prosecute a friend for killing a friend. He requested a special prosecutor.

The Michigan Attorney General's Criminal Division decided to prosecute and assigned Assistant Attorney General Mark Blumer. Circuit Judge Dennis Kolenda presided over the trial, which was tried to a jury made up of nine men and three women. The defense essentially tried Carol Irons while defending Ratliff. The defense alleged that Ratliff was hurting inside because his wife was seeing another man, a border patrol agent. They put a bartender on the witness stand who said Ratliff had told him that it was "pretty hard when your wife's a judge and a whore at the same time."

Psychologist Daniel Rosen examined Ratliff while the case was pending. During the trial, the psychologist testified that Ratliff was a "passive-dependent" person. Ratliff suffered from a diminished mental capacity when he shot his wife. He thought he was "a bad guy in a police training drill" and "when I saw the blood in the office I realized it wasn't a drill." Rosen said that Ratliff felt inferior to his wife because she had a superior education and social position to his own. He had been raised poor in a coal mining town. Ratliff failed to confront his wife over alleged infidelities because of his insecurities. On the day of the murder, he went to his attorney's office after having worked a ten-hour shift, and after having gone to several bars drinking with friends. At his attorney's office, he read a letter that said his desired property settlement was jeopardized. Rosen also testified that Ratliff suffered from sexual dysfunction problems.

Defense attorneys also argued that Ratliff was normally a happy drunk and was intoxicated at the time of the shooting. His inebriation contributed to his diminished capacity.

The jury was not allowed to hear evidence that Ratliff had struck and threatened to kill his first wife. He had been suspended from his job for five days without pay, but his first wife failed to file charges. They also didn't hear that he had tapped the judge's phone and threatened her, though she didn't want to make trouble for him on his job and didn't file any motions for her own protection.

The jury deliberated for about six hours over two days. They ended up convicting him of voluntary manslaughter in her death saying by their verdict that his reason was clouded by "undue excitement" at the time of the shooting, that an average person's reason would have been similarly excited, and that Ratliff had no time to "cool off" before the killing. The sentence range was zero to fifteen years in prison. In the other cases, he was convicted of two counts of assault with intent to murder because he shot at Officer John DenBoer and Sheriff's Deputy Robert Maier. The possible sentence in those two cases: one year to life in prison. He was also found guilty of assault with a firearm, reduced from assault with intent to murder, which meant that jurors felt Ratliff shot at Police Captain Daniel Ostapowicz and intended to injure or put him in fear of being hurt but not kill him. The maximum he could get for that charge: four years. Lastly, he was convicted of felony firearm: using a firearm during the commission of a felony, which carried a mandatory two-year prison term.

The outcome of his trial brought a stream of protests from women's groups, who were shocked and outraged that the murder of a woman was considered less serious than attempting to shoot and missing a man (the police officer). They felt that the verdicts sent the wrong message to the community: tacit approval of spousal battering. (In fact, news reports show that in subsequent years shelters were underfunded and had to close.)

Jurors tried to justify their verdict by saying that Judge Irons "provoked" her husband into shooting her by doing the following things:

1. Dating during the divorce separation. Ratliff was having trouble sexually and she probably "rubbed that into him";
2. Not agreeing to the settlement that he wanted, that being his cottage and his truck.

Later some of the jurors said that had they known some of the things they were not allowed to hear, the verdict probably would have been different.

On June 12, 1989, Circuit Judge Dennis Kolenda, after receiving over 1,000 cards and letters, and after hearing from the deceased judge's friends and family, and of course, after hearing from attorneys for both sides, sentenced Ratliff as follows:

- two life terms on the attempted murder charges,
- ten to fifteen years for shooting Judge Irons,
- up to four years for assaulting the third officer,
- and two years for using a gun to commit a felony offense.

Ratliff began serving his prison term at State Prison of Southern Michigan in Jackson, where he went for processing. A month later, he was transferred to Marquette Branch Prison. In January 1990, Ratliff was sent to Carson City Regional Facility, then back to Marquette a week later. April 5, 1990, he was moved to Michigan Reformatory at Ionia, then returned to Marquette on April 26. August 16, he was moved to Huron Valley Men's Facility at Ypsilanti. At the end of October 1990, he was transferred to a federal prison in Texas after receiving death threats due to his being a police officer. There were reputedly 200 inmates in the Michigan prison at the same time as Ratliff. Still later, he was transferred to a prison in Pennsylvania. The earliest he could be released was the year 2000.

In the meantime, under an unusual civil statute, the state of Michigan sued Ratliff to pay for the costs of his incarceration out of certain assets of his estate. In Ratliff's case, ninety percent of his pension could be seized, as well as any savings.

In May 1990, after a trial, the judge ruled in favor of Ratliff, stating that another law passed later in time cancelled out the first one. The state appealed and won a reversal. In January 1993, Ratliff's attorneys sued him for back attorney's fees in an effort to block the state from seizing his pension, seeking $80,610. The lawsuit stated that Ratliff had paid them $7,389 in cash and signed over a cottage in Newaygo County with equity of $12,000 and a market value of $52,000. Subsequent to their filing suit, Kent County Circuit Judge Dennis Kolenda approved a settlement with the state of Michigan of sixty percent of Ratliff's $1,200 per month pension to offset the cost of his imprisonment. He also approved a settlement giving the state 55 percent of the $47,000 that had accrued since January 1990. The state had paid between $56 and $59 per day for his incarceration.

In April 1991, the Michigan Court of Appeals heard Ratliff's appeal. Ratliff's attorney, Grant Gruel, argued that if Ratliff's mental capacity was diminished by alcohol and stress from his impending divorce such that he wasn't able to form the intent necessary to sustain a verdict of first- or second-degree murder, then it was completely illogical for the jury to find that he had the ability to form the requisite intent to murder the police officers who had come to his wife's aid. It was a creative argument designed to reduce Ratliff's sentence and included an argument that, at the very least, the trial judge should reduce Ratliff's sentence if the Court of Appeals didn't give him a new trial. The Court of Appeals didn't buy it. It affirmed the jury's verdict. The Michigan Supreme Court refused to consider the case.

Chapter 38

Judge Jack Dooley
Palacios, Matagorda County, Texas
April 7, 1989

Palacios, Texas, sun-drenched in the summers, wind-blown in the winters, is a coastal village southeast of Houston where everyone is acquainted with one another. Life moves at a slow pace. Fishermen abound. There is only a bit of a tourist trade and no real industry.

On April 7, 1989, in the tiny courthouse annex in what passes for downtown in a village that small, a masked gunman walked into the tax office where construction worker Dwain Koening carried on a conversation with Matagorda County Justice of the Peace T. J. "Jack" Dooley. A few minutes later, Judge Dooley and the gunman lay dead.

Koening had gone there to obtain Dooley's advice when the killer came in and stuck a gun in Koening's back. Pam Gaslight, the police chief's wife, was the only tax office employee present. She thought she recognized the gunman from earlier in the day when he inquired about obtaining a Texas driver's license. Police Dispatcher Teresa Spradlen was operating the computer from behind a bulletproof window. She thought he looked familiar, too. Assistant Chief Emmett Greene was standing in the doorway behind Teresa when the masked man

(*Courtesy Nick West*, Palacios Beacon)

Matagorda County Courthouse annex. (Photo by author)

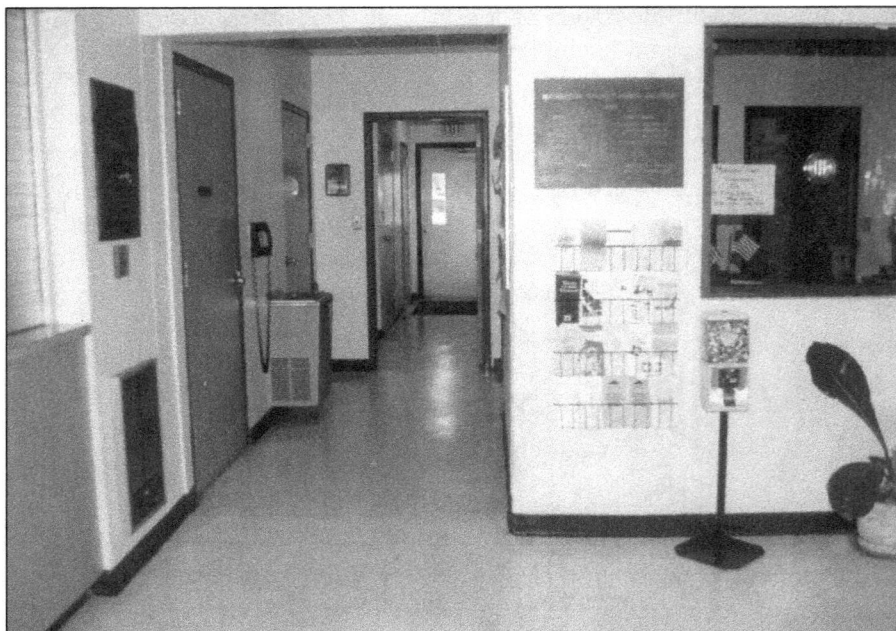

Lobby in Matagorda County Courthouse annex where shootout occurred. (Photo by author)

opened the glass door and walked inside. Also in the building was Elizabeth Brumley, secretary to Justice of the Peace Dooley.

The killer, Nga Duc Nguyen, twenty-seven, was of Vietnamese descent. He had recently returned from Garden City, Kansas, where he had lived for about eighteen months. Before that, he had been a shrimper in the Palacios area. He lived in his van, was a loner, and had very little contact with the rest of the world. Armed with a 7.65 Mauser semi-automatic pistol, Nguyen, who was wearing a baseball cap, a mask made from a piece of white sheet which only partially covered his face, and a backpack containing an odd assortment of items such as handcuffs and a four of clubs, walked in, pointed the gun at Koening, and said, "Move, move." Koening took a few steps, then dropped to the floor.

Assistant Chief Greene saw Nguyen through the plate glass window, pulled his gun, and yelled, "Drop it." A hail of gunfire erupted over Koening's head. When it was over, Judge Dooley had taken a shot in the heart, Nguyen lay dead, and a bullet had pierced Greene's abdomen.

Jack Dooley, seventy-nine, was a former marine, father of two sons, grandfather of seven, and a great-grandfather of three. A devout Catholic, Dooley was preparing to travel with one of his sons in Italy, where he had a meeting set up with the Pope. Earlier on the day of his death, Judge Dooley had been telling everyone that he had his clothes laid out, ready to pack and go.

Judge Dooley was born in LaGrange, Illinois, in 1909. Before moving to Palacios in 1969, he was a meat and poultry broker in Houston, Texas. He retired to the country for a more peaceful way of life and ran for justice of the peace in 1976. His wife, Margaret, had passed away three years earlier, but Jack continued to do the things he loved, and that was work with people every day, helping them with their problems.

Chapter 39

Judge John C. Fairbanks
Newport, Sullivan County, New Hampshire
March 27, 1994

Former Newport, New Hampshire, district judge and attorney John C. Fairbanks, seventy, disappeared in 1989. He had been indicted on December 28, 1989, by the Sullivan County Grand Jury for theft by unauthorized taking, a felony. He had embezzled client funds for over twenty years. During the summer before his indictment, Fairbanks had been disbarred.

The day following the indictment, the then-sixty-six-year-old white male read a story to his grandson, closed the book, and drove away into oblivion. He and his wife of thirty-five years owned two homes, one in Newport, New Hampshire, and one in Ogunquit, Maine. Numerous children and other relatives lived on the East Coast, but the New Hampshire Attorney General's Office, the New Hampshire State Police, and other authorities were unable to locate him.

John Fairbanks had been well respected in Newport, New Hampshire, a town of about 6,000 people in the western part of the state. He had practiced law for forty years, specializing in estates and trusts. In 1964, he was appointed a district judge. In New Hampshire, district judges could maintain a law practice.

Judge Fairbanks' family dated back to the earliest settlers in the area. His grandfather, George A. Fairbanks, co-owned Fairbanks and Dorr Woolen Mill in Guilld. His father, Harold Fairbanks, had been a state senator and owned a Chevrolet dealership in Newport.

Fairbanks and his three sisters attended local schools, where he was a "B" student. He was also an avid snow skier. He was described as an ordinary boy, well liked by everyone. He served in the army in World War II. He graduated from Dartmouth College after the war in 1946 and obtained his law degree from Boston University. In 1951, he married Miriam Bull, the sister of his Dartmouth College roommate.

By 1956, the Fairbanks had three daughters and a son. The daughters were named after three of the sisters in *Little Women*, Amy, Beth, and Meg. His son, Jim, lived in Colorado.

Fairbanks was described as a devoted father who lavished everything he could on his children, even to the detriment of those who worked for him, whom he paid low wages. His children always had nice cars. The daughters had elaborate lawn weddings with over 200 guests in attendance.

Some local residents described Fairbanks as an eccentric. He would go jogging at 2:00 A.M., arrive at the office at 5:00 A.M., and depart for home at 2:00 P.M., explaining that he could get more done in the quiet. One of his daughters described him as a control freak, who wanted to keep up his image above anything else. He often gave his wife instructions and expected them to be carried out to the letter. He objected to her doing volunteer work or anything that took her away from what he wanted.

Fairbanks was also a closet homosexual, though associates said it was a poorly kept secret. His wife knew and chose to stay with him. The children didn't find out until after he'd disappeared, when everyone was talking about it.

The general consensus of the authorities and his family members seems to be that although Fairbanks was very good with interpersonal relations in dealing with the kids and adults who came before him in his thirty-three years as part-time district judge, he was terrible at investments. He had access to funds through estates and trusts. He invested the funds, including his own, and not very well. He lost money and then invested more, dipping into client accounts and playing higher stakes to make up for what he'd lost. His daughter described him as an addictive personality.

With the stock market dip of 1987, Fairbanks couldn't recover. Witnesses described how the judge would recess court and go into his chambers, where they could hear him talking in a loud voice to his stockbroker on the telephone.

The grand jury indictment in 1989 alleged that as early as 1983, Fairbanks had begun taking client funds, including those of insurance companies, businesses, and trust funds for a small town of 500, Washington.

His sisters claimed he took over $500,000 of their money. One investigator believes that Fairbanks had been taking money illegally since the 1950s and that the total stolen exceeded $1,000,000, though no one will ever know for sure. Lawsuits that were filed against his estate alleged over $6,000,000. In 1992, the New Hampshire Bar Association established a fund to repay

Fairbanks' debts and managed to repay fifteen cents on every dollar. After his property was sold, the clients who sued him got twenty-one cents on the dollar.

When his thievery came out and he was indicted, Fairbanks couldn't bring himself to face time in prison with the very people he'd sentenced. His friends knew that he would either commit suicide or run. In the end, authorities allege, he did both. His truck was found in a parking lot near his vacation home in Ogunquit, Maine, but nothing pointed to where he'd gone.

Ten months after Fairbanks fled, he was in Quebec City, Canada, where the majority of people spoke French. He assumed the name of a former client and friend, Richard Mansfield. He told everyone that he was a retired Harvard history professor who moved to Canada to take advantage of its liberal medical benefits. He also used another alias, Harry Tilton. Fairbanks first rented a nice apartment in a waterfront complex. In October 1990, he bought a condominium in the suburb of Charlesbourg. He put down $8,000 and made monthly payments of $616.

He later sold the first condominium and bought a more expensive one for $112,500 from the same developer. He had difficulty over time making the payments. The rooms in his apartment were described as bizarre, each one painted a bright color. They were decorated with artwork and antiques.

Fairbanks was able to obtain a driver's license with the help of a young man named Walter Pares, who befriended him when he stopped him to ask directions. Pares drove him to the airport on March 21, 1994. From Quebec, Fairbanks flew to Vancouver, British Columbia, spent the night, and then flew to Las Vegas with a stop in Salt Lake City.

In late March, Fairbanks telephoned his family and asked for money. They refused. He also told them that he was suffering from prostate difficulties and was in a lot of pain but wouldn't see a physician.

Police in Las Vegas report the following conclusions: On March 27, 1994, former judge John Fairbanks wrote out a suicide note, taped it to a mirror, placed a plastic bag over his head, and went to sleep. He died of suffocation at the MGM Grand Hotel and Casino in Las Vegas, Nevada. Security personnel at the casino hotel found Fairbanks' body in his twenty-first-floor room. The Clarke County, Nevada, coroner, Ron Flud, concluded that Fairbanks died of asphyxiation and that it was self-inflicted.

Fairbanks died a pauper with only $15 in a bank account. Though he did own some properties, he was in debt (other than what he stole) over $150,000, and his credit cards were all run up to their limits.

Some of the reasons Fairbanks was never located are:

- He was ordinary-looking.

- He led a quiet life.
- He wore a beard and a toupee, and most of the time a hat.
- He told acquaintances that his doctor advised him to wear a hat because of possible skin cancer.
- He attended a small Episcopal church of about eighty-five English-speaking members.

Chapter 40

Judge Robert Smith Vance
Mountain Brook, Jefferson County, Alabama
December 16, 1989

On a quiet Saturday afternoon during the Christmas season in 1989, Judge Robert S. "Bob" Vance, fifty-eight, one of ten judges on the United States Court of Appeals, 11th Circuit, received a package from the U.S. Postal Service. His wife, Helen Rainey Vance, had been wrapping Christmas presents while he had been out running errands. Upon his return, Judge Vance took the package into the kitchen to open it, believing it contained horse-breeding magazines. The return address appeared to be that of Judge Lewis "Pete" Morgan, a colleague on the 11th Circuit bench, who had sent similar materials earlier. The package exploded, killing him and severely wounding his wife. Their white, two-story brick colonial home was in the suburbs of Birmingham, Alabama, on a four-acre estate-sized lot, so neighbors did not hear the explosion. The pipe bomb blast tore part of Judge Vance's torso and threw him on the kitchen floor in a corner. Mrs. Vance, who was not immediately next to him at the time the package was opened, suffered internal injuries and severe cuts and bruising all over her body but was able to stumble outside and drive to the neighbor's for help. She had returned and sat bloodied and dazed in the family van when police arrived.

The package had appeared harmless enough on the outside. It had been wrapped with brown paper and bore a red-and-white mailing sticker and stamps of the American flag flying over the Yosemite National Park. It had been mailed in Georgia and had excess postage, like all mail bombs, since the killers have no desire to take their bombs to the post office for proper weighing. Inside, it contained aluminum pie plate pieces, flashlight batteries, high explosives, steel pipe, and eighty nails, one of which embedded itself inside Helen Vance's body.

Immediately after the incident, authorities suspected that criminals behind drug-related cases might be responsible for the bombing, since Judge Vance had been assigned recently to preside over such cases in Miami. Two days later, though, on December 18, another mail bomb arrived in another office. At about 5:00 P.M., Robert "Robbie" Robinson, a black city alderman and a lawyer in Savannah, Georgia, was killed after a package blew up in his face. He also thought he recognized the return address. He sat down at his desk to open the package, which ordinarily would have been opened by his secretary. Robinson's secretary had the day off, and her replacement wasn't comfortable with opening the mail.

A third mail bomb went unopened when Jacksonville, Florida, NAACP chapter president Willye Dennis left the package while she went to a news conference. By the time she got to the office the next day and saw it sitting there, she had heard of the other bombings. She immediately called the authorities.

Steven Grant, a court security officer, spotted a fourth bomb as it moved along the conveyor belt in the boxy x-ray machine at the Atlanta county courthouse. In a complicated and dangerous procedure, bomb technicians removed it and rendered it safe before it could do any damage.

A fifth package bomb wounded a Maryland state circuit court judge during the same time period, but that incident turned out to be unrelated to the others.

The bombings were clearly racially motivated and directed at individuals and systems that participated in the civil rights movement in the South. Judge Vance had ruled against segregationists several times since his elevation to the bench.

In his extraordinary true-crime book about this case, *Priority Mail,* Mark Winne detailed the entire investigation, summarized on the following pages, as well as Moody's trials.

The FBI, ATF, U.S. marshals, postal inspectors, Georgia Bureau of Investigation, fire department investigators, and local policing authorities in each affected city and county were all involved in the investigation of the assassination of Judge Vance, Robert Robinson, and the attempted murders of the others.

Within a short period, an ATF agent recognized Walter Leroy Moody, Jr., fifty-seven, as a person who had made a bomb of the same style as the one that had been found in the Atlanta courthouse. In 1972 in Macon, Georgia, Hazel Moody had opened a package that had been addressed, but not mailed, to a car dealer who had repossessed her husband's car. The explosion inflicted first and second-degree burns on Mrs. Moody, a maimed hand, and an eye injury. Because of the technical difficulties of the case, authorities were only able to get a conviction on Moody for constructive possession of the bomb rather than for building the bomb. However, Moody's behavior during the case, together with his style of bomb making, was difficult to forget.

In the meantime, authorities began looking at other evidence. The bomber had sent missives with the NAACP bomb in which he referred to the "Americans for a Competent Federal Judicial System" as the group that would be committing the assassinations. The messages each gave the code 010187 as the identifier, which would enable police to credit it as the responsible "hate group." Federal judges, NAACP offices, and other places received more letters. At the end of December, the "Americans for a Competent Federal Judicial System" sent a letter to an anchorwoman at Atlanta's CBS television affiliate in which it gave her orders and threatened her life. The letter also made clear that the bombings were race related.

Over a period of months, investigators kept turning up leads to Roy Moody from people who had been involved with him over the years. Moody had attended law school for two years and had used that training to represent himself and sue various people, including his siblings in an estate case, and various entities time and time again. Investigators heard from attorneys who had dealings with Moody, defendants in lawsuits he had filed, relatives, and women with whom he'd had relationships. No one had anything good to say about Roy Moody.

Since expert analysis of the writings from the "Americans for a Competent Federal Judicial System" had indicated that the writer had some legal training or experience with the law and courts, the FBI had been focusing on individuals who had represented themselves before the 11th Circuit Court of Appeals. In January 1990, the FBI zeroed in on such a man. A lab had concluded that an envelope and two notices of appeal from him had been typed on the same typewriter as the labels on the mail bombs. Search warrants were sworn out, a search of the man's salvage store ensued, blood samples were taken from him for DNA testing, and investigators did a thorough investigation. The man's business included buying and selling salvage, junk, and used property. If he'd had the typewriter, he had sold it. It was not his practice to keep records on everyone who came in and made a purchase.

Investigators then focused on a couple who had a business called the Printing Press. The first individual had used their copier for his 11th Circuit court case papers. More search warrants were obtained; more searches took place. Nothing turned up.

Meanwhile, other investigators had been shadowing Roy Moody. The man had been a regular patron of several hardware and building stores. All of them sold most of the materials needed to build and mail a bomb. At the end of January, the group focusing on Moody began preparing for a search of Moody's premises. Agents purchased the bomb materials themselves for analysis at the lab. The warrant affidavit began to be drafted under the strictest scrutiny. Surveillance of Moody continued twenty-four hours a day. Finally, in February, investigators, armed with a lengthy search warrant, raided Moody's home. They found one room totally empty with fresh paint on the walls and new carpet on the floor. His wife, Susan Moody, had in her possession a Federal Express overnight envelope and the same twenty-five-cent stamps that had been on the bombs. Agents found other evidence, but not enough to convict Roy Moody.

The investigation continued with phones being tapped, people being wired, investigators trailing suspects, and finally, after the couple's arrests, assistance from Susan McBride-Moody.

Finally, on July 10, 1990, Roy and Susan Moody were arrested on indictments for obstruction of justice, bribery, subornation of perjury, witness tampering, and obstructing a criminal investigation. The majority of the charges related to bribing witnesses to testify falsely in other cases as well as threatening them in the instant case. Roy Moody was held without bond. Susan Moody was released on bond under the condition that she have no contact with Roy.

Roy was held in Atlanta at the High Security Unit of the Atlanta Federal Penitentiary in solitary confinement until his trial. He tried, without success, not only to get Susan to violate the conditions of her parole by coming to see him but to direct her defense. He contacted her attorney with suggestions, but her attorney had other ideas. Susan started counseling with a family violence social worker, Dr. Marti Loring, who reported that Susan suffered from Battered Woman Syndrome. After a time, Susan began communicating with investigators. And, in the fall of 1990, Susan filed for divorce. It appeared from her *pro se* pleadings (she represented herself) that she and Roy had been married only two months before Judge Vance's murder, though they had been together for ten years.

Roy's original attorneys quit. He asked the judge to appoint counsel for him, but the government opposed the appointment, since Roy had property he could sell to raise money for his own defense. His property included two planes, two sailboats, a motorcycle, a Datsun 280Z sports car, and a 1985 pickup truck. He had also cashed an inheritance check of $43,000 earlier in the year. The judge decided Moody's property would be held as collateral for his legal bills and appointed a very able criminal defense attorney by the name of Ed Tolley to defend Roy.

In October, the judge who would have heard the case and who had heard the 1972 case recused himself. District Judge Anthony A. Alaimo of Brunswick, Georgia, replaced him. Before the obstruction case could be tried, however, Roy Moody was indicted by a federal grand jury for the two mail bomb murders, sending the threatening letters, and other offenses.

In the first case, Ed Tolley thought Moody's only chance was an insanity defense, but Moody objected to the submission of a charge that included a provision that the jury could find him "insane of this crime." The provision was removed before the charge was submitted to the jury. The jury deliberated for less than four hours before rendering a verdict of guilty on all counts. For obstruction of justice, subornation of perjury, witness tampering, and other related charges, Judge Alaimo sentenced Moody to 125 months in prison, a $400,000 fine, and three years' supervised parole.

In the mail-bomb murder case, the federal judges in Atlanta recused themselves, resulting in Senior Judge Edward Devitt of St. Paul, Minnesota, being named to the case. Judge Devitt had first become a judge in 1935, a federal judge in 1954, and was a legal scholar. Judge Devitt granted a change of venue to St. Paul. Ed Tolley had again been appointed to represent Moody, after the government objected to his original attorney on the basis that the man had also represented Susan McBride-Moody in the early stages of the prosecution. Moody's defense counsel's first line of defense was insanity. Moody, however, had other ideas. He insisted, against Tolley's advice, on withdrawing his insanity defense. Susan testified against him, as did others who had been involved with him over the years. Prosecutors decided, though, that Walter Leroy Moody was his own worst enemy when he insisted on testifying in his own defense, again against legal advice.

It was clear that Moody still thought, as in 1972 when he did the same thing, he was smarter than everyone else. He spent two days concocting a creative defense. The jury deliberated for about two days before convicting him on all seventy-one counts. Judge Dewitt sentenced him to seven life sentences without parole plus 400 years for killing Judge Bob Vance and Attorney Robbie Robinson, sending threatening letters to seventeen judges and television stations nationwide, and the two other mail bombs that were intercepted.

Following federal prosecution, Moody was sent to state court, where he was tried for the murder and assault for Judge Vance's death. The jury recommended the electric chair.

Ironically, Judge Vance had been an outspoken advocate for the Alabama Capital Representation Resource Center in Montgomery, which had been created in response to a need for more and better representation of death row prisoners and assistance to attorneys handling capital cases. At the time, Alabama had one of the largest and fastest-growing death row populations and a very low lawyer-to-inmate ratio. The private criminal defense bar had long ago lost the ability to handle the sheer numbers of defendants. Alabama often had to rely on out-of-state counsel.

On November 12 and 13, 1989, a month before his murder, Judge Vance was one of two judges who represented federal judges at the Alabama State Bar's Capital Representation Resource Center Conference in Birmingham. He was quoted in *The Alabama Lawyer* as saying, "I believe that participation in the capital representation program is one of the finest examples of how the practicing bar can demonstrate a meaningful commitment to exercising professional responsibility. This type of service separates lawyers as professionals from managers of the marketplace." His advocacy for adequate representation could have very well been of assistance to Walter Leroy Moody, his own murderer, in the defense of his case. From Vance's reputation, it is clear that he would not have had it any other way.

In his memorial to Judge Vance in *The Alabama Lawyer*, the Honorable R. Clifford Fulford, U.S. Bankruptcy Court, Birmingham, Alabama, reported that Vance's "insistence on a level playing field for contending parties in our judicial process was well-known." He described Judge Vance as "a man who was the antithesis of outrage . . . ," who led "a noble life," who "revered our Constitution" and "never lost sight of his goal to resolve disputes reasonably and peacefully." Judge Vance "had the unique ability to draw his circles to include his adversaries and to join them in the search for common ground on which both could honorably stand."

Indeed, an attorney with whom he clerked after law school at the Alabama Supreme Court said of Judge Vance, when Vance was a candidate for nomination to the federal bench, that Vance was completely unbiased. Even though they were of different political parties, he would recommend him without reservation as a person who would be an outstanding jurist and a valuable addition to the United States court system. "No wonder that his assassins, who lacked his capacity and belief in the rule of law, could not tolerate such a man in their presence," Judge Fulford later stated.

Judge Vance was a native of Talladega, Alabama, where he graduated from Woodlawn High School at fifteen. While in high school, he worked as a page for the House of Representatives from 1945 to 1947. He was student body president at the University of Alabama, where he earned a B.S. degree in business and commerce in 1950 at nineteen and an LL.B. at twenty-one, which was later converted to a J.D. He earned a Master of Laws (LL.M.) from George Washington University in Washington, D.C., in 1955.

Vance entered the U.S. Army as a second lieutenant in August 1952 and served on active duty until December 1954. He attended the Judge Advocate General Corps School, and his active service was in the JAG Office handling criminal or "military justice" cases. He obtained the rank of lieutenant colonel by his retirement from the reserves in 1971 at forty.

An active Democrat from the time of his youth, Vance was called "a voice of sanity in turbulent times and a leader of reasoned action" by U.S. Senator Howell Heflin, who knew Judge Vance for thirty years, dating back to when they were young lawyers together. He was highly influential in Alabama Democratic Party politics from the middle 1960s to the middle 1970s, rivaling George Wallace.

When Vance was Alabama Democratic Party chairman, Wallace ran a conservative ally against Vance every election cycle but was unable to unseat Vance, who ended Wallace's control of the state Democratic executive committee of conservative states'-righters and dixiecrats. Vance was a people person and a pro-Democrat who believed that there were two parties in the United States. His position was that the Democratic Party believes in people and trusts people, and that the role of government is to give people the opportunity to better themselves and their lives. Vance was responsible for integrating the all-white Alabama Democratic Party. *The Birmingham News* reported that one of Vance's first moves as state Democratic Party chair was to remove the rooster from the top of the Democratic Party ballot. (The rooster was a symbol of white supremacy.) Vance was a leader in election law reform and campaign finance disclosure. He also pushed through a reform in the way presidential electors were selected in Alabama. He was a delegate to the 1968, 1972, and 1976 Democratic national conventions, where he was responsible for keeping the Democratic Party intact and in the national Democratic Party. There was a move by Wallaceites to take over the Alabama party and seat their own delegates at the 1968 convention, but Vance was able to thwart it and get the duly elected Democratic delegates seated.

Robert S. Vance, the attorney, served as law clerk for a year to Justice James J. Mayfield, Supreme Court of Alabama, from December 1954 to December 1955. In January 1956, he was employed as a trial attorney in the U.S. Labor Department in Birmingham. In November 1956, he took a position with the firm of Hogan & Callaway, to which later he became a name partner. That firm, as most law firms do, metamorphosized several times over and was Vance, Thompson & Brown at the time of Vance's judicial appointment. The firm was engaged in the civil practice of law, with Vance handling trial and appellate cases including miscellaneous cases and complicated litigation. He served as general counsel for a national bank he formed, general counsel of an insurance company, and as municipal attorney and school board attorney for a town of 15,000. His firm represented businesses in manufacturing, trucking, mining, real estate development, and marketing. He handled class actions, consumer cases, securities, antitrust, contract, fraud, and other business cases representing plaintiffs and defendants. Half his caseload was in federal and half in state court, and about forty percent were jury trials.

One of Mr. Vance's major civil cases involved the first large recovery in a bank credit card case in the 1970s, where BankAmericard and Master Charge operators were imposing usurious charges on credit card accounts in violation of the National Bank Act. The eventual settlement was a refund of approximately $4.5 million to credit card holders.

Another case in which Mr. Vance was involved was the "one man–one vote" case decided by the U.S. Supreme Court. (*Reynolds v. Sims; Vann and Vance v. Baggett*, 377 U.S. 533, [1964] reh. Denied 379 U.S. 870.) Mr. Vance and Mr. Vann were intervenors because of being local Democratic Party officials. On appeal, Mr. Vance was the principal author of the jurisdictional statement and the brief of intervenor-appellants. That case resulted in the reapportionment of the Alabama legislature for the first time in over sixty years, shifting control of the state government from sparsely populated rural counties to the middle and larger counties. This is now the law of the United States.

Mr. Vance also filed a fraud case for the plaintiff in the first automobile speedometer case in Alabama, which resulted in a substantial award of punitive damages. This was before federal legislation prohibited the practice of dealers running back speedometers on used cars. His client had bought a car, which was represented as new. It had, in fact, been a demonstrator. The dealer had disconnected the speedometer.

From 1967 until 1970, Mr. Vance taught a course in federal procedure at the Cumberland School of Law at Samford University.

President Jimmy Carter appointed Vance to the 5th Circuit Court of Appeals in 1977, and when the 11th Circuit, based in Atlanta, Georgia, was created, Judge Vance was assigned there. After Judge Vance took the bench, he was involved in some very controversial cases, including election and desegregation cases. In one case in 1987, he and two other members of a three-judge panel removed a U.S. district judge from a seven-year-old college-desegregation case and threw out that judge's ruling, which had to do with Alabama officials continuing to segregate some state colleges and universities.

Judge and Mrs. Vance had been married thirty-six years and were the parents of two sons, Robert S. Vance, Jr., a Birmingham attorney, and Charles R. Vance, who, at the time, was working on his doctorate.

Chapter 41

Vickie Bunnell
Colebrook, Coos County, New Hampshire
August 19, 1997

In rural New Hampshire one warm Tuesday afternoon, a white male named Carl Drega, sixty-seven, set his home on fire and then drove to a grocery store just outside the tiny town of Colebrook, nine miles south of Canada. He entered the store and started a ruckus. When two New Hampshire state troopers arrived, he shot and killed them both before stealing a patrol car and driving to the offices of the weekly newspaper, the *News and Sentinel of Colebrook*. Not just the newspaper was housed in that building. The law office of part-time district court judge Vickie Bunnell was located there. Drega had a dispute with Judge Bunnell dating back six years, to the time when, as a selectwoman in the town of Columbia, she had once had him removed from the town hall in handcuffs. She was well aware that Drega was dangerous. She had also ruled against him in court on several occasions.

Bunnell spotted Drega, whom she had often called a "walking time bomb" and against whom she had once taken out a restraining order. She screamed and ran through the newspaper offices yelling, "It's Drega! He's got a gun." Drega shot Judge Bunnell in the back with an assault rifle as she ran, killing her instantly.

The *News and Sentinel of Colebrook* editor, Dennis Joos, struggled with the assassin as people fled out of the back of the building. Drega shot the newspaper editor eight times during the altercation. Joos dies of his wounds.

Drega then got back into the stolen police car and sped to the other side of the Connecticut River to Bloomfield, Vermont, where he stopped under the overpass, got out of the cruiser, and shot at two sheriff's deputies. He wounded one, who lost control of his vehicle and careened into some trees.

The trees probably saved his life; otherwise his car would have run off the road and into the river.

Drega disappeared into the area around Maidstone Lake, Vermont, south of Bloomfield, where he was chased by innumerable police officers of every kind. He somehow found his way back to New Hampshire and then hid out in the woods at Stratford. Police officers armed themselves heavily and, wearing bulletproof clothing, went after him. Early in the evening, around 7:00 P.M., Drega and approximately twenty officers engaged in a shootout. A U.S. Border Patrol officer was wounded, as well as two other officers. Drega was killed.

After the shootout, authorities roped off and searched Drega's property in Bow, New Hampshire, where the assailant had lived for close to thirty years. They found bomb-making manuals, weapons, hundreds of pounds of explosives, and an elaborate system of tunnels. Police burned Drega's barn the following day to set off explosives.

Carl Drega had worked for a contractor at the Vermont Yankee nuclear power plant twice, in 1992 and again in 1995. His sister, Jane Drega of Connecticut, reportedly said that Carl Drega said police and other officials in New Hampshire had been harassing him. She said he told her he couldn't take it anymore. She talked to him the Saturday before the shooting. He had spent the winter working as a carpenter in Massachusetts, New York, and Ohio, and had just returned home in the summer.

Authorities found a "hit" list in Drega's truck. One of the names on Drega's hit list was Superior Court Judge Harold Perkins, who was in court in Lancaster during the shootings. He was placed under police protection, but no other incidents occurred.

Vickie Bunnell's funeral was held the Sunday following her murder. She was described as one who always went out of her way to help people. She constantly wore a smile.

The townspeople, as well as people in the region, honored the victims by not only erecting a black marble monument outside the newspaper building where Judge Bunnell and editor Joos were killed, and Blue Mountain in Columbia was renamed after Bunnell. The library in West Stewartstown was renamed after Joos. Sections of the main highway in the region were named after the murdered troopers.

A joint resolution by the New Hampshire legislature better describes the type of person Judge Bunnell was:

No. R-191. Joint Resolution in Memory of Vickie Bunnell

Offered by: Representatives Johnson of Canaan, Peaslee of Guildhall and Weiss of Northfield.

Whereas, Vickie Bunnell spent her childhood in Canaan, Vermont, and graduated from Canaan High School, Plymouth State College, Plymouth, New Hampshire, and the University of Puget Sound Law School in Tacoma, Washington, where she received her law degree with honors, and

Whereas, she returned home to work with Attorney Phil Waystack of Colebrook, New Hampshire, and

Whereas, she hung out her own shingle in Colebrook, quietly establishing a practice dedicated to cases involving child custody, adoption, family abuse, sexual abuse, and victims' rights, and

Whereas, she served two terms as Selectwoman of the Town of Columbia, New Hampshire, and served on many community service boards and committees, and

Whereas, in 1995 she was appointed as the first woman associate judge to the Colebrook District Court by then Governor Steve Merrill, and

Whereas, she was a dedicated and caring judge whose service to the law and her community were marked by integrity, intelligence and courage, and

Whereas, the loss of Vickie Bunnell is immeasurable and she will be remembered for her friendship and her love and appreciation of the great outdoors, as well as for her dedication to the legal profession, now therefore be it

Resolved by the Senate and House of Representatives:

That the General Assembly extends its condolences to the family of Judge Vickie Bunnell, and be it further

Resolved: That the Secretary of State be directed to send a copy of this resolution to Mr. and Mrs. Earl Bunnell of Canaan, Vermont.

Chapter 42

Judge and Mrs. H. George Taylor
Rancho Cucamonga, San Bernardino County, California
March 18, 1999

At about 9:30 P.M. on Thursday, March 18, 1999, Judge H. George Taylor, sixty-eight, called a "Commissioner" in California because he was appointed by, and served at the pleasure of, the judges of the Los Angeles Superior Court, was shotgunned to death. On his return from a party for a retiring judge, Judge Taylor pulled his Mercedes-Benz into his unlit driveway. The killer didn't even wait for the judge to turn off his engine. He fired three times at close range, hitting Taylor in the head and chest. Lynda Taylor, the judge's wife, heard the shotgun blasts and ran to see what it was. She was hit by two blasts to the chest as well and killed. The murderer made a clean getaway, with neighbors hearing the sounds of the gunfire and seeing a small white car but nothing further.

Dressed only in her bathrobe, Mrs. Taylor lay dead on the floor of the garage. Judge Taylor still sat in his car. Clearly, the Taylors were not expecting anyone. The motive is uncertain, but authorities assume the murders were related to the judge's area of expertise, family law. Nothing was stolen, although the Taylors lived a comfortable life in an exclusive subdivision.

Judge Taylor was appointed in 1986. He'd heard criminal, civil, and family cases. At the time of his death, he was assigned to Norwalk, California. He had practiced law in the private sector for twenty-four years and had been a deputy prosecutor for seven years before his appointment. He was raised in Pasadena, California, and graduated from UCLA Law School.

Peers described Judge Taylor as "a wonderful human being and a very good judge."

Three grown children survived the judge, and two children survived Mrs. Taylor, all by first marriages.

Investigators were attempting to ascertain whether the judge's murder could be connected to a series of fires in the area. An arsonist had set fire to an attorney's home a few days before the murders as well as fires near the attorney's law office.

Additionally, detectives have reviewed hundreds of pending cases, hoping to find a suspect. Although they have developed some leads, no one has been charged.

A $50,000 reward has been posted by the Los Angeles County Board of Supervisors and the Superior Court for information leading to the arrest and conviction of the killer(s).

The case remains unsolved.

Acknowledgments

I would like to express deep appreciation to Barbara Bienkowski and all the other employees of the Rosenberg Library, Galveston, Texas, for all their help in the years I was conducting my research for this book.

My gratitude goes also to my friends Benjamin Troia, the Honorable Beth McGregor, and Donald M. Waterbury for their assistance in my research, friendship, and emotional support.

I also want to thank the following persons for their aid in my research:
- Dean P. Agee, Circuit Court Clerk, Louisa Courthouse, Louisa, VA.
- Antonio Alvarado, Executive Dir., State Bar of Texas, Austin.
- Lennis Anderson, State Library Division, Dept. of Community and Economic Development, Utah State Historical Society.
- Stephen Anderson, Director of Communications, Illinois State Bar Association.
- Susan H. Andres, Director of Communications, Alabama State Bar Association, Montgomery, AL.
- W. Alford, Office of JoAnne Holman, Clerk of Circuit Court, St. Lucie County, FL.
- Atlantic City Free Public Library employees, Atlantic City, NJ.
- Victor Bailey, Mississippi Department of Archives & History.
- Diana L. Balch, Director of Membership, Virginia State Bar.
- Alan Barnett, State History Division, Utah Department of Community and Economic Development, Division of State History, Utah State Historical Society.
- LeRoy Barnett, Archivist, Michigan Department of State.
- Alice Jackson Baughn, *The Sun Herald,* Biloxi, MS.
- Birmingham Alabama Public Library employees.
- Martha Bloem, Grand Rapids Public Library, Grand Rapids, MI.

- Carol Boeckmann, Head of Reference, Kirkwood Public Library, Kirkwood, MO.
- James S. Boyd, Archives Technician, National Personnel Records Center, Military Personnel Records, St. Louis, MO.
- Breathett County Public Library employees, Jackson, KY.
- Breathett County Courthouse employees, Jackson, KY.
- Margaret Buerk, Clerical Asst., *Texas Bar Journal*, Austin, TX.
- Joe Cameron, Webmaster, Bland County, VAGenWeb pages.
- Gilbert R. Campbell, Jr., Executive Director of the Tennessee Bar Association.
- Kenneth S. Carlson, Reference Archivist, Rhode Island State Archives and Pubic Records Administration, Providence, RI.
- Pat Carmichael, Douglas County Historical & Genealogical Society, Inc., Ava, MO.
- Joe Chadwell, Circuit Clerk, Wright County, Hartville, MO.
- *Chicago Sun Times* staff.
- *Chicago Tribune*.
- Rose Marie Christensen, Chief, Freedom of Information and Privacy Acts Office, Department of the Army, Arlington, VA.
- Sue Jett Clair, Jackson, KY.
- Kendall O. Clay, Radford, VA.
- George K. Combs, Reference Librarian/Archivist, Lloyd House, Library of Virginia History and Genealogy, Alexandria, VA.
- Barbara S. Cook, Reference Librarian, McClung Historical Collection, Knox County Public Library.
- Craig D. Dahle, FBI, Birmingham, AL.
- John Daly, Director, Illinois State Archives.
- Dept. of Human Services, Augusta, ME.
- Constance Dove, California Judges Association.
- Penelope Dukes-Williams, Texas State Library and Archives Commission.
- Tim Eckert, Regional Archivist, Washington Secretary of State's Office, Ellensburg.
- William R. Ellis, Jr., Archivist, Archives 1 Reference Branch, Textual Reference Division, National Archives, Washington, D.C.
- Diana M. Gerling, Administrative Assistant, The Missouri Bar Association, Jefferson City, MO.
- Grainger County Courthouse employees, Rutledge, TN.
- Lynn Gilmer Guilford, Louisa County Historical Society, VA.
- Ronald B. Hall, Clerk, Circuit Court of Bland County, Bland, VA.

- Rhonda Hamrick, *The Sun Herald,* Biloxi, MS.
- Michael "Mickey" Hammer, County Executive, Grainger County, Rutledge, TN.
- Reginald T. Hammer, Past Executive Director, Alabama State Bar Association, Montgomery, AL.
- Beth S. Harris, Archivist and Special Collections Librarian, Hollins College, Roanoke, VA.
- Catherine Harris, Texas State Law Library.
- Stephen C. Harris, Attorney at Law, Louisa, VA.
- Adele Head, Bay County Public Library, Panama City, FL.
- James Helms, Florida State Archives.
- Richard J. Hill, Newspapers Librarian, Commonwealth Libraries, Harrisburg, PA.
- Ina L. Horton, Publisher, *The Carroll News,* Hillsville, VA.
- Sarah Huggins, Reference Librarian, The Library of Virginia, Richmond.
- Helen B. Hummel, Volunteer, Franklin County Historical Society, Pasco, WA.
- Janice Ishmael, Illinois State Bar Association.
- Carol James, Meridian-Lauderdale County Public Library, MS.
- Edward L. Johnson, Jr., Executive Director, Connecticut Bar Association.
- Bernard Judge, Editor, *Chicago Daily Law Bulletin.*
- Mary B. Kegley, Attorney and Historian, Wytheville, VA.
- Fred Keller, *Deseret News* Library, P.O. Box 1257, Salt Lake City.
- Norwood A. Kerr, Archival Reference, Department of Archives and History, State of Alabama.
- Susan Kosinski (and staff), Prothonotary/Clerk of Courts, 37th Judicial District, Warren, PA.
- Susan M. LaGore, *The News Herald,* Panama City, FL.
- Christine Lamar, Genealogical Researcher, Providence, RI
- Sandi Lee, Reference Librarian, Concord Public Library.
- Benny C. Lister, Clerk, Gulf County Courts, FL.
- Nicole Luongo, Special Collection Librarian, Portsmouth Public Library, Portsmouth, NH.
- Jeannine L. McCoy, New Hampshire Bar Association.
- Lodena McCoy, Probate Clerk, Wright County, Hartville, MO.
- Helen Desmond McDonald, Exe. Director, Rhode Island Bar Association, Providence, RI.
- Judy McGehee, Louisa, VA.

- Jack McGoldrick, Rutledge, TN.
- Thomas Marusin, Director Freedom of Information, Department of the Treasury, IRS, Washington, D.C.
- Patricia Martinez, Deputy Court Clerk, 2nd District Court, Ogden.
- Doris R. Martinson, Head, Knox County Archives.
- Katherine Menz, Supervisor, Adult Service, St. Louis County Library.
- Frank C. Mevers, New Hampshire Department of State.
- Linda Miller, *The Grand Rapids Press.*
- Mississippi State Bar Association staff.
- Joan Koster Morales, Windham, NY.
- Nebraska State Historical Society, Lincoln, NB.
- Margaret Murphy, Managing Editor, *The Alabama Lawyer,* Alabama State Bar Association.
- Keith B. Norman, Executive Director, Alabama State Bar Association.
- J. Kevin O'Brien, Chief, Freedom of Information-Privacy Acts Section, Information Resources Division, U.S. Department of Justice, FBI, Washington, D.C.
- Lt. Kevin P. O'Brien, State Police, New Hampshire Department of Safety.
- Judson H. Orrick, Editor, *Florida Bar Journal Florida Bar News.*
- Gene Overall, Saint Louis County Circuit Court, Clayton, Mo.
- Fred Pernell, Assistant Chief for Reference, Still Picture Branch, National Archives, College Park, MD.
- Carolyn M. Picciano, Library specialist, History and Genealogy Unit, Connecticut State Library.
- Chase Putnam, Editor, Warren County Historical Society, PA.
- Julia Rather, Archivist II, Tennessee Department of State, Tennessee State Library and Archives.
- Pat Reinhard, Archives Staff, Missouri Office of Secretary of State.
- Charles Riley, Breathett County Public Library, Jackson, KY.
- Phyllis Rippee, Office Supervisor, Wright County Historical Society, Hartville, MO.
- Shirley A. Rittenhouse, Librarian III, Maryland State Law Library, Annapolis.
- Dorothy Roberts, Supervisor, Board of County Commissioners, St. Lucie County, FL.

- Fred J. Romanski, Archives II, Textual Reference Branch, National Archives at College Park, MD.
- Andrew F. Shick, Passaic County Historical Society, Paterson, NJ.
- Mary Jane Slipsky, Weber County Law Librarian, Weber County Library System, Ogden.
- Kevin J. Swanson, Director, State and Local Records, Maryland State Archives, Annapolis, MD.
- Jean Therrien, Reference Assistant, The Rhode Island Historical Society, Providence.
- Inez Thompson, Curator, Benton County Museum and Historical Society, Inc., Prosser, WA.
- Ann Toplinich, Executive Director, The Tennessee Historical Society.
- Sue Troyan, Reference/Documents Librarian, Texas State Library, Austin.
- Ron Tyler, Director, The Texas State Historical Association.
- United States Department of Justice, Federal Bureau of Investigation.
- Administrative Services, Utah State Archives and Records Service, Archives Building, State Capitol, Salt Lake City.
- John K. Vandereedt, Archivist, Archives I Reference Branch, Textual Reference Division, National Archives, Washington, D.C.
- Karen Warren, Austin History Center.
- Tommy L. Waters, Head of Special Collections, Government of the Virgin Islands of the United States Department of Planning and Natural Resources, Division of Libraries, Archive and Museums, St. Thomas, U.S. Virgin Islands.
- Minor T. Weisiger, Archivist, Library of Virginia, Richmond, VA.
- Nick West, Publisher, *The Palacios Beacon*, Palacios, TX.
- Marilyn D. Wick, Marin County Historical Society, CA.
- Penny Wolboldt, Warren Library Association, Warren, PA.
- Lois Worrell, Meridian-Lauderdale County Public Library, MS.
- Kim of Kim's Flowers and Gifts, Jackson, KY.
- Laurel Yatsko, St. Louis Public Library, St. Louis, MO.
- Jean Zajac, Librarian, New Jersey Historical Society.

Most of all I thank my husband, John E. Hunger, for his love, support, patience, and advice.

Bibliography

(Alphabetically)

JUDGE BAILEY

Florida Department of Health and Rehabilitative Services, State Office of Vital Statistics, Jacksonville, Florida.

Galveston Daily News, 9 May 1988.

Lanier, A.C. Interview, August 1997.

New York Times, 29 July 1987.

Official Court Records in Cause No. 86-112, IN RE: The Marriage of Eleanor Inez Melvin, Petitioner/Wife, and Clyde M. Melvin, Respondent/Husband, In the Circuit Court, Fourteenth Judicial Circuit of the State of Florida, In and For Gulf County.

Official Court Records in Cause Nos. 87-149, 87-150, 87-151, 87-152, *State of Florida vs. Clyde M. Melvin,* Defendant, In Circuit Court, Fourteenth Judicial Circuit, In and For Gulf County, Florida.

20-20, August 21, 1992.

JUDGE BUNNELL

Associated Press, 17, 19 Aug., 17 Dec. 1998.

Fort Worth Star-Telegram, 24 Aug. 1997.

Galveston County Daily News, 20, 22, 24 Aug. 1997.

The Joplin Globe, 21 Aug. 1997

Texas City Sun, 20 Aug. 1997.

JUDGE AND MRS. CHILLINGWORTH

Bishop, Jim. *The Murder Trial of Judge Peel.* New York: Simon and Schuster, 1962.

Lester, Donald G. "The End of Our Innocence: The Chillingworth Murder Case," *Broward Legacy: A Journal of South Florida History* 16, Summer–Fall, 1993.

"The Missing Judge," *Newsweek,* 29 Aug. 1955: 20.

New York Times, 1955, 1957, 1960, 1961, 1982.

Panama City Herald, 16, 18, 19, 29 June and 13 Aug. 1955.

"The Scoutmaster & the Judge," *Time* Magazine, 14 Nov. 1960: 25.

"When 'Lucky' Babbled," Newsweek, 17 Oct. 1960: 39-40.

JUDGE COLASANTO

Alexandria Gazette (Alexandria, VA), 24, 25, 26, 27 Nov. 1970.

New York Times, 24, 25, 26 Nov. 1970.

JUDGE CRATER

Crater, Stella, Oscar Fraley. *The Empty Robe.* Garden City, New York: Doubleday & Company, 1961.

Dept. of Justice Case File No. 95-51-11.

Lee, Henry. "The Mystery of the Vanished Judge." *Coronet,* February 1951.

Manning, Gordon. "The Most Tantalizing Disappearance of Our Time." *Colliers,* 29 July 1950.

New York Daily News, 16 April 1931.

New York Times, Aug.-Dec. 1930; 1, 2, 3, 4 Mar., 6 Aug. 1931; 2 May, 5 Aug., 6, 7, 8 Sept., 28, 29 Nov. 1935; 22, 23, 24, 25, 26, 27, 30 July, 5, 7 Aug., 22 Nov. 1937; 6 Aug. 1947; 29 July 1955; 21 June, 6 Aug. 1960; 26, 27 June 1964; 25 Sept. 1971.

New York Times Magazine, 7, 28 Aug. 1960.

Official Court Records: No. 2936, Estate of Joseph Force Crater, Deceased, In The Surrogate's Court, County of New York, NY.

JUDGE CRESCENTE

New York Times, 5, 6, 8, 9, 13 Nov. 1974; 11, 22, 23 Mar., 18 April, 2 May 1975; 31 Mar. 1977.

JUDGE CUNNINGHAM

Atlanta Constitution, 14 Feb. 1975.

Louisa County Courthouse records in the case of *Commonwealth of Virginia vs. Curtis Darnell Poindexter,* Register No. 39622, In the General District Court of Louisa County.

Louisa County Courthouse records in the case of *Commonwealth of Virginia vs. Curtis Darnell Poindexter,* Felony Case #523, In the Circuit Court of Louisa County.

New York Times, 14 Feb. 1975.

Richmond News-Leader, 14 Feb., 7 Mar. 1975.
Richmond Times-Dispatch, 14, 15 Feb. 1975.
Virginia Law & Order, April 1975.

JUDGE DARONCO

Kasindorf, Jeanie. "Last Judgment," *New York,* 1 Aug. 1988.
New York Times, 22 May 1988.

JUDGE DOOLEY

Palacios Beacon, 12 April 1989.

JUDGE FAIRBANKS

Boston Globe, 29 Mar. 1994.
Concord Monitor, 29, 30, 31 Mar. 1994; 2, 3, 4, 5, 6, 10, 14, 15, 27, 30
April; 8 May, 30 Dec. 1994; 2, 3, 14 June 1995.
Ladies Home Journal, Mar. 1992.
New Hampshire State Police Wanted Flyer.
FBI field reports.

JUDGE FISHMAN

Brown, Chip. *Washington Post,* 4 Dec. 1980; 26, 27, 28 Ap. 1981.
Maryland DEPARTMENT OF HEALTH AND MENTAL HYGIENE
POSTMORTEM EXAMINERS COMMISSION (Autopsy Reports) Box 80-
38, file 124318, Frederick Fishman, 28 November 1980 [MSA T1258; 2-60-
3-23].
Meyer, Eugene L. *Washington Post,* 30 Nov. 1980.
New York Times 30 Nov. 1980.
Official Montgomery County, Maryland, Court Records in Cause
Number 25,413, *State of Maryland v. Lawrence W. Fishman.*
Stevens, Joann, Martin Weil. *Washington Post,* 29 Nov. 1980.

JUDGE GENTILE

Chicago Daily Law Bulletin, 21, 24, 25, 26 Oct. 1983.
New York Times, 22, 27 Oct. 1983.

JUDGE HALEY

Arnold, Kenneth James. *California Courts and Judges Handbook,* 2nd ed.
San Francisco: Law Book Service Company.
Independent-Journal, San Rafael, California. 7 Aug. 1970.
Life, 11 Sept. 1970.

Mahoney, Jean. "Portrait of Judge Harold J. Haley," *Rose Valley Reporter,* 4 Aug. 1971.

New York Times, 1970, 1971, 1972, 1973, 1974.

San Francisco Chronicle, Obituaries, 8 June 2002.

JUDGE HARGIS

Bowling, Archie, ed. "Tales of Captain Bill Strong."

Hayes, Charles. *The Hanging of "Bad Tom" Smith and The Events Leading to His Hanging Including a Brief Account of the French and Eversole Feud.* Vol. 1, Breathitt County History Series, Jackson, Kentucky, 1969.

Kozee, William C. *Early Families of Eastern and Southeastern Kentucky and Their Descendants.* Baltimore: Genealogical Publishing, 1979.

New York Times, 1908, 1909, 1913.

Pearce, John Ed. "The Last and Bloodiest Feud." *Days of Darkness.* University Press of Kentucky, 1994.

Schweitzer, George K. *Kentucky Genealogical Research.* Knoxville: 1981.

Trimble, J. Green. "Recollections of Breathitt," *The Jackson Times,* 1924.

JUDGE HELFANT

New York Times, 16, 17, 22 Feb., 15 June 1978.

The Press (Atlantic City), 16, 17, 18 Feb. 1978.

Tomlinson, Gerald. *Murdered in Jersey.* New Jersey: Rutgers University Press, 1994.

JUDGE IRONS

Grand Rapids Press, 5 Apr., 20, 21, 22, 23, 25, 26 Oct., 3, 22, 30 Nov., 1 Dec. 1988; 4, 13, 14 Feb., 2, 15 Mar., 14, 16, 18, 25, 26, 27, 28 Apr., 2, 3, 4, 5, 9, 10, 11, 12, 13, 14, 17, 25, 31 May, 1, 6, 11, 13 June, 13 Aug., 28 Sept., 16, 20 Oct. 1989; 13 Feb., 13 Apr., 15 May, 26 Oct. 1990; 10 Apr., 26 Oct. 1991; 6, 11 June, 1992; 15 Jan., 24 Mar., 17 Oct. 1993.

New York Times, 20 Oct. 1988; 4 June 1989.

JUDGE JACKSON

Bishop, Esther Downs, ed. *State of Missouri, Official Manual,* "The Blue Book," 1947-1948.

Journal of the Missouri Bar, May 1948.

Mountain Grove Journal (Missouri), 1, 8 Apr., 17, 24 June, 1, 8 July, 5, 12 Aug. 1948; 10 Feb., 26 Sept., 3, 7 Nov. 1949.

Springfield Leader (Camdenton, Missouri), 1 Apr. 1948.

Wright County, Missouri, Official Probate Records.

Wright County Republican (Hartville, Missouri), 1, 15 April, 27 May, 3, 17 June, 8 July, 12 August, 1948.

JUDGE JOHNSON

McGoldrick, Jack. Personal interview, July 1996.
Knoxville Journal, 19, 20 June 1937.
New York Times, 19 June 1937.
Official Court Records, Granger County, Tennessee.

JUDGE KEGLEY

Kegley, Clinton. Telephone interview, November 2000.
Kegley, Robert. Telephone interview, November 2000.
Official Court Records. Commonwealth of *Virginia vs. Charles Edward Jarrell.* Bland Circuit Court, Bland, Virginia.
Roanoke Times, 2 Apr. 1970.
Southwest Virginia Enterprise, 2 Apr. 1970.

JUDGE KEITH

New York Times 1, 2 Mar. 1933.

JUDGES KNOWLES

Hufbauer, Virginia Knowles, ed. *Descendents of Richard Knowles 1637-1973.* San Diego: Ventures International, 1974.
Providence Journal (Rhode Island), 7, 8, 9, 10, 11, 12, 13, 14, 16, 17, 18, 19, 20, 21, 22, 23, 24, 25, 26, 27, 28, 29, 30 Sept., 2, 4, 5, 8, 14, 21, 22, 26 Oct., 7, 9, 28, Nov. 1915; 15, 17 Mar., 24 May 1916; 17 July 1937.
Manual with Rules and Orders for the use of the General Assembly of the State of Rhode Island. J. Fred Parker, Secretary of State. Providence: E.L. Freeman Co., State Printers, 1915.
Official Court Records: Cause No. 1916, Will and Probate Records of Willis S. Knowles, Cranston City Hall.
Rhode Island State Archives. DEATHS Registered in the Town Of Johnston. Providence, R.I.

JUDGE LAWLER

Birmingham Age-Herald, 19, 20, 21, 22, 23, 24, 25, 26, 27, 28, 29, 30 Nov., 1, 2, 3, 6 Dec. 1916; 21, 22, 23, 24 Mar. 1917.
Birmingham News 24 June, 22, 23, 24, 25, 26, 27, 28, 29, 30 Nov. 1, 9 Dec. 1916; 20, 21, 22, 23, 24 Mar. 1917.
Kean, David. "Death Dooms the Judge," *Daring Detective,* April 1943.

Huntsville Weekly Democrat, 28 June, 5, 26 July, 27, 27 Sept., 4, 11, 24 Oct., 15, 22, 29 Nov., 6 Dec. 1916; 21 Mar. 1917.

New York Times, 18, 24 June, 16 July 1916.

JUDGE LAWLESS

New York Times, 3 June, 2 Dec. 1974, 19 July 1975.

Tri-City Herald, 3 June 1976.

JUDGE MASSIE

Allen, J. Sidna. Memoirs of J. Sidna Allen, *A True Narrative of What Really Happened at Hillsville, Virginia.* Mt. Airy, N.C.: F.H. Lamb, 1929.

Burt, Olive Wooley. *American Murder Ballads and Their Stories.* New York: Oxford University Press, 1958.

DuBose, Louise Jones. "The Fatal Doom of the Allens," reprinted in *The Southwest Virginia Enterprise,* Wytheville, VA, July-December 1981.

Gardner, Rufus L. *The Courthouse Tragedy, Hillsville, Virginia.* Nu-line Printing, 5th Edition, 1991.

Hooker, Patricia F. "The History and Mystery of the Hillsville Courthouse Shootout." Master's Thesis, Hollins College, Roanoke, VA. 1986.

Nash, Jay Robert. *Bloodletters and Badmen, A Narrative Encyclopedia of American Criminals from the Pilgrims to the Present,* New York: M. Evans and Company, 1973, 1995.

New York Times, 15, 31 Mar., 1 Apr. 1912; 16 Jan., 6, 7, 24, 25, 29 Mar. 1913; 19 Mar. 1916.

The Roanoke Times, 14 March 1912.

JUDGE MORNING

Lincoln Star, 18 Feb. 1924.

New York Times, 19 Feb. 1924.

JUDGE PARKER

Meridian Star, 7, 8 Nov. 1920; 2, 4, 5 Mar. 1921.

JUDGE PARKINSON

Chicago Daily Law Bulletin, 29, 30 Oct., 2 Nov. 1959.

Judges of the United States, 2nd ed., Published under the Auspices of the Bicentennial Committee of The Judicial Conference of the United States, 1983.

New York Times, 28, 29, 30, 31 Oct., 1, 3, 5, 8, 15 Nov. 1959; 20 Jan., 25 Apr., 3 May 1960.

JUDGE PARTRIDGE

New York Times, 30 Sept. 1982.

Official Court Records, *State v. Meyer*, Greene County, New York.

JUDGE PIERSON

Austin American, 27 Apr., 21, 28 Oct. 1935; 12 Oct. 1940; 12 Sept., 16, 21 Nov. 1963.

Austin Statesman, 13 June, 1963.

Dallas Morning News, 25 Apr. 1935; 17 Dec. 1955.

New York Times, 25, 26 Apr. 1935; 17 Dec. 1955.

Anonymous statement from a friend to authorities, on file at Austin History Center.

Oral History Interview, Justice Thomas Morrow Reavley, Ret., on file at Texas State Cemetery.

Profile, Justice Thomas Morrow Reavley, Ret., Texas State Cemetery. (www.cemetery.state.tx.us/pub/user)

JUDGE PRICE

Dover, Karen L. Personal interview, July 1996.

Lauderdale County Deed Records and Probate Records, Lauderdale County Courthouse, Meridian, MS.

Meridian Police Department.

MERIDIAN STAR, 14 January 1921–January 15, 1922.

Mississippi Department of Archives and History, Archives and Library Division, P.O. Box 571, Jackson, MS.

Mississippi State Bar Association, Jackson, MS.

New York Times, 15 Jan. 1921.

Rush, Fonda. Personal interview, July 1996.

Yarbrough, Carmelita. Personal interview, July 1996.

JUDGE PRIZZIA

New York Times, 22, 23 Jan., 17 Feb. 1976.

JUDGE RABENAU

Kirkwood Messinger (Missouri), 2 Jan. 1935.

New York Times, 30 Dec. 1934.

Saint Louis Post Dispatch, 29 Dec. 1934.

Judge & Mrs. Sherry

Aynesworth, Hugh. "Slaying of Judge Tied to Lonely-Hearts Scam." *Washington, Post* 27 Sept. 1990.

Baker, James N., Vern E. Smith. "The Murder and the Mayor," *Newsweek,* 23 Oct. 1989.

Bradley, John Ed. "The Life and Crimes of the Dixie Mafia," *Esquire,* Sept. 1991.

Humes, Edward. *Mississippi Mud, Southern Justice, and the Dixie Mafia.* New York: Simon & Schuster, 1994.

Jackson Mississippi Clarion Ledger, 1987-1990.

New York Times, 24 Oct. 1996.

Ocean Springs Record, 1989.

Smith, Vern E. "The Jailbird's Song," *Southpoint.* Apr. 1990.

Sun Herald (Biloxi, MS), 1987-1997.

Washington Times 1989.

Judge Smith

New York Times, 1, 2 Sept. 1926.

Weekly Herald (Wetumpka, Alabama), 2, 9, 16 Sept., 21 Oct. 1926; 10, 12 Mar., 16, 30 June, 7, 21 July 1927.

Judge Sullivan

Hartford Courant, 21 Apr. 1975.

New York Times, 21 Apr., 11 Nov. 1975.

Judge Taylor

Associated Press, 20 Mar. 1999.

Los Angeles Times, 20 Mar. 1999, 12 July 2002.

San Bernardino County Sheriff's Department, Wanted Poster, San Bernardino, CA.

United Press International. 20 Mar. 1999.

Judge Travers

New York Times, 10 June 1978.

St. Croix Auis (U.S. Virgin Islands), 10 June 1978.

Virgin Islands Daily News, 10, 12 June 1978.

Judge Trueman

Cox v. Utah, 147 P.2d 848, 1944.

Deseret News (Salt Lake City), 24 July 1943.

Minute Book, 2nd Judicial District Court, Weber County, Utah, July Term 1943, Vol. 51, p. 39, Utah State Archives.

New York Times, 25 July 1943.

Ogden Standard-Examiner (Utah), 24 July 1943; 16 Aug. 1987.

Salt Lake Tribune, 11 May, 25, 29 July 1943.

JUDGE VANCE

Birmingham News, 17 Dec. 1989.

Fulford, Honorable R. Clifford. "In Memoriam," *The Alabama Lawyer,* Montgomery, Alabama, January 1990.

Galveston County Daily News, 6 Nov. 1996.

Hackett, George, Frank Washington, Howard Manly, Clara Bingham, and Mark Miller. "Terror in the South," *Newsweek,* Jan. 1, 1990.

Investigative File (redacted), Freedom of Information Privacy Acts Section, Office of Public and Congressional Affairs, U.S. Department of Justice, Federal Bureau of Investigation, Washington, D.C.

Military Personnel Records, National Personnel Records Center, St. Louis, MO.

Winn, Mark. *Priority Mail: The Investigation and Trial of a Mail Bomber Obsessed with Destroying Our Justice System.* New York: Scribner, 1995.

JUDGE WADE

McIntyre, Bruce. "Jury of One," *INSIDE Detective,* 25 May 1954.

New York Times, 14 Jan., 25 May 1954.

Observer (Warren, PA), 13 Jan. 1954.

Official Court Records: Quarter Sessions Docket, November Term, 1952, No. 20, *Commonwealth of Pennsylvania vs. Norman W. Moon,* "Nonsupport of Wife." Tracy M. Greenlund, Justice of the Peace.

Official Court Records: Oyer and Terminer Docket, February Sessions, 1954, No. 1, *Commonwealth of Pennsylvania vs. Norman W. Moon,* In the Court of Oyer & Terminer of Warren County, Pennsylvania. (Murder trial and Insanity proceedings).

Warren Times-Mirror (Warren Times-Observer) 13, 14, 18, 19, 20 Jan., 30 Apr., 10 May 1954; 22 Nov. 1957; 18 Apr., 8 Dec., 1958; 26 Oct. 1973; 23 July 1987; 29 Feb., 2, 3, 5, 6, 17 Mar., 11 May, 9 June 1992.

JUDGE WILLIAMS

Gilmer, John. Personal interview, July 1996.

Official Court Records, Louisa County Circuit Court Clerk, Louisa County, Virginia.

JUDGE WOOD

"Assault," *Time*, 11 June 1979.

Associated Press, 13 Feb. 1999.

Austin American-Statesman, 2, 3, 17 June 1979; 13 Sept. 1981; 6 Aug. 1998.

Cartwright, Gary. "The Black Striker Gets Hit," *Texas Monthly*, Dec. 1981.

———. *Dirty Dealing: A True Story of Smuggling, Murder, and the FBI's Biggest Investigation*. New York: Atheneum, 1984.

———. *Dirty Dealing: Drug Smuggling on the Mexican Border and the Assassination of a Federal Judge: An American Parable*. El Paso: Cinco Puntos Press, 1998.

———. "Good Fella," *Texas Monthly*, Feb. 1997.

———. "The Man Who Killed Judge Wood," *Texas Monthly*, Sept. 1982.

———. "The Sins of the Father," *Texas Monthly*, Nov. 1994.

Dallas Morning News 31 May 1979; 20, 21, 23, 25 March 1981; 6, 10 Aug. 1998.

Fort Worth Star-Telegram, 28 Oct. 1983.

Galveston County Daily News, 6 Oct. 1987; 7 July 1995; 9 Dec. 1996.

"Hitting a Hitman," *Time*, 27 Dec. 1982.

Houston Chronicle, 6, 9 Aug. 1998.

Investigative File (redacted), Freedom of Information Privacy Acts Section, Office of Public and Congressional Affairs, U.S. Department of Justice, Federal Bureau of Investigation, Washington, D.C.

Memorials: "J.H. Wood, Jr.," *Texas Bar Journal*, Dec. 1979.

National Law Journal, 14 June 1982.

New York Times, 1979-1988.

Reuters News Service, 3 Aug. 1998.

San Antonio Express, 19 Aug. 1970.

"Some Excuse," *Time*, 6 Dec. 1982.

"Texas: Killing a Federal Judge," *Newsweek*, 11 June 1979.

Texas Lawyer, 20 Apr., 6 July 1992; 21 Feb., 7 Mar. 1994; 17 Aug., 14 Dec. 1998.

"Texas Sniper," *Time*, 25 Oct. 1982.

www.ingramcontent.com/pod-product-compliance
Lightning Source LLC
Chambersburg PA
CBHW052126270326
41930CB00012B/2776